The

NORTON MIX

NORTON
CUSTOM

W · W · NORTON & COMPANY · *New York · London*

The

NORTON MIX

A CUSTOM PUBLICATION

BERGEN COMMUNITY COLLEGE

WRITING 101

W. W. Norton & Company has been independent since its founding in 1923, when William Warder Norton and Mary D. Herter Norton first published lectures delivered at the People's Institute, the adult education division of New York City's Cooper Union. The firm soon expanded its program beyond the Institute, publishing books by celebrated academics from America and abroad. By mid-century, the two major pillars of Norton's publishing program— trade books and college texts—were firmly established. In the 1950s, the Norton family transferred control of the company to its employees, and today—with a staff of four hundred and a comparable number of trade, college, and professional titles published each year— W. W. Norton & Company stands as the largest and oldest publishing house owned wholly by its employees.

Editor: Katie Hannah
Developmental editors: Mike Fleming and Erin Granville
Managing editor: Marian Johnson
Project editor: Melissa Atkin
Editorial assistant: Sophie Hagen
Production managers: Eric Pier-Hocking and Ashley Horna
Permissions editor: Nancy Rodwan
Photo permissions editor: Trish Marx, Stephanie Romeo
Designer: Toni Krass
Cover designs: Debra Morton-Hoyt
Emedia editor: Eileen Connell
Marketing manager: Scott Berzon
Proofreaders: Paulette McGee, Ben Reynolds
Composition: RR Donnelley
Manufacturing: RR Donnelley

ISBN-13 978-0-393-51931-0

W. W. Norton & Company, Inc., 500 Fifth Avenue, New York, N.Y. 10110
www.wwnorton.com
W. W. Norton & Company Ltd., Castle House, 75/76 Wells Street, London W1T 3QT

GENERAL EDITORS

ELIZABETH RODRIGUEZ KESSLER
COORDINATING EDITOR
University of Houston

JEFFREY ANDELORA
Mesa Community College

MELISSA GOLDTHWAITE
St. Joseph's University

CHARLES HOOD
Antelope Valley College

KATHARINE N. INGS
Manchester College

ANGELA L. JONES
Western Kentucky University

CHRISTOPHER KELLER
University of Texas–Pan American

WITH CONTRIBUTIONS FROM

CEDRIC BURROWS
University of Kansas

LORI CHASTAINE
Boise State University

MICHELLE L. CHESTER
Towson University

DENNIS McGLOTHIN
*University of North Carolina
at Pembroke*

WANDA FRIES
Somerset Community College

HOLLY HASSEL
*University of Wisconsin–
Marathon County*

BETH DINATALE JOHNSON
Ursuline College

Contents

Culture and Identity

PAUL CHAAT SMITH
*The Big Movie (from Everything You Know About Indians Is
Wrong)*   *1*

JHUMPA LAHIRI
This Blessed House   *13*

CHANG-RAE LEE
Coming Home Again   *33*

JERALD WALKER
Dragon Slayers   *46*

BELL HOOKS
Talking Back   *55*

JUNOT DIAZ
Fiesta, 1980   *63*

School and Education

WILLIAM M. CHACE
A Question of Honor   *81*

Contents

JAMES BARSZCZ
Can You Be Educated from a Distance?   98

T. ALLEN CULPEPPER
The Myth of Inferiority   103

SEAMUS HEANEY
Mid-Term Break   109

TOM WAYMAN
Did I Miss Anything?   112

TRIP GABRIEL
Plagiarism Lines Blur for Students in Digital Age   115

ANNE PERRIN
Stop Blaming Teachers   121

Gender

NATALIE ANGIER
Men, Women, Sex, and Darwin   132

MARGARET ATWOOD
The Female Body   147

NAOMI WOLF
The Beauty Myth   153

DAVE BARRY
A GPS Helps a Guy Always Know Where His Couch Is   168

ANNA QUINDLEN
Still Needing the F Word   172

GUY TREBAY
The Vanishing Point   177

KATHA POLLITT
Why Boys Don't Play with Dolls   183

Contents

Globalization

CECILIA BALLÍ
Ciudad de la Muerte   188

FAREED ZAKARIA
The Islamic Threat   211

THOMAS FRIEDMAN
Globalization: The Super-Story   220

PICO IYER
The Burning House   226

Cyberspace

BRENT STAPLES
What Adolescents Miss When We Let Them Grow Up in Cyberspace   246

THOMAS FRIEDMAN
Generation Q   250

ROB FISHMAN
The Generation of Generation Q   255

MOTOKO RICH
Literacy Debate: Online, R U Reading?   260

JESSICA BENNETT
The Flip Side of Internet Fame   272

MARK BITTMAN
I Need a Virtual Break. No, Really   277

MICHAL OZIBKO
iDeath   313

Contents

Appendix

NORTON
Using Sources in Your Writing   *283*

Index   311

PAUL CHAAT SMITH ⎰ *The Big Movie*

PAUL CHAAT SMITH (b. 1954), a member of the Comanche Tribe of
Oklahoma, serves as an associate curator of the National Museum of the
American Indian in Washington, DC. He is the founding editor of the
American Indian Movement's *Treaty Council News* and writes on issues
related to American Indian art, politics, history, and culture. Smith is the
author, with Robert Warrior, of *Like a Hurricane: The Indian Movement
from Alcatraz to Wounded Knee* (1996), a study of the awakening of Native
American political activism in the 1960s and '70s.

"The Big Movie," a chapter from his book *Everything You Know about
Indians Is Wrong* (2009), mixes memoir and cultural commentary to help
readers reflect upon the highly political and hotly disputed place of Native
Americans in the United States, past and present. Known for a straightforward prose style, Smith is frequently sarcastic, even scathing, in his
approach. Notice how Smith uses easily recognizable references to popular
culture as a means to express views and arguments that many readers may
be less likely to recognize or accept. Smith presents American Indians in
ways that disrupt readers' previously held views and stereotypes, allowing
them to consider fresh perspectives on the history that all Americans share.

---

*Our Indians are no longer dangerous. We understand today better than
ever that we have wronged them much and often, that we have misjudged
and slandered them in the past. Now the reaction has set in, and it is surely
a curious phase of the white man's civilization that his latest invention is
helping to set the red man right in history. All of the more artistic Indian
films exalt the Indian, depict the noble traits in his character and challenge*

1

for him and his views and his manner of life the belated admiration of his white brother.

—*The Moving Picture World*, AUGUST 1911

ABOUT FIVE YEARS AGO I realized that I had no memories of seeing Indians at the movies or on television while I was growing up.

Even now I recall nothing of the thousands of hours of Hollywood westerns I must have watched during the late 1950s and 1960s, in Oklahoma and the suburbs of Washington, D.C. It certainly wasn't because I found the medium lacking. I love television and always have. To this day I learn from it constantly, but somehow the thousands of flickering Indians that must have entered my consciousness disappeared without a trace.

There was no shortage of hardware, either. We had multiple televisions, my family being the kind of consumers whom advertising agencies classify as "early adopters." Televisions were in the kitchen and the den, and later I often smuggled a portable black-and-white set into my room and watched late into the night, using earphones to subvert curfew.

The amnesia is selective. I remember *The Twilight Zone, Mayberry RFD, Lost in Space, The Mod Squad, The Man from U.N.C.L.E.,* and *The Ghost and Mrs. Muir.* I remember the assassinations, *Apollo 8,* and the night Lyndon Johnson told us he would not run for reelection, peace being more important.

Indians, sure. Uncle Sly and Aunt Maude, Grandma telling us how   5
glad she is not to live in a tipi, and the Comanche Reformed Church (a sign near the door proudly announces last week's take: $82.50) packed with the faithful, singing Indian hymns where the only words I could ever make out were "Jesus Christ." As befits a people classified as prisoners of war and raised in a military fort, those of my grandparents' generation didn't talk much about the old days. I never heard them discuss *The Searchers* or *Two Rode Together*, tales of Comanche rape and kidnapping and murder that critics agree are among the best American films ever made.

Not that I remember, anyway.

The first moving pictures of Indians that anyone knows about were made by Thomas Edison in 1894. One was a little kinetoscope number called *Sioux Ghost Dance*, and even though it showed no such thing it was nonetheless a hit on the penny arcade peep-show circuit. Modern cinema was still years in the future, but Indians were already establishing market share.

More than two thousand Hollywood features and hundreds of radio and television series later, the western rocks on. Critics through the ages have pronounced it dead and buried, but most of them are the ones dead and buried while the western is still here.

Cars replace horses, flying machines turn into 747s, communism rises and falls. Through it all the western escaped obsolescence by brilliantly reinventing itself time and time again.

So adaptable is the western, an art form as supremely American as 10 jazz or baseball, that in the 1960s the Italians rode to its rescue, breathing new life into a format that seemed hopelessly old-fashioned by creating the spaghetti western: brutal, ironic, and up-to-the-minute cool. Synonymous with Indian bashing, the number-one moneymaking western of all time is *Dances with Wolves*.

We're coming up on the second century of westerns, but even that understates their importance. They have always been with us and always will be. Flip channels if you want, try self-induced amnesia, but these efforts are useless, because the western is encoded in our cultural DNA. If you live in North America, westerns are the Book of Genesis, the story of our lives.

Attention must be paid.

Investigations of the western begin with a man named William F. Cody. He's our Moses, a self-made legend, partly fact and partly fiction, the genius who shaped the myth. In 1869 Ned Buntline, whose given name was Edward Z. C. Judson, famed writer of dime novels, traveled to Nebraska in search of a hero. He found the twenty-three-year-old William Cody, already a veteran of gold rushes, the Pony Express, and the Union Army. His nickname was a result of employment as a hunter-supplier for the Union Pacific Railroad.

Cody became a national figure through reports of his exploits in the *New York Weekly*. He appeared in stage productions based on his life, but it was a part-time affair. Mostly, he continued with being Buffalo Bill.

In 1883 he created Buffalo Bill's Wild West show and hired out-of-work Indians and cowboys. Troupe members included such all-star veterans of the Indian Wars as Sitting Bull, Black Elk, Gall, and Gabriel Dumont.

Why'd they do it? Here's one explanation, from a 1980 essay by Ward Churchill, Mary Anne Hill, and Norbert S. Hill: "Sitting Bull and other plainsmen who participated in spectacles such as Cody's and those of Pawnee Bill and Colonel Frederick T. Cummins had their reasons. There was a pressing need for revenue for their impoverished peoples, an ingrained desire for mobility, perhaps a hope of communicating some sense of their cultural identity to an ignorant and overbearing race of conquerors. But surely if the latter is the case they failed . . . before the prejudgemental myopia of their land- and mineral-hungry hosts."

Well, could be. Maybe they felt Bill's circus was a chance for cross-cultural exchange and went for it. Maybe they had to just keep moving, although this "ingrained desire for mobility" business sounds to me a bit like saying "all God's chillun got happy feet." Some believe that Indians would never in their right mind choose to participate in kitsch like Buffalo Bill's Wild West. However, I speak from personal experience in arguing that Indians are as likely to have bad taste as everyone else.

Most accounts indicate Cody was liked and respected by his Indian employees, who knew exactly what they were doing. Like Cody, the Indians were part-time entertainers and full-time legends. They made history, then re-created the history they made in popular entertainments that toured America and Europe.

Just as art critic Philip Monk makes the case that Canadian contemporary art "passed from pre-modernism to so-called post-modernism without a history of modernism," so too can it be argued that our leaders anticipated the impact of the information age. Never given much of a chance with industrialism, we moved straight into ironic, cartoonish media experiments. If some prefer to see them as gullible dupes (let's see, Sitting Bull was a brilliant leader who forced the United States to sue for peace, and definitely nobody's fool, except of course for that embarrassing business with Cody), I see them as pioneers, our first explorers of the information age.

Unlike in the movies, everything was fabulous confusion. Here's an example: It's December 1890 on Pine Ridge Reservation in the southwest corner of South Dakota. The Ghost Dance religion was sweeping Indian Country. Wovoka, the Paiute some called Messiah, promised to vanquish the whites and return the buffalo. Indians were leaving the reservation for the Black Hills. The government was spooked and sent thousands of soldiers to put down a possible uprising.

They worried most about Sitting Bull, now back on the reservation after his vacation in Canada. General Nelson Miles called up Sitting Bull's friend and sometime boss William Cody. He was on staff with the governor of Nebraska and just back from another boffo European tour. In a bizarre confluence of show biz and diplomacy, General Miles asked Cody to talk some sense into Sitting Bull.

The meeting never happened. It's said Cody stayed up late the night before drinking with cavalry officers. Instead of Cody, an Indian agent with agendas of his own sent Indian cops to arrest Sitting Bull. The cops were terrified, and when the Sioux leader refused to submit he was shot. Sitting Bull's white horse, a gift from Cody, was trained to kneel at the sound of gunfire. This the horse did, as his master lay dying.

Two weeks later, the massacre at Wounded Knee.[1]

And twenty-three years after Wounded Knee, General Miles, Cody, and dozens of Indians who were there the first time re-created the events of that unfortunate December. The government cooperated in the film, hoping it would help with recruitment in a possible war with Mexico. Miles played himself and served as the film's technical adviser, which drove everyone nuts because he insisted on complete authenticity. This meant that because eleven thousand troops participated in a review after the hostiles surrendered, eleven thousand troops were going to be used in the movie. His demands that the Badlands sequence be shot in the Badlands, despite the enormous cost of

[1] Wounded Knee Creek in South Dakota, where, on December 29, 1890, members of the U.S. Seventh Cavalry killed 150 Lakota Sioux, an event generally regarded as one of the most horrific in Native American history.

moving the camp, caused so much bitterness that it finally ended his friendship with Cody.

General Miles also worked as a press agent for the movie, saying 25 in one interview, "The idea is to give the whole thing from the start—the Indian dissatisfaction, their starving condition, the coming of the false 'Messiah' who stirred them to revolt, the massing of the troops, the death of Sitting Bull and, finally, the surrender. All of these incidents will be gone over, just as they happened. Some of the Indians will be there who fought against us. They will fight again, but there will be no bullets. All that is over."

They shot Sitting Bull again, and General Miles insisted on shooting the Battle of Wounded Knee just where it had originally happened, on the mass grave of Big Foot's band.

The night before, rumors swept the camp that some of the Indian extras were going to use live ammunition. Cody called a midnight meeting and told the Indians that the movie would celebrate their resistance. The next morning, although both sides were extremely reluctant to begin firing, they managed to reenact the battle/massacre.

Many Indians broke into tears.

After filming was completed, they spent six months editing. This was during a time when studios turned out movies by the week. Finally it was shown before the secretary of the interior and other top officials of the Wilson administration, who said they loved it.

Other reviews were mixed. One critic called the film "war itself, 30 grim, unpitying and terrible . . . no boy or girl should be allowed to miss these pictures. If you are a lonely man or woman pick up some equally lonely kiddie and take him for an afternoon with the great leaders of our army, with the great chiefs of our Indian tribes and two hours in the open world that has been made sacred by heroic blood of the nation's fighting heroes." A Lakota named Chauncey Yellow Robe trashed the movie in a speech to the Society of American Indians, reserving particular scorn for Miles and Cody, "who were not even there when it happened, went back and became heroes for a moving picture machine."

After a few screenings it mysteriously disappeared. Cody died in 1917, and for nearly a century the film was nowhere to be found. Even the title wasn't known for sure: at various times Buffalo Bill's lost masterpiece was called *The Indian Wars Refought, The Last Indian Battles; or, From the Warpath to the Peace Pipe, The Wars for Civilization in America*, and *Buffalo Bill's Indian Wars*.

The most expensive, elaborate western of its day was the victim of its own identity crisis. For Cody, it was the most spectacular movie ever made, the triumph of a fabled career. For Miles, it was part documentary, part training film. For the government, it was a recruiting device. For the critics, it was a battle showing the victory of Western civilization.

The final result must have been too close, too real. Critical distance could not be established when original combatants were actors, and when the set was the site of battle and massacre. It was a movie, but it was no western.

The films we know came later, as Hollywood matured (or at least got its act together). From the 1920s through the 1950s, cowboys and Indians were a lucrative staple of the industry.

The United States also was just getting its act together. National identity was still shaky, with the Civil War over but not resolved, a frontier still largely untamed, and vast regional differences. Reports of armed resistance by Apaches, Cherokees, Yaquis, and others circulated into the 1920s. In 1909 a Paiute accidentally killed an in-law and vengeful whites chased him across Southern California. The accompanying hysteria made it clear many Americans were not convinced the Indian Wars were over, and even if they were, many wished they weren't. (This event became the subject of a 1969 pro-Indian movie called *Tell Them Willie Boy Was Here*, starring Robert Redford, Katharine Ross, and Robert Blake.)

The directors who pioneered the modern western grew up when the Indian Wars were recent, even current events. D. W. Griffith was born in 1875, Cecil B. DeMille in 1881, Raoul Walsh in 1887, and King Vidor in 1894. John Ford, born in 1894, said "I had four uncles in the Civil War. I used to ask my Uncle Mike to tell me about the Battle of Gettysburg. All Uncle Mike would say was, 'It was horrible. I went six whole days without a drink.'"

Geronimo, Wounded Knee, Sitting Bull, and Custer were no more distant to these guys than Vietnam and Watergate are to many of us.

The form they invented has several characteristics. First, it's set in the past. The films are implicitly about America's history. Second, they are set on the frontier. (This could be almost anywhere, since every inch of the continent was frontier at one time.) Third, westerns set up a language that extends the metaphor of the frontier into paired opposites of, for example, the wilderness versus civilization, the individual versus community, savagery versus humanity.

John Ford, the king of westerns, set his most famous movies about Indians in Monument Valley, a landscape that might be described as Martian, to contrast the alienness of the land with the flimsy covered wagons and lonely outposts. Often the Indians seemed alien as well, but they seemed to belong there, while the Americans looked like intruders, or tourists.

Some westerns demonstrate a real interest in Indians, but in most 40 we exist as a metaphor. The definitive moment in *The Searchers* is at the movie's close. The search is over, the rescue accomplished. Ethan (the rescuer, played by John Wayne) is asked to stay with the family he has reunited against all odds. Framed by a doorway, half in sunlight, half in darkness, the tormented Ethan says no. Still at war with demons from his past, he can't submit to a domestic life. His personal war goes on, and as he leaves the cabin to take his place in the wilderness we know it has nothing to do with Indians. The Comanches he's been fighting for two hours are simply a plot device to get to this moment of terrible pain and alienation.

Imagine something instead of Western history. For most of us, it can't be done. We think, okay, these movies are not exactly accurate (not that they ever claimed to be), and maybe we get closer to the truth if we turn them upside down. Maybe Indians didn't yelp. Maybe the whites were bloodthirsty savages. The master narrative will admit good Indians and bad whites; a western may even present the Long Knives[2] as supremely vicious and evil and the Indian cause just, yet still not challenge the basic premise of a frontier, a wilderness, an inevitable clash of cultures that ends in conquest.

[2] That is, whites.

In *Dances with Wolves*,[3] for example, there exists not a single positive white character. Many of the whites are physically disgusting. The film's title is the name of the protagonist, who becomes Indian and marries a white captive who is also now Indian. The government forces are incompetent, cowardly, and brutal. The message is delivered with all the subtlety of a sledgehammer. The Americans are portrayed as primitive Nazis with bad table manners.

Reduced to its essentials in this way, *Dances with Wolves* seems to be a devastating, revisionist history. In effect, however, the film is a moving, patriotic hymn to all that is majestic about the United States, which includes the beautiful Lakota and their tragic passing. The achievement of *Dances with Wolves* is extraordinary. It turns an indictment of genocide into a valentine to America. Audiences identify with the Indians as part of their heritage, a kind of national mascot. (In the fall of 1992, according to press reports, McDonald's, a corporation synonymous with patriotic values, was close to a deal to sell videocassettes of the movie with purchases of hamburgers and fries. These promotions are called tie-ins, and the phrase couldn't be more appropriate.)

One might ask, okay, maybe it is one-sided and overblown, but aren't we entitled to a little of that after thousands of one-sided and overblown racist westerns? It's a fair question. The night of the Academy Awards in the spring of 1991, one television network showed the ecstatic reaction of children from the Pine Ridge Reservation in South Dakota. Who can argue that those kids who desperately need positive images and role models are not uplifted, even with all the movie's flaws?

Well, I won't argue with that. I think it is positive for many. I also   45
think it leads to a dead end, because the opposite of a lie isn't necessarily true or useful. The master narrative thrives on us/them oppositions.

The 1992 remake of *Last of the Mohicans*[4] provides another illustration of what is permitted and what isn't. Director Michael Mann,

[3] Academy Award–winning film (1990) starring Kevin Costner and Graham Greene. The movie follows a Civil War Lieutenant to a remote Western outpost where he befriends members of a Lakota tribe and ultimately joins them, rejecting his white American background.

[4] James Fenimore Cooper's 1826 novel has been adapted several times for film, radio, and television.

the inventor of television's *Miami Vice*, gave interviews describing his uncompromising research of the eighteenth century, his obsession with getting everything right, and the importance of showing the complex politics of the era. He said back then, if you were an American settler, the Mohawks were your rich neighbors.

I see no reason to doubt that Mann had every intention of including this idea in his movie, but he didn't. It can't be done, because the master narrative does not include settled, prosperous farming towns of Indians. Pictures of Indian towns challenge the idea of settlers clearing a wilderness and instead raise the possibility that Europeans invaded and conquered and pillaged heavily populated, developed real estate. (*Dances with Wolves* offered us an inviting and warm village, but temporary villages with tipis are acceptable. They do not represent property.)

This isn't because some studio boss got a call from the Trilateral Commission.[5] It's because the audience knows about Indians, and knows Indians didn't live in settled farming towns. To be outside the narrative, then, is not to exist. A film that attempted to show something more historically accurate would appear to audiences to be like science fiction, a tale from a parallel universe.

The master narrative (let's call it the Big Movie) is like an infinitely elastic spider web that grows stronger with every change of pattern and wider after each assault. Subversion appears impossible.

Collectively, this is the accomplishment of westerns: they reconcile 50 horrible truths and make them understandable, acceptable, and even uplifting. And because they execute this reconciliation in a way that reinforces status quo values they are a powerful mechanism that serves and strengthens the dominant ideology.

The Big Movie is always up-to-date and these days is an equal opportunity employer. Indians are welcome to amplify or change aspects of the story, and with talent, luck, and the right contacts they have as much chance to succeed as anyone else. It won't be easy, but it's pos-

[5] Private organization founded in 1973 to promote closer relations among the United States, Europe, and Japan. Because its proceedings are closed and many of its members are wealthy, powerful, and well connected, the Trilateral Commission has become the focus of numerous conspiracy theories.

sible and in the long run inevitable that we will see westerns written and directed by Indians.

For those who want not a piece of the pie but a different pie altogether, the task is both urgent and far more difficult. It requires invention, not rewriting. Instead of a reimagined western, it means a final break with a form that really was never about us in the first place.

The stories of the continent must be told. A vacuum is impossible, and humans demand an explanation. So far, the only one that exists is the Big Movie. It says with perfect consistency that we are extinct, were never here anyway, that it was our fault because we couldn't get with the program. It says we are noble, are savage, and noble savages.

There's another narrative waiting to be written. It tells Sitting Bull's story: Did he complain about his agent? Did he really propose marriage to his secretary, a rich white woman from Brooklyn named Catherine Weldon, who lived in his camp in those final days? And let's say they did get hitched, could it have worked? It fully imagines that mysterious cipher Crazy Horse[6] (as a kid his nickname was "Curly") and Almighty Voice and Poundmaker and gives voice to the women nobody remembers.

Even more important, it tells the story of our all-too-human parents 55 and brothers and sisters and uncles and aunts, just plain folks who were nothing like the Indians in the movies even though some of us tried hard to be like them. It tells a story of resistance, of laughter and tears in a doomed land cursed by the legacy of slavery and genocide, a place that's perhaps forever beyond redemption but still the only place we've got.

It's a long shot but worth a try. Besides, in the Big Movie, we'll always be extras. In our movie, we could be stars.

[6] Lakota Sioux warrior who was one of the Indian leaders at the Battle of the Little Big Horn. Almighty Voice and Poundmaker are important historical figures from the Cree tribe.

STUDY QUESTIONS

1. In Paul Chaat Smith's view, how does the movie *Dances with Wolves* differ from earlier movies featuring Native Americans? Does he find the movie satisfying? Why or why not?

2. Smith DESCRIBES and EVALUATES a number of movies, old and new, that depict Native Americans in both positive and negative ways. He also uses the phrase "The Big Movie" many times in a less literal sense. Explain in your own words what Smith means by the phrase "The Big Movie." How does he use this phrase to make a larger ARGUMENT?

3. How does Smith's focus on movies give us a sense of his intended AUDIENCE? Do you feel that you are part of this audience? Even if you have never heard of or seen the movies he discusses, does his ANALYSIS of these movies and "The Big Movie" behind them seem clear and well argued?

4. Toward the end of the selection, Smith writes, "The stories of this continent must be told. A vacuum is impossible, and humans demand an explanation. So far, the only one that exists is the Big Movie. It says with perfect consistency that we are extinct, were never here anyway, that it was our fault because we couldn't get with the program. It says we are noble, are savage, and noble savages." Who are "we" in this passage? What is implied by the phrase "noble savage"? What specific kinds of stories is he talking about here and why are they so necessary?

5. *For Writing.* In his discussion of the movie *Dances with Wolves*, Smith writes that it "turns an indictment of genocide into a valentine to America. Audiences identify with the Indians as part of their heritage, a kind of national mascot." Watch *Dances with Wolves* and write an essay that evaluates Smith's critique of the movie. Are you able to identify with the American Indians in the movie? With Kevin Costner's character? In what ways do you agree or disagree with Smith's claims about the movie? Be sure to cite specific passages from the text and refer to specific scenes from the movie in order to support your points.

JHUMPA LAHIRI { *This Blessed House*

JHUMPA LAHIRI (b. 1967) moved with her Bengali Indian immigrant family from London, England, to Kingston, Rhode Island, at the age of three. Educated at Barnard College and Boston University, where she earned three master's degrees and a PhD in Renaissance studies, Lahiri writes mostly fiction, including her collection *Interpreter of Maladies* (1999), which won the Pulitzer Prize for fiction. The *New Yorker* named Lahiri one of the twenty best writers under the age of forty, and she serves on the President's Committee on the Arts and Humanities. "Writing," she says, "is the hardest thing I do. But it's a struggle I enjoy on some level. I have very little choice. If I don't write, I feel dreadful. So I write."

The following selection was published in *Interpreter of Maladies.* As occurs frequently in Lahiri's writing, it depicts characters confronted with a divided sense of belonging in different places and cultures. "It's what I've struggled with," Lahiri says. "In India, I'm told, 'You look Indian, you speak Bengali, but you're really American.' In America, I'm told, 'You sound and act American, but you're really Indian.'" While reading "This Blessed House" pay particular attention to the challenges facing the newlywed couple as they try to reconcile family and religious traditions, married and work lives, and to establish a home in unfamiliar terrain.

THEY DISCOVERED THE FIRST ONE in a cupboard above the stove, beside an unopened bottle of malt vinegar. "Guess what I found." Twinkle walked into the living room, lined from end to end with taped-up packing boxes, waving the vinegar in one hand and a white porcelain effigy of Christ, roughly the same size as the vinegar bottle, in the other.

Sanjeev looked up. He was kneeling on the floor, marking, with ripped bits of a Post-it, patches on the baseboard that needed to be retouched with paint. "Throw it away."

"Which?"

"Both."

"But I can cook something with the vinegar. It's brand-new." 5

"You've never cooked anything with vinegar."

"I'll look something up. In one of those books we got for our wedding."

Sanjeev turned back to the baseboard, to replace a Post-it scrap that had fallen to the floor. "Check the expiration. And at the very least get rid of that idiotic statue."

"But it could be worth something. Who knows?" She turned it upside down, then stroked, with her index finger, the minuscule frozen folds of its robes. "It's pretty."

"We're not Christian," Sanjeev said. Lately he had begun noticing 10 the need to state the obvious to Twinkle. The day before he had to tell her that if she dragged her end of the bureau instead of lifting it, the parquet floor would scratch.

She shrugged. "No, we're not Christian. We're good little Hindus." She planted a kiss on top of Christ's head, then placed the statue on top of the fireplace mantel, which needed, Sanjeev observed, to be dusted.

By the end of the week the mantel had still not been dusted; it had, however, come to serve as the display shelf for a sizable collection of Christian paraphernalia. There was a 3-D postcard of Saint Francis done in four colors, which Twinkle had found taped to the back of the medicine cabinet, and a wooden cross key chain, which Sanjeev had stepped on with bare feet as he was installing extra shelving in Twinkle's study. There was a framed paint-by-number of the three wise men, against a black velvet background, tucked in the linen closet. There was also a tile trivet depicting a blond, unbearded Jesus, delivering a sermon on a mountaintop, left in one of the drawers of the built-in china cabinet in the dining room.

"Do you think the previous owners were born-agains?" asked Twinkle, making room the next day for a small plastic snow-filled dome containing a miniature Nativity scene, found behind the pipes of the kitchen sink.

Sanjeev was organizing his engineering texts from MIT[1] in alphabetical order on a bookshelf, though it had been several years since he had needed to consult any of them. After graduating, he moved from Boston to Connecticut, to work for a firm near Hartford, and he had recently learned that he was being considered for the position of vice president. At thirty-three he had a secretary of his own and a dozen people working under his supervision who gladly supplied him with any information he needed. Still, the presence of his college books in the room reminded him of a time in his life he recalled with fondness, when he would walk each evening across the Mass. Avenue bridge to order Mughlai chicken with spinach from his favorite Indian restaurant on the other side of the Charles,[2] and return to his dorm to write out clean copies of his problem sets.

"Or perhaps it's an attempt to convert people," Twinkle mused.   15

"Clearly the scheme has succeeded in your case."

She disregarded him, shaking the little plastic dome so that the snow swirled over the manger.

He studied the items on the mantel. It puzzled him that each was in its own way so silly. Clearly they lacked a sense of sacredness. He was further puzzled that Twinkle, who normally displayed good taste, was so charmed. These objects meant something to Twinkle, but they meant nothing to him. They irritated him. "We should call the Realtor. Tell him there's all this nonsense left behind. Tell him to take it away."

"Oh, Sanj." Twinkle groaned. "Please. I would feel terrible throwing them away. Obviously they were important to the people who used to live here. It would feel, I don't know, sacrilegious or something."

---

[1] Massachusetts Institute of Technology, in Cambridge.

[2] The river that separates the cities of Cambridge and Boston.

"If they're so precious, then why are they hidden all over the house? 20
Why didn't they take them with them?

"There must be others," Twinkle said. Her eyes roamed the bare
off-white walls of the room, as if there were other things concealed
behind the plaster. "What else do you think we'll find?"

But as they unpacked their boxes and hung up their winter clothes
and the silk paintings of elephant processions bought on their honey-
moon in Jaipur, Twinkle, much to her dismay, could not find a thing.
Nearly a week had passed before they discovered, one Saturday afternoon, a larger-than-life-sized watercolor poster of Christ, weeping
translucent tears the size of peanut shells and sporting a crown of
thorns, rolled up behind a radiator in the guest bedroom. Sanjeev had
mistaken it for a window shade.

"Oh, we must, we simply must put it up. It's too spectacular."
Twinkle lit a cigarette and began to smoke it with relish, waving it
around Sanjeev's head as if it were a conductor's baton as Mahler's
Fifth Symphony roared from the stereo downstairs.

"Now, look. I will tolerate, for now, your little biblical menagerie in
the living room. But I refuse to have this," he said, flicking at one of
the painted peanut-tears, "displayed in our home."

Twinkle stared at him, placidly exhaling, the smoke emerging in 25
two thin blue streams from her nostrils. She rolled up the poster slowly,
securing it with one of the elastic bands she always wore around her
wrist for tying back her thick, unruly hair, streaked here and there
with henna. "I'm going to put it in my study," she informed him.
"That way you don't have to look at it."

"What about the housewarming? They'll want to see all the rooms.
I've invited people from the office."

She rolled her eyes. Sanjeev noted that the symphony, now in its
third movement, had reached a crescendo, for it pulsed with the tell-
tale clashing of cymbals.

"I'll put it behind the door," she offered, "That way, when they peek
in, they won't see. Happy?"

He stood watching her as she left the room, with her poster and her
cigarette; a few ashes had fallen to the floor where she'd been standing.
He bent down, pinched them between his fingers, and deposited them

in his cupped palm. The tender fourth movement, the *adagietto*, began. During breakfast, Sanjeev had read in the liner notes that Mahler had proposed to his wife by sending her the manuscript of this portion of the score. Although there were elements of tragedy and struggle in the Fifth Symphony, he had read, it was principally music of love and happiness.

He heard the toilet flush. "By the way," Twinkle hollered, "if you want to impress people, I wouldn't play this music. It's putting me to sleep." 30

Sanjeev went to the bathroom to throw away the ashes. The cigarette butt still bobbed in the toilet bowl, but the tank was refilling, so he had to wait a moment before he could flush it again. In the mirror of the medicine cabinet he inspected his long eyelashes—like a girl's, Twinkle liked to tease. Though he was of average build, his cheeks had a plumpness to them; this, along with the eyelashes, detracted, he feared, from what he hoped was a distinguished profile. He was of average height as well, and had wished ever since he had stopped growing that he were just one inch taller. For this reason it irritated him when Twinkle insisted on wearing high heels, as she had done the other night when they ate dinner in Manhattan. This was the first weekend after they'd moved into the house; by then the mantel had already filled up considerably, and they had bickered about it in the car on the way down. But then Twinkle had drunk four glasses of whiskey in a nameless bar in Alphabet City,[3] and forgot all about it. She dragged him to a tiny bookshop on St. Mark's Place, where she browsed for nearly an hour, and when they left she insisted that they dance a tango on the sidewalk in front of strangers.

Afterward, she tottered on his arm, rising faintly over his line of vision, in a pair of suede three-inch leopard-print pumps. In this manner they walked the endless blocks back to a parking garage on Washington Square, for Sanjeev had heard far too many stories about the terrible things that happened to cars in Manhattan. "But I do nothing all day except sit at my desk," she fretted when they were driving home, after he had mentioned that her shoes looked uncomfortable and suggested that perhaps she should not wear them. "I can't exactly wear heels when I'm typing." Though he abandoned the argument, he knew

---

[3] A section of lower Manhattan where numbered streets intersect lettered avenues.

for a fact that she didn't spend all day at her desk; just that afternoon, when he got back from a run, he found her inexplicably in bed, reading. When he asked why she was in bed in the middle of the day she told him she was bored. He had wanted to say to her then, You could unpack some boxes. You could sweep the attic. You could retouch the paint on the bathroom windowsill, and after you do it you could warn me so that I don't put my watch on it. They didn't bother her, these scattered, unsettled matters. She seemed content with whatever clothes she found at the front of the closet, with whatever magazine was lying around, with whatever song was on the radio—content yet curious. And now all of her curiosity centered around discovering the next treasure.

A few days later when Sanjeev returned from the office, he found Twinkle on the telephone, smoking and talking to one of her girlfriends in California even though it was before five o'clock and the long-distance rates were at their peak. "Highly devout people," she was saying, pausing every now and then to exhale. "Each day is like a treasure hunt. I'm serious. This you won't believe. The switch plates in the bedrooms were decorated with scenes from the Bible. You know, Noah's Ark and all that. Three bedrooms, but one is my study. Sanjeev went to the hardware store right away and replaced them, can you imagine, he replaced every single one."

Now it was the friend's turn to talk. Twinkle nodded, slouched on the floor in front of the fridge, wearing black stirrup pants and a yellow chenille sweater, groping for her lighter. Sanjeev could smell something aromatic on the stove, and he picked his way carefully across the extra-long phone cord tangled on the Mexican terra-cotta tiles. He opened the lid of a pot with some sort of reddish brown sauce dripping over the sides, boiling furiously.

"It's a stew made with fish. I put the vinegar in it," she said to him, 35 interrupting her friend, crossing her fingers. "Sorry, you were saying?" She was like that, excited and delighted by little things, crossing her fingers before any remotely unpredictable event, like tasting a new flavor of ice cream, or dropping a letter in a mailbox. It was a quality he did not understand. It made him feel stupid, as if the world contained hidden wonders he could not anticipate, or see. He looked at her face, which, it occurred to him, had not grown out of its girlhood, the eyes untroubled, the pleasing features unfirm, as if they still had to settle into some sort of permanent expression. Nicknamed after a nursery rhyme, she had yet to shed a childhood endearment. Now, in the second month of their marriage, certain things nettled him—the way she sometimes spat a little when she spoke, or left her undergarments after removing them at night at the foot of their bed rather than depositing them in the laundry hamper.

They had met only four months before. Her parents, who lived in California, and his, who still lived in Calcutta, were old friends, and across continents they had arranged the occasion at which Twinkle and Sanjeev were introduced—a sixteenth birthday party for a daughter in their circle—when Sanjeev was in Palo Alto on business. At the restaurant they were seated side by side at a round table with a revolving platter of spareribs and egg rolls and chicken wings, which, they concurred, all tasted the same. They had concurred too on their adolescent but still persistent fondness for Wodehouse[4] novels, and their dislike for the sitar, and later Twinkle confessed that she was charmed by the way Sanjeev had dutifully refilled her teacup during their conversation.

And so the phone calls began, and grew longer, and then the visits, first he to Stanford, then she to Connecticut, after which Sanjeev would save in an ashtray left on the balcony the crushed cigarettes she had smoked during the weekend—saved them, that is, until the next time she came to visit him, and then he vacuumed the apartment, washed the sheets, even dusted the plant leaves in her honor. She was twenty-seven and recently abandoned, he had gathered, by an American who had tried and failed to be an actor; Sanjeev was lonely, with an excessively generous income for a single man, and had never been in love. At the urging of their matchmakers, they married in India, amid hundreds of well-wishers whom he barely remembered from his childhood, in incessant August rains, under a red and orange tent strung with Christmas tree lights on Mandeville Road.

---

[4] P. G. Wodehouse (1881–1975), English novelist best known for a series of comedic novels featuring a wealthy, blithely bumbling young man, Bertie Wooster, and his ever-faithful and impossibly competent valet, Jeeves.

"Did you sweep the attic?" he asked Twinkle later as she was folding paper napkins and wedging them by their plates. The attic was the only part of the house they had not yet given an initial cleaning.

"Not yet. I will, I promise. I hope this tastes good," she said, planting the steaming pot on top of the Jesus trivet. There was a loaf of Italian bread in a little basket, and iceberg lettuce and grated carrots tossed with bottled dressing and croutons, and glasses of red wine. She was not terribly ambitious in the kitchen. She bought preroasted chickens from the supermarket and served them with potato salad prepared who knew when, sold in little plastic containers. Indian food, she complained, was a bother; she detested chopping garlic, and peeling ginger, and could not operate a blender, and so it was Sanjeev who, on weekends, seasoned mustard oil with cinnamon sticks and cloves in order to produce a proper curry.

He had to admit, though, that whatever it was that she had cooked 40 today, it was unusually tasty, attractive even, with bright white cubes of fish, and flecks of parsley, and fresh tomatoes gleaming in the dark brown-red broth.

"How did you make it?"

"I made it up."

"What did you do?"

"I just put some things into the pot and added the malt vinegar at the end."

"How much vinegar?" 45

She shrugged, ripping off some bread and plunging it into her bowl.

"What do you mean you don't know? You should write it down. What if you need to make it again, for a party or something?"

"I'll remember," she said. She covered the bread basket with a dish-towel that had, he suddenly noticed, the Ten Commandments printed on it. She flashed him a smile, giving his knee a little squeeze under the table. "Face it. This house is blessed."

The housewarming party was scheduled for the last Saturday in October, and they had invited about thirty people. All were Sanjeev's acquaintances, people from the office, and a number of Indian couples in the Connecticut area, many of whom he barely knew, but who had regularly invited him, in his bachelor days, to supper on Saturdays. He often wondered why they included him in their circle. He had little in common with any of them, but he always attended their gatherings, to eat spiced chickpeas and shrimp cutlets, and gossip and discuss politics, for he seldom had other plans. So far, no one had met Twinkle; back when they were still dating, Sanjeev didn't want to waste their brief weekends together with people he associated with being alone. Other than Sanjeev and an ex-boyfriend who she believed worked in a pottery studio in Brookfield, she knew no one in the state of Connecticut. She was completing her master's thesis at Stanford, a study of an Irish poet whom Sanjeev had never heard of.

Sanjeev had found the house on his own before leaving for the wedding, for a good price, in a neighborhood with a fine school system. He was impressed by the elegant curved staircase with its wrought-iron banister, and the dark wooden wainscoting, and the solarium overlooking rhododendron bushes, and the solid brass 22, which also happened to be the date of his birth, nailed impressively to the vaguely Tudor facade. There were two working fireplaces, a two-car garage, and an attic suitable for converting into extra bedrooms if, the Realtor mentioned, the need should arise. By then Sanjeev had already made up his mind, was determined that he and Twinkle should live there together, forever, and so he had not bothered to notice the switch plates covered with biblical stickers, or the transparent decal of the Virgin on the half shell, as Twinkle liked to call it, adhered to the window in the master bedroom. When, after moving in, he tried to scrape it off, he scratched the glass.

The weekend before the party they were raking the lawn when he heard Twinkle shriek. He ran to her, clutching his rake, worried that she had discovered a dead animal, or a snake. A brisk October breeze stung the tops of his ears as his sneakers crunched over brown and yellow leaves. When he reached her, she had collapsed on the grass, dissolved in nearly silent laughter. Behind an overgrown forsythia bush was a plaster Virgin Mary as tall as their waists, with a blue painted hood draped over her head in the manner of an Indian bride. Twinkle grabbed the hem of her T-shirt and began wiping away the dirt staining the statue's brow.

21

"I suppose you want to put her by the foot of our bed," Sanjeev said.

She looked at him, astonished. Her belly was exposed, and he saw that there were goose bumps around her navel. "What do you think? Of course we can't put this in our bedroom."

"We can't?"

"No, silly Sanj. This is meant for outside. For the lawn."   55

"Oh God, no. Twinkle, no."

"But we must. It would be bad luck not to."

"All the neighbors will see. They'll think we're insane."

"Why, for having a statue of the Virgin Mary on our lawn? Every other person in this neighborhood has a statue of Mary on the lawn. We'll fit right in."

"We're not Christian."   60

"So you keep reminding me." She spat onto the tip of her finger and started to rub intently at a particularly stubborn stain on Mary's chin. "Do you think this is dirt, or some kind of fungus?"

He was getting nowhere with her, with this woman whom he had known for only four months and whom he had married, this woman with whom he now shared his life. He thought with a flicker of regret of the snapshots his mother used to send him from Calcutta, of prospective brides who could sing and sew and season lentils without consulting a cookbook. Sanjeev had considered these women, had even ranked them in order of preference, but then he had met Twinkle. "Twinkle, I can't have the people I work with see this statue on my lawn."

"They can't fire you for being a believer. It would be discrimination."

"That's not the point."

"Why does it matter to you so much what other people think?"   65

"Twinkle, please." He was tired. He let his weight rest against his rake as she began dragging the statue toward an oval bed of myrtle, beside the lamppost that flanked the brick pathway. "Look, Sanj. She's so lovely."

He returned to his pile of leaves and began to deposit them by handfuls into a plastic garbage bag. Over his head the blue sky was cloudless. One tree on the lawn was still full of leaves, red and orange, like the tent in which he had married Twinkle.

He did not know if he loved her. He said he did when she had first asked him, one afternoon in Palo Alto as they sat side by side in a darkened, nearly empty movie theater. Before the film, one of her favorites, something in German that he found extremely depressing, she had pressed the tip of her nose to his so that he could feel the flutter of her mascara-coated eyelashes. That afternoon he had replied, yes, he loved her, and she was delighted, and fed him a piece of popcorn, letting her finger linger an instant between his lips, as if it were his reward for coming up with the right answer.

Though she did not say it herself, he assumed then that she loved him too, but now he was no longer sure. In truth, Sanjeev did not know what love was, only what he thought it was not. It was not, he had decided, returning to an empty carpeted condominium each night, and using only the top fork in his cutlery drawer, and turning away politely at those weekend dinner parties when the other men eventually put their arms around the waists of their wives and girlfriends, leaning over every now and again to kiss their shoulders or necks. It was not sending away for classical music CDs by mail, working his way methodically through the major composers that the catalogue recommended, and always sending his payments in on time. In the months before meeting Twinkle, Sanjeev had begun to realize this. "You have enough money in the bank to raise three families," his mother reminded him when they spoke at the start of each month on the phone. "You need a wife to look after and love." Now he had one, a pretty one, from a suitably high caste, who would soon have a master's degree. What was there not to love?

That evening Sanjeev poured himself a gin and tonic, drank it and 70 most of another during one segment of the news, and then approached Twinkle, who was taking a bubble bath, for she announced that her limbs ached from raking the lawn, something she had never done before. He didn't knock. She had applied a bright blue mask to her face, was smoking and sipping some bourbon with ice and leafing through a fat paperback book whose pages had buckled and turned gray from the water. He glanced at the cover; the only thing written on it was the word "Sonnets" in dark red letters. He took a breath, and then he informed her very calmly that after finishing his drink he was going to put on his shoes and go outside and remove the Virgin from the front lawn.

"Where are you going to put it?" she asked him dreamily, her eyes closed. One of her legs emerged, unfolding gracefully, from the layer of suds. She flexed and pointed her toes.

"For now I am going to put it in the garage. Then tomorrow morning on my way to work I am going to take it to the dump."

"Don't you dare." She stood up, letting the book fall into the water, bubbles dripping down her thighs. "I hate you," she informed him, her eyes narrowing at the word "hate." She reached for her bathrobe, tied it tightly about her waist, and padded down the winding staircase, leaving sloppy wet footprints along the parquet floor. When she reached the foyer, Sanjeev said, "Are you planning on leaving the house that way?" He felt a throbbing in his temples, and his voice revealed an unfamiliar snarl when he spoke.

"Who cares? Who cares what way I leave this house?"

"Where are you planning on going at this hour?" 75

"You can't throw away that statue. I won't let you." Her mask, now dry, had assumed an ashen quality, and water from her hair dripped onto the caked contours of her face.

"Yes, I can. I will."

"No," Twinkle said, her voice suddenly small. "This is our house. We own it together. The statue is a part of our property." She had begun to shiver. A small pool of bathwater had collected around her ankles. He went to shut a window, fearing that she would catch cold. Then he noticed that some of the water dripping down her hard blue face was tears.

"Oh, God, Twinkle, please, I didn't mean it." He had never seen her cry before, had never seen such sadness in her eyes. She didn't turn away or try to stop the tears; instead she looked strangely at peace. For a moment she closed her lids, pale and unprotected compared to the blue that caked the rest of her face. Sanjeev felt ill, as if he had eaten either too much or too little.

She went to him, placing her damp toweled arms about his neck, 80 sobbing into his chest, soaking his shirt. The mask flaked onto his shoulders.

In the end they settled on a compromise: the statue would be placed in a recess at the side of the house, so that it wasn't obvious to passersby, but was still clearly visible to all who came.

The menu for the party was fairly simple: there would be a case of champagne, and samosas from an Indian restaurant in Hartford, and big trays of rice with chicken and almonds and orange peels, which Sanjeev had spent the greater part of the morning and afternoon preparing. He had never entertained on such a large scale before and, worried that there would not be enough to drink, ran out at one point to buy another case of champagne just in case. For this reason he burned one of the rice trays and had to start it over again. Twinkle swept the floors and volunteered to pick up the samosas; she had an appointment for a manicure and a pedicure in that direction, anyway. Sanjeev had planned to ask if she would consider clearing the menagerie off the mantel, if only for the party, but she left while he was in the shower. She was gone for a good three hours, and so it was Sanjeev who did the rest of the cleaning. By five-thirty the entire house sparkled, with scented candles that Twinkle had picked up in Hartford illuminating the items on the mantel, and slender stalks of burning incense planted into the soil of potted plants. Each time he passed the mantel he winced, dreading the raised eyebrows of his guests as they viewed the flickering ceramic saints, the salt and pepper shakers designed to resemble Mary and Joseph. Still, they would be impressed, he hoped, by the lovely bay windows, the shining parquet floors, the impressive winding staircase, the wooden wainscoting, as they sipped champagne and dipped samosas in chutney.

Douglas, one of the new consultants at the firm, and his girlfriend Nora were the first to arrive. Both were tall and blond, wearing matching wire-rimmed glasses and long black overcoats. Nora wore a black hat full of sharp thin feathers that corresponded to the sharp thin angles of her face. Her left hand was joined with Douglas's. In her right hand was a bottle of cognac with a red ribbon wrapped around its neck, which she gave to Twinkle.

"Great lawn, Sanjeev," Douglas remarked. "We've got to get that rake out ourselves, sweetie. And this must be . . ."

"My wife. Tanima." 85

"Call me Twinkle."

"What an unusual name," Nora remarked.

Twinkle shrugged. "Not really. There's an actress in Bombay named Dimple Kapadia. She even has a sister named Simple."

Douglas and Nora raised their eyebrows simultaneously, nodding slowly, as if to let the absurdity of the names settle in. "Pleased to meet you, Twinkle."

"Help yourself to champagne. There's gallons." 90

"I hope you don't mind my asking," Douglas said, "but I noticed the statue outside, and are you guys Christian? I thought you were Indian."

"There are Christians in India," Sanjeev replied, "but we're not."

"I love your outfit," Nora told Twinkle.

"And I adore your hat. Would you like the grand tour?"

The bell rang again, and again and again. Within minutes, it 95 seemed, the house had filled with bodies and conversations and unfamiliar fragrances. The women wore heels and sheer stockings, and short black dresses made of crepe and chiffon. They handed their wraps and coats to Sanjeev, who draped them carefully on hangers in the spacious coat closet, though Twinkle told people to throw their things on the ottomans in the solarium. Some of the Indian women wore their finest saris, made with gold filigree that draped in elegant pleats over their shoulders. The men wore jackets and ties and citrus-scented aftershaves. As people filtered from one room to the next, presents piled onto the long cherry-wood table that ran from one end of the downstairs hall to the other.

It bewildered Sanjeev that it was for him, and his house, and his wife, that they had all gone to so much care. The only other time in his life that something similar had happened was his wedding day, but somehow this was different, for these were not his family, but people who knew him only casually, and in a sense owed him nothing. Everyone congratulated him. Lester, another coworker, predicted that Sanjeev would be promoted to vice president in two months maximum. People devoured the samosas, and dutifully admired the freshly painted ceilings and walls, the hanging plants, the bay windows, the silk paintings from Jaipur. But most of all they admired Twinkle, and her brocaded *salwar-kameez*,[5] which was the shade of a persimmon with a low scoop in the back, and the little string of white rose petals she had coiled cleverly around her head, and the pearl choker with a sapphire at its center that adorned her throat. Over hectic jazz records, played under Twinkle's supervision, they laughed at her anecdotes and observations, forming a widening circle around her, while Sanjeev replenished the samosas that he kept warming evenly in the oven, and getting ice for people's drinks, and opening more bottles of champagne with some difficulty, and explaining for the fortieth time that he wasn't Christian. It was Twinkle who led them in separate groups up and down the winding stairs, to gaze at the back lawn, to peer down the cellar steps. "Your friends adore the poster in my study," she mentioned to him triumphantly, placing her hand on the small of his back as they, at one point, brushed past each other.

Sanjeev went to the kitchen, which was empty, and ate a piece of chicken out of the tray on the counter with his fingers because he thought no one was looking. He ate a second piece, then washed it down with a gulp of gin straight from the bottle.

"Great house. Great rice." Sunil, an anesthesiologist, walked in, spooning food from his paper plate into his mouth. "Do you have more champagne?"

"Your wife's wow," added Prabal, following behind. He was an unmarried professor of physics at Yale. For a moment Sanjeev stared at him blankly, then blushed; once at a dinner party Prabal had pronounced that Sophia Loren was wow, as was Audrey Hepburn. "Does she have a sister?"

Sunil picked a raisin out of the rice tray. "Is her last name Little Star?"   100

---

[5] Traditional South Asian attire, worn by both men and women, consisting of baggy trousers and a long shirt.

The two men laughed and started eating more rice from the tray, plowing through it with their plastic spoons. Sanjeev went down to the cellar for more liquor. For a few minutes he paused on the steps, in the damp, cool silence, hugging the second crate of champagne to his chest as the party drifted above the rafters. Then he set the reinforcements on the dining table.

"Yes, everything, we found them all in the house, in the most unusual places," he heard Twinkle saying in the living room. "In fact we keep finding them."

"No!"

"Yes! Every day is like a treasure hunt. It's too good. God only knows what else we'll find, no pun intended."

That was what started it. As if by some unspoken pact, the whole 105 party joined forces and began combing through each of the rooms, opening closets on their own, peering under chairs and cushions, feeling behind curtains, removing books from bookcases. Groups scampered, giggling and swaying, up and down the winding staircase.

"We've never explored the attic," Twinkle announced suddenly, and so everybody followed.

"How do we get up there?"

"There's a ladder in the hallway, somewhere in the ceiling."

Wearily Sanjeev followed at the back of the crowd, to point out the location of the ladder, but Twinkle had already found it on her own. "Eureka!" she hollered.

Douglas pulled the chain that released the steps. His face was flushed 110 and he was wearing Nora's feather hat on his head. One by one the guests disappeared, men helping women as they placed their strappy high heels on the narrow slats of the ladder, the Indian women wrapping the free ends of their expensive saris into their waistbands. The men followed behind, all quickly disappearing, until Sanjeev alone remained at the top of the winding staircase. Footsteps thundered over his head. He had no desire to join them. He wondered if the ceiling would collapse, imagined, for a split second, the sight of all the tumbling drunk perfumed bodies crashing, tangled, around him. He heard a shriek, and then rising, spreading waves of laughter in discordant tones. Something fell, something else shattered. He could hear them babbling about a trunk. They seemed to be struggling to get it open, banging feverishly on its surface.

He thought perhaps Twinkle would call for his assistance, but he was not summoned. He looked about the hallway and to the landing below, at the champagne glasses and half-eaten samosas and napkins smeared with lipstick abandoned in every corner, on every available surface. Then he noticed that Twinkle, in her haste, had discarded her shoes altogether, for they lay by the foot of the ladder, black patent-leather mules with heels like golf tees, open toes, and slightly soiled silk labels on the instep where her soles had rested. He placed them in the doorway of the master bedroom so that no one would trip when they descended.

He heard something creaking open slowly. The strident voices had subsided to an even murmur. It occurred to Sanjeev that he had the house all to himself. The music had ended and he could hear, if he concentrated, the hum of the refrigerator, and the rustle of the last leaves on the trees outside, and the tapping of their branches against the windowpanes. With one flick of his hand he could snap the ladder back on its spring into the ceiling, and they would have no way of getting down unless he were to pull the chain and let them. He thought of all the things he could do, undisturbed. He could sweep Twinkle's menagerie into a garbage bag and get in the car and drive it all to the dump, and tear down the poster of weeping Jesus, and take a hammer to the Virgin Mary while he was at it. Then he would return to the empty house; he could easily clear up the cups and plates in an hour's time, and pour himself a gin and tonic, and eat a plate of warmed rice and listen to his new Bach CD while reading the liner notes so as to understand it properly. He nudged the ladder slightly, but it was sturdily planted against the floor. Budging it would require some effort.

"My God, I need a cigarette," Twinkle exclaimed from above.

Sanjeev felt knots forming at the back of his neck. He felt dizzy. He needed to lie down. He walked toward the bedroom, but stopped short when he saw Twinkle's shoes facing him in the doorway. He thought of her slipping them on her feet. But instead of feeling irritated, as he had ever since they'd moved into the house together, he felt a pang of anticipation at the thought of her rushing unsteadily down the winding staircase in them, scratching the floor a bit in her path. The pang intensified as he thought of her rushing to the bathroom to brighten her lipstick, and eventually rushing to get people their coats, and finally rushing to the cherry-wood table when the last guest had left, to begin opening their housewarming presents. It was the same pang he used to feel before they were married, when he would hang up the phone after one of their conversations, or when he would drive back from the airport, wondering which ascending plane in the sky was hers.

"Sanj, you won't believe this." 115

She emerged with her back to him, her hands over her head, the tops of her bare shoulder blades perspiring, supporting something still hidden from view.

"You got it, Twinkle?" someone asked.

"Yes, you can let go."

Now he saw that her hands were wrapped around it: a solid silver bust of Christ, the head easily three times the size of his own. It had a patrician bump on its nose, magnificent curly hair that rested atop a pronounced collarbone, and a broad forehead that reflected in miniature the walls and doors and lampshades around them. Its expression was confident, as if assured of its devotees, the unyielding lips sensuous and full. It was also sporting Nora's feather hat. As Twinkle descended, Sanjeev put his hands around her waist to balance her, and he relieved her of the bust when she had reached the ground. It weighed a good thirty pounds. The others began lowering themselves slowly, exhausted from the hunt. Some trickled downstairs in search of a fresh drink.

She took a breath, raised her eyebrows, crossed her fingers. "Would 120 you mind terribly if we displayed it on the mantel? Just for tonight? I know you hate it."

He did hate it. He hated its immensity, and its flawless, polished surface, and its undeniable value. He hated that it was in his house, and that he owned it. Unlike the other things they'd found, this contained dignity, solemnity, beauty even. But to his surprise these qualities made him hate it all the more. Most of all he hated it because he knew that Twinkle loved it.

"I'll keep it in my study from tomorrow," Twinkle added. "I promise."

She would never put it in her study, he knew. For the rest of their days together she would keep it on the center of the mantel, flanked on either side by the rest of the menagerie. Each time they had guests Twinkle would explain how she had found it, and they would admire her as they listened. He gazed at the crushed rose petals in her hair, at the pearl and sapphire choker at her throat, at the sparkly crimson polish on her toes. He decided these were among the things that made Prabal think she was wow. His head ached from gin and his arms ached from the weight of the statue. He said, "I put your shoes in the bedroom."

"Thanks. But my feet are killing me." Twinkle gave his elbow a little squeeze and headed for the living room.

Sanjeev pressed the massive silver face to his ribs, careful not to let the feather hat slip, and followed her.

125

STUDY QUESTIONS

1. Provide brief character DESCRIPTIONS of both Sanjeev and Twinkle. In particular, focus on their character traits as well as the ways each seems to adapt to married life in their new house in Connecticut. How well do Sanjeev and Twinkle understand each other? How does each seem to feel about their parental and ancestral culture? What conflicts do they have aside from their disagreement about the Christian objects they find?

2. "This Blessed House" NARRATES the story of a newlywed couple trying to establish a new home (yet notice that the title of the story refers to a "house," not a home). How does each of the characters seem to understand this new space? That is, what beliefs does each have about the meaning and significance of the new house? How do the religious artifacts they keep finding help to shape their understanding of what it means to establish a home?

3. On one level, this is a story about global living, the disjunctions that can occur when a first-generation Indian couple begins married life together in a new geographic location. What does the story suggest about transplanting culture and community from one area of the world to another, about the ability to retain one's culture yet assimilate to another one in a different part of the world? Refer to specific passages in the text to develop and support your ideas.

4. *For Writing.* Notice how frequently descriptions, thoughts, and talk of food arise in the story, particularly Sanjeev's references to authentic Indian food. Reread "This Blessed House" and write an essay that explains why Indian food is so significant to Sanjeev and so central to many scenes in the story, particularly the housewarming party. Why does eating Indian food matter so much to Sanjeev, and why does Twinkle's inability to cook it seem to bother him? And conversely, does Twinkle's lack of concern about cooking indicate anything about her cultural identity? You may also wish to consider the various guests at the housewarming party: what seems to be their connection to food and to Indian culture?

CHANG-RAE LEE { *Coming Home Again*

CHANG-RAE LEE (b. 1965) came to New York State from South Korea
with his family at age three. He graduated from Yale University in 1987 and
worked in the finance industry before changing course and earning his MFA
in creative writing from the University of Oregon, where he also taught.
Currently he directs the program in creative writing at Princeton University.
Lee is also a frequent contributor to magazines, including the *New Yorker*
and *Time*. His novels include *Native Speaker* (1995), which won the
PEN/Hemingway Award, *A Gesture Life* (1999), *Aloft* (2004), and
The Surrendered (2010).

In "Coming Home Again," Lee explores the adjustments that parents and
children must make when they are together again after a significant period of
separation. As Lee prepares food that his mother, ill with cancer, cannot eat,
he reflects on how food was the thread that connected their family through
his years away at boarding school. And as Lee's mother lies dying, he real-
izes that her recipes, passed on orally and through practice, will continue to
forge that connection when she has passed on. As you read, think about the
significance of food in your family or among your friends.

WHEN MY MOTHER BEGAN USING the electronic pump that fed her liq-
uids and medication, we moved her to the family room. The bedroom
she shared with my father was upstairs, and it was impossible to carry
the machine up and down all day and night. The pump itself was attached to a metal stand on casters, and she pulled it along wherever she
went. From anywhere in the house, you could hear the sound of the

wheels clicking out a steady time over the grout lines of the slate-tiled foyer, her main thoroughfare to the bathroom and the kitchen. Sometimes you would hear her halt after only a few steps, to catch her breath or steady her balance, and whatever you were doing was instantly suspended by a pall of silence.

I was usually in the kitchen, preparing lunch or dinner, poised over the butcher block with her favorite chef's knife in my hand and her old yellow apron slung around my neck. I'd be breathless in the sudden quiet, and, having ceased my mincing and chopping, would stare blankly at the brushed sheen of the blade. Eventually, she would clear her throat or call out to say she was fine, then begin to move again, starting her rhythmic *ka-jug*; and only then could I go on with my cooking, the world of our house turning once more, wheeling through the black.

I wasn't cooking for my mother but for the rest of us. When she first moved downstairs she was still eating, though scantily, more just to taste what we were having than from any genuine desire for food. The point was simply to sit together at the kitchen table and array ourselves like a family again. My mother would gently set herself down in her customary chair near the stove. I sat across from her, my father and sister to my left and right, and crammed in the center was all the food I had made—a spicy codfish stew, say, or a casserole of gingery beef, dishes that in my youth she had prepared for us a hundred times.

It had been ten years since we'd all lived together in the house, which at fifteen I had left to attend boarding school in New Hampshire. My mother would sometimes point this out, by speaking of our present time as being "just like before Exeter," which surprised me, given how proud she always was that I was a graduate of the school.

My going to such a place was part of my mother's not so secret plan 5 to change my character, which she worried was becoming too much like hers. I was clever and able enough, but without outside pressure I was readily given to sloth and vanity. The famous school—which none of us knew the first thing about—would prove my mettle. She was right, of course, and while I was there I would falter more than a few times, academically and otherwise. But I never thought that my leaving home then would ever be a problem for her, a private quarrel she would have even as her life waned.

Now her house was full again. My sister had just resigned from her job in New York City, and my father, who typically saw his psychiatric patients until eight or nine in the evening, was appearing in the driveway at four-thirty. I had been living at home for nearly a year and was in the final push of work on what would prove a dismal failure of a novel. When I wasn't struggling over my prose, I kept occupied with the things she usually did—the daily errands, the grocery shopping, the vacuuming and the cleaning, and, of course, all the cooking.

When I was six or seven years old, I used to watch my mother as she prepared our favorite meals. It was one of my daily pleasures. She shooed me away in the beginning, telling me that the kitchen wasn't my place, and adding, in her half-proud, half-deprecating way, that her kind of work would only serve to weaken me. "Go out and play with your friends," she'd snap in Korean, "or better yet, do your reading and homework." She knew that I had already done both, and that as the evening approached there was no place to go save her small and tidy kitchen, from which the clatter of her mixing bowls and pans would ring through the house.

I would enter the kitchen quietly and stand beside her, my chin lodging upon the point of her hip. Peering through the crook of her arm, I beheld the movements of her hands. For *kalbi*,[1] she would take up a butchered short rib in her narrow hand, the flinty bone shaped like a section of an airplane wing and deeply embedded in gristle and flesh, and with the point of her knife cut so that the bone fell away, though not completely, leaving it connected to the meat by the barest opaque layer of tendon. Then she methodically butterflied the flesh, cutting and unfolding, repeating the action until the meat lay out on her board, glistening and ready for seasoning. She scored it diagonally, then sifted sugar into the crevices with her pinched fingers, gently rubbing in the crystals. The sugar would tenderize as well as sweeten the meat. She did this with each rib, and then set them all aside in a large shallow bowl. She minced a half-dozen cloves of garlic, a stub of gingerroot, sliced up a few scallions, and spread it all over the meat. She wiped her hands and took out a bottle of sesame oil, and, after

[1] Korean-style ribs.

pausing for a moment, streamed the dark oil in two swift circles around the bowl. After adding a few splashes of soy sauce, she thrust her hands in and kneaded the flesh, careful not to dislodge the bones. I asked her why it mattered that they remain connected. "The meat needs the bone nearby," she said, "to borrow its richness." She wiped her hands clean of the marinade, except for her little finger, which she would flick with her tongue from time to time, because she knew that the flavor of a good dish developed not at once but in stages.

Whenever I cook, I find myself working just as she would, readying the ingredients—a mash of garlic, a julienne of red peppers, fantails of shrimp—and piling them in little mounds about the cutting surface. My mother never left me any recipes, but this is how I learned to make her food, each dish coming not from a list or a card but from the aromatic spread of a board.

I've always thought it was particularly cruel that the cancer was in   10
her stomach, and that for a long time at the end she couldn't eat. The last meal I made for her was on New Year's Eve, 1990. My sister suggested that instead of a rib roast or a bird, or the usual overflow of Korean food, we make all sorts of finger dishes that our mother might fancy and pick at.

We set the meal out on the glass coffee table in the family room. I prepared a tray of smoked-salmon canapés, fried some Korean bean cakes, and made a few other dishes I thought she might enjoy. My sister supervised me, arranging the platters, and then with some pomp carried each dish in to our parents. Finally, I brought out a bottle of champagne in a bucket of ice. My mother had moved to the sofa and was sitting up, surveying the low table. "It looks pretty nice," she said. "I think I'm feeling hungry."

This made us all feel good, especially me, for I couldn't remember the last time she had felt any hunger or had eaten something I cooked. We began to eat. My mother picked up a piece of salmon toast and took a tiny corner in her mouth. She rolled it around for a moment and then pushed it out with the tip of her tongue, letting it fall back onto her plate. She swallowed hard, as if to quell a gag, then glanced up to see if we had noticed. Of course we all had. She attempted a bean cake, some cheese, and then a slice of fruit, but nothing was any use.

She nodded at me anyway, and said, "Oh, it's very good." But I was already feeling lost and I put down my plate abruptly, nearly shattering it on the thick glass. There was an ugly pause before my father asked me in a weary, gentle voice if anything was wrong, and I answered that it was nothing, it was the last night of a long year, and we were together, and I was simply relieved. At midnight, I poured out glasses of champagne, even one for my mother, who took a deep sip. Her manner grew playful and light, and I helped her shuffle to her mattress, and she lay down in the place where in a brief week she was dead.

My mother could whip up most anything, but during our first years of living in this country we ate only Korean foods. At my harangue-like behest, my mother set herself to learning how to cook exotic American dishes. Luckily, a kind neighbor, Mrs. Churchill, a tall, florid young woman with flaxen hair, taught my mother her most trusted recipes. Mrs. Churchill's two young sons, palish, weepy boys with identical crew cuts, always accompanied her, and though I liked them well enough, I would slip away from them after a few minutes, for I knew that the real action would be in the kitchen, where their mother was playing guide. Mrs. Churchill hailed from the state of Maine, where the finest Swedish meatballs and tuna casserole and angel food cake in America are made. She readily demonstrated certain techniques—how to layer wet sheets of pasta for a lasagna or whisk up a simple roux, for example. She often brought gift shoeboxes containing curious ingredients like dried oregano, instant yeast, and cream of mushroom soup. The two women, though at ease and jolly with each other, had difficulty communicating, and this was made worse by the often confusing terminology of Western cuisine ("corned beef," "deviled eggs"). Although I was just learning the language myself, I'd gladly play the interlocutor, jumping back and forth between their places at the counter, dipping my fingers into whatever sauce lay about.

I was an insistent child, and, being my mother's firstborn, much too 15 prized. My mother could say no to me, and did often enough, but anyone who knew us—particularly my father and sister—could tell how much the denying pained her. And if I was overconscious of her indulgence even then, and suffered the rushing pangs of guilt that she could inflict upon me with the slightest wounded turn of her lip, I was too happily obtuse and venal to let her cease. She reminded me daily that I was her sole son, her reason for living, and that if she were to lose me, in either body or spirit, she wished that God would mercifully smite her, strike her down like a weak branch.

In the traditional fashion, she was the house accountant, the maid, the launderer, the disciplinarian, the driver, the secretary, and, of course, the cook. She was also my first basketball coach. In South Korea, where girls' high school basketball is a popular spectator sport, she had been a star, the point guard for the national high school team that once won the all-Asia championships. I learned this one Saturday during the summer, when I asked my father if he would go down to the schoolyard and shoot some baskets with me. I had just finished the fifth grade, and wanted desperately to make the middle school team the coming fall. He called for my mother and sister to come along. When we arrived, my sister immediately ran off to the swings, and I recall being annoyed that my mother wasn't following her. I dribbled clumsily around the key, on the verge of losing control of the ball, and flung a flat shot that caromed wildly off the rim. The ball bounced to my father, who took a few not so graceful dribbles and made an easy layup. He dribbled out and then drove to the hoop for a layup on the other side. He rebounded his shot and passed the ball to my mother, who had been watching us from the foul line. She turned from the basket and began heading the other way.

"*Um-mah,*"[2] I cried at her, my exasperation already bubbling over, "the basket's over here!"

After a few steps she turned around, and from where the professional three-point line must be now, she effortlessly flipped the ball up in a two-handed set shot, its flight truer and higher than I'd witnessed from any boy or man. The ball arced cleanly into the hoop, stiffly popping the chain-link net. All afternoon, she rained in shot after shot, as my father and I scrambled after her.

When we got home from the playground, my mother showed me the photograph album of her team's championship run. For years I kept it in my room, on the same shelf that housed the scrapbooks I made of

[2]Mommy (Korean).

basketball stars, with magazine clippings of slick players like Bubbles Hawkins and Pistol Pete and George (the Iceman) Gervin.

It puzzled me how much she considered her own history to be im- 20 material, and if she never patently diminished herself, she was able to finesse a kind of self-removal by speaking of my father whenever she could. She zealously recounted his excellence as a student in medical school and reminded me, each night before I started my homework, of how hard he drove himself in his work to make a life for us. She said that because of his Asian face and imperfect English, he was "working two times the American doctors." I knew that she was building him up, buttressing him with both genuine admiration and her own brand of anxious braggadocio, and that her overarching concern was that I might fail to see him as she wished me to—in the most dawning light, his pose steadfast and solitary.

In the year before I left for Exeter, I became weary of her oft-repeated accounts of my father's success. I was a teenager, and so ever inclined to be dismissive and bitter toward anything that had to do with family and home. Often enough, my mother was the object of my derision. Suddenly, her life seemed so small to me. She was there, and sometimes, I thought, *always* there, as if she were confined to the four walls of our house. I would even complain about her cooking. Mostly, though, I was getting more and more impatient with the difficulty she encountered in doing everyday things. I was afraid for her. One day, we got into a terrible argument when she asked me to call the bank, to question a discrepancy she had discovered in the monthly statement. I asked her why she couldn't call herself. I was stupid and brutal, and I knew exactly how to wound her.

"Whom do I talk to?" she said. She would mostly speak to me in Korean, and I would answer in English.

"The bank manager, who else?"

"What do I say?"

"Whatever you want to say." 25

"Don't speak to me like that!" she cried.

"It's just that you should be able to do it yourself," I said.

"You know how I feel about this!"

"Well, maybe then you should consider it *practice*," I answered lightly, using the Korean word to make sure she understood.

Her face blanched, and her neck suddenly became rigid, as if I were   30
throttling her. She nearly struck me right then, but instead she bit her
lip and ran upstairs. I followed her, pleading for forgiveness at her
door. But it was the one time in our life that I couldn't convince
her, melt her resolve with the blandishments of a spoiled son.

When my mother was feeling strong enough, or was in particularly
good spirits, she would roll her machine into the kitchen and sit at the
table and watch me work. She wore pajamas day and night, mostly old
pairs of mine.

She said, "I can't tell, what are you making?"

"*Mahn-doo*[3] filling."

"You didn't salt the cabbage and squash."

"Was I supposed to?"   35

"Of course. Look, it's too wet. Now the skins will get soggy before
you can fry them."

"What should I do?"

"It's too late. Maybe it'll be OK if you work quickly. Why didn't you
ask me?"

"You were finally sleeping."

"You should have woken me."   40

"No way."

She sighed, as deeply as her weary lungs would allow.

"I don't know how you were going to make it without me."

"I don't know, either. I'll remember the salt next time."

"You better. And not too much."   45

We often talked like this, our tone decidedly matter-of-fact, chin up,
just this side of being able to bear it. Once, while inspecting a potato
fritter batter I was making, she asked me if she had ever done anything
that I wished she hadn't done. I thought for a moment, and told her no.
In the next breath, she wondered aloud if it was right of her to have let
me go to Exeter, to live away from the house while I was so young. She
tested the batter's thickness with her finger and called for more flour.
Then she asked if, given a choice, I would go to Exeter again.

[3]Korean dumplings.

I wasn't sure what she was getting at, and I told her that I couldn't be certain, but probably yes, I would. She snorted at this and said it was my leaving home that had once so troubled our relationship. "Remember how I had so much difficulty talking to you? Remember?"

She believed back then that I had found her more and more ignorant each time I came home. She said she never blamed me, for this was the way she knew it would be with my wonderful new education. Nothing I could say seemed to quell the notion. But I knew that the problem wasn't simply the *education*; the first time I saw her again after starting school, barely six weeks later, when she and my father visited me on Parents Day, she had already grown nervous and distant. After the usual campus events, we had gone to the motel where they were staying in a nearby town and sat on the beds in our room. She seemed to sneak looks at me, as though I might discover a horrible new truth if our eyes should meet.

My own secret feeling was that I had missed my parents greatly, my mother especially, and much more than I had anticipated. I couldn't tell them that these first weeks were a mere blur to me, that I felt completely overwhelmed by all the studies and my much brighter friends and the thousand irritating details of living alone, and that I had really learned nothing, save perhaps how to put on a necktie while sprinting to class. I felt as if I had plunged too deep into the world, which, to my great horror, was much larger than I had ever imagined.

I welcomed the lull of the motel room. My father and I had nearly 50 dozed off when my mother jumped up excitedly, murmured how stupid she was, and hurried to the closet by the door. She pulled out our old metal cooler and dragged it between the beds. She lifted the top and began unpacking plastic containers, and I thought she would never stop. One after the other they came out, each with a dish that traveled well—a salted stewed meat, rolls of Korean-style sushi. I opened a container of radish kimchi and suddenly the room bloomed with its odor, and I reveled in the very peculiar sensation (which perhaps only true kimchi lovers know) of simultaneously drooling and gagging as I breathed it all in. For the next few minutes, they watched me eat. I'm not certain that I was even hungry. But after weeks of pork

41

parmigiana and chicken patties and wax beans, I suddenly realized that I had lost all the savor in my life. And it seemed I couldn't get enough of it back. I ate and I ate, so much and so fast that I actually went to the bathroom and vomited. I came out dizzy and sated with the phantom warmth of my binge.

And beneath the face of her worry, I thought, my mother was smiling.

From that day, my mother prepared a certain meal to welcome me home. It was always the same. Even as I rode the school's shuttle bus from Exeter to Logan airport, I could already see the exact arrangement of my mother's table.

I knew that we would eat in the kitchen, the table brimming with plates. There was the *kalbi*, of course, broiled or grilled depending on the season. Leaf lettuce, to wrap the meat with. Bowls of garlicky clam broth with miso and tofu and fresh spinach. Shavings of cod dusted in flour and then dipped in egg wash and fried. Glass noodles with onions and shiitake. Scallion-and-hot-pepper pancakes. Chilled steamed shrimp. Seasoned salads of bean sprouts, spinach, and white radish. Crispy squares of seaweed. Steamed rice with barley and red beans. Homemade kimchi. It was all there—the old flavors I knew, the beautiful salt, the sweet, the excellent taste.

After the meal, my father and I talked about school, but I could never say enough for it to make any sense. My father would often recall his high school principal, who had gone to England to study the methods and traditions of the public schools, and regaled students with stories of the great Eton man. My mother sat with us, paring fruit, not saying a word but taking everything in. When it was time to go to bed, my father said good night first. I usually watched television until the early morning. My mother would sit with me for an hour or two, perhaps until she was accustomed to me again, and only then would she kiss me and head upstairs to sleep.

During the following days, it was always the cooking that started our conversations. She'd hold an inquest over the cold leftovers we ate at lunch, discussing each dish in terms of its balance of flavors or what might have been prepared differently. But mostly I begged her to leave the dishes alone. I wish I had paid more attention. After her death, when my father and I were the only ones left in the house, drifting through the rooms like ghosts, I sometimes tried to make that meal for him. Though it was too much for two, I made each dish anyway, taking as much care as I could. But nothing turned out quite right—not the color, not the smell. At the table, neither of us said much of anything. And we had to eat the food for days.

I remember washing rice in the kitchen one day and my mother's saying in English, from her usual seat, "I made a big mistake."

"About Exeter?"

"Yes. I made a big mistake. You should be with us for that time. I should never let you go there."

"So why did you?" I said.

"Because I didn't know I was going to die." 60

I let her words pass. For the first time in her life, she was letting herself speak her full mind, so what else could I do?

"But you know what?" she spoke up. "It was better for you. If you stayed home, you would not like me so much now."

I suggested that maybe I would like her even more.

She shook her head. "Impossible."

Sometimes I still think about what she said, about having made a 65 mistake. I would have left home for college, that was never in doubt, but those years I was away at boarding school grew more precious to her as her illness progressed. After many months of exhaustion and pain and the haze of the drugs, I thought that her mind was beginning to fade, for more and more it seemed that she was seeing me again as her fifteen-year-old boy, the one she had dropped off in New Hampshire on a cloudy September afternoon.

I remember the first person I met, another new student, named Zack, who walked to the welcome picnic with me. I had planned to eat with my parents—my mother had brought a coolerful of food even that first day—but I learned of the cookout and told her that I should probably go. I wanted to go, of course. I was excited, and no doubt fearful and nervous, and I must have thought I was only thinking ahead. She agreed wholeheartedly, saying I certainly should. I walked them to the car, and perhaps I hugged them, before saying goodbye. One day, after she died, my father told me what happened on the long drive home to Syracuse.

He was driving the car, looking straight ahead. Traffic was light on the Massachusetts Turnpike, and the sky was nearly dark. They had driven for more than two hours and had not yet spoken a word. He then heard a strange sound from her, a kind of muffled chewing noise, as if something inside her were grinding its way out.

"So, what's the matter?" he said, trying to keep an edge to his voice.

She looked at him with her ashen face and she burst into tears. He began to cry himself, and pulled the car over onto the narrow shoulder of the turnpike, where they stayed for the next half hour or so, the blank-faced cars droning by them in the cold, onrushing night.

Every once in a while, when I think of her, I'm driving alone some-   70
where on the highway. In the twilight, I see their car off to the side, a blue Olds coupe with a landau top, and as I pass them by I look back in the mirror and I see them again, the two figures huddling together in the front seat. Are they sleeping? Or kissing? Are they all right?

STUDY QUESTIONS

1. Why is food an important part of Lee's relationship with his mother?

2. Lee tells his NARRATIVE out of CHRONOLOGICAL ORDER, with FLASHBACKS. What is the effect of breaking up the story in this manner? How effective is this STRATEGY?

3. *For Writing.* Write a PERSONAL ESSAY in which you explore the significance of food in your family. What kinds of food define your family? Do you have special meals? If food is not important, then what is the significance of that lack of a clear relationship?

JERALD WALKER { *Dragon Slayers*

JERALD WALKER (b. 1964) earned his MFA in creative writing from the
Iowa Writers' Workshop and his PhD in interdisciplinary studies from the
University of Iowa. He is cofounder of *The Bridge*, a literary/arts journal
that, since it was first published in 2003, has received some fifty national
awards. Walker's work has appeared in numerous periodicals, including *The
North American Review* and *The Chronicle of Higher Education*, as well as in
anthologies such as *Best American Essays* (2007) and *Best African American
Essays* (2009). His memoir, *Street Shadows,* appeared in 2010.

In "Dragon Slayers," published in the *Iowa Review* in 2006, Walker
writes of his experiences as a student at the Iowa Writer's Workshop,
relating events that changed not only the way he wrote but also the way he
viewed African Americans—not as victims, but as heroes. The author never
explicitly names either the dragons or the dragon slayers referred to in his
title, but leaves the reader to infer who they are, opening up the possibility
for multiple ways of reading his essay. As you read, think about Walker's
ethos and how he presents his younger self.

I WAS AT A CHRISTMAS party with a man who wanted me to hate him.
I should hate *all* whites, he felt, for what they have done to me. I
thought hard about what whites have done to me. I was forty, old
enough to have accumulated a few unpleasant racial encounters, but
nothing of any significance came to mind. The man was astonished at
this response. "How about *slavery*?" he asked. I explained, as politely

as I could, that I had not been a slave. "But you *feel* its effects," he snapped. "Racism, discrimination, and prejudice will *always* be a problem for you in this country. White people," he insisted, "are your *oppressors.*" I glanced around the room, just as one of my oppressors happened by. She was holding a tray of canapés. She offered me one. I asked the man if, as a form of reparations, I should take two.

It was mid-way through my third year in academia. I had survived mountains of papers, apathetic students, cantankerous colleagues, boring meetings, sleep deprivation, and two stalkers, and now I was up against a man who had been mysteriously transported from 1962. He even looked the part, with lavish sideburns and solid, black-rimmed glasses. He wasn't an academic, but rather the spouse of one. In fact, he had no job at all, a dual act of defiance, he felt, against a patriarchal and capitalistic society. He was a fun person to talk with, especially if, like me, you enjoyed driving white liberals up the wall. And the surest way to do that, if you were black, was to deny them the chance to pity you.

He'd spotted me thirty minutes earlier while I stood alone at the dining room table, grazing on various appetizers. My wife Brenda had drifted off somewhere, and the room buzzed with pockets of conversation and laughter. The man joined me. I accepted his offer of a gin and tonic. We talked local politics for a moment, or rather he talked and I listened, because it wasn't something I knew much about, before moving on to football, our kids, and finally my classes. He was particularly interested in my African American Literature course. "Did you have any black students?" he inquired.

"We started with two," I said, "but ended with twenty-eight." I let his puzzled expression linger until I'd eaten a stuffed mushroom. "Everyone who takes the course has to agree to be black for the duration of the semester."

"Really?" he asked, laughing. "What do they do, smear their faces 5 with burnt cork?"

"Not a bad idea," I said. "But for now, they simply have to think like blacks, but in a way different from what they probably expect." I told him that black literature is often approached as records of oppression, but that my students don't focus on white cruelty, but rather its flip side: black courage. "After all," I continued, "slaves and their immediate descendants were by and large heroic, not pathetic, or I wouldn't be standing here."

The man was outraged. "You're letting whites off the hook," he said. "You're absolving them of responsibility, of the obligation to atone for past and present wrongs. . . ." He went on in this vein for a good while, and I am pleased to say that I goaded him until he stormed across the room and stood with his wife who, after he'd spoken with her, glanced in my direction to see, no doubt, a traitor to the black race. That was unfortunate. I'd like to think I betray whites, too.

More precisely, it's the belief that blacks are primarily victims that I betray, a common view held by both races. I, too, held it for many years. When I was in my early twenties and making my first crude attempts at writing fiction, I'd sit at my word processor and pound out stories brimming with blacks who understood only anger and pain. My settings were always ghettoes, because that was what I knew, and the plots centered on hardship and suffering, because I knew that, too. And I also knew this: white society was responsible for the existence of this miserable world, and it was my duty, as a black artist, to make this clear. Three of these stories gained me acceptance into the Iowa Writers' Workshop. It was there that my awakening occurred.

My first course was with Frank Conroy,[1] the program's director. He was brutally honest and harbored a militant obsession with clarity. Most of the two-hour long classes were spent with him shredding the stories and our egos. We squirmed in our seats and wiped our brows as he did his infamous line-by-line, zeroing in on words and phrases that confused the work's meaning or failed to make unequivocal sense. It was the most intense and best writing class that I'd ever had. I went into the second semester confident that my prose had improved, and that the most difficult course was behind me.

Randomly, I decided to take a workshop with James Alan McPherson.[2] During the break before classes resumed, I read for the

10

---

[1]American author (1936–2005), best known for the memoir *Stop-Time* (1967).
[2]American author (b. 1943), winner of the Pulitzer Prize for his short-story collection *Elbow Room* (1978).

first time his books *Hue and Cry* and *Elbow Room*. The impact his writing had on me was profound. He, too, chronicled the lives of African Americans, and he had done it in short story form, my genre of choice; this was the model I'd been searching for. I read the stories over and over again, convinced that I had found my literary father.

The contrast between Conroy and McPherson could not have been more stark. Conroy was tall, white, and boisterous; McPherson was short, black, and shy. Conroy cursed, yelled, laughed, and joked, McPherson rarely spoke at all, and when he did his voice was so quiet you often couldn't hear him. The students dominated his workshops. I was disappointed. McPherson was a Pulitzer Prize winner, after all, the first African American to receive that honor for fiction. He was the recipient of a MacArthur "Genius" grant, as well as countless other awards. I wanted his wisdom. I wanted his insight. He gave it mid-semester, when it was time to workshop my first story.

"Before we begin today," he said, "I'd like to make a few comments." This was new; he'd never prefaced a story before. A smile crept on my face as I allowed myself to imagine him praising me for my depiction of a den of heroin addicts, for this was not easy to do, requiring, among other things, an intimate knowledge of heroin addicts and a certain flair for profanity.

"Are you all familiar with gangster rap?" McPherson asked. We were, despite the fact that, besides me, all of the students were white and mostly middle- to upper-class. While we each nodded our familiarity with the genre, McPherson reached into a shopping bag he'd brought and removed a magazine. He opened it to a pre-marked page, on which was a picture of a rapper, cloaked in jewelry and guns and leaning against the hood of a squad car. Behind him was a sprawling slum. "This person raps about the ghetto," McPherson said, "but he doesn't live in the ghetto. He lives in a wealthy white suburb with his wife and daughter. His daughter attends a predominantly white, private school. That's what this article is about." He closed the magazine and returned it to the bag. "What some gangster rappers are doing is using black stereotypes because white people eat that stuff up. But these images are false, they're dishonest. Some rappers are selling out their race for personal gain." He paused again, this time to hold up my story.

"That's what this writer is doing with his work." He sat my story back on the table. "Okay, that's all I have to say. You can discuss it now."

For a few seconds, the only sound in the room was of my labored breathing. And then someone said, "McPherson's right. The story is garbage."

"Complete rubbish," said another. 15

And so it went from there.

I did not sleep that night. At 8 a.m., when I could hold out no longer, I called McPherson at home and demanded a conference. He agreed to meet me in his office in ten minutes.

He was there when I arrived, sitting behind his desk. The desk was bare except for a copy of my story, and the office was bare except for the desk and two chairs. The built-in bookshelves held nothing, and nothing hung on the walls. There was no dressing on the window, no telephone, and no computer. It might have been the janitor's office, a place to catch a few winks while the mopped floors dried. And McPherson might have been the janitor. His blue shirt was a mass of wrinkles and his eyes were bloodshot. His trademark hat, a straw, beige Kangol, seemed to rest at an odd angle on his head; from beneath it a single, long braid had worked its way free and dangled rebelliously behind his right ear. He noticed me staring at it and poked it back into concealment.

"Are you okay?" he asked. His voice was gentle, full of concern. "You sounded like a crazy man on the phone."

"Well, I'm *not* a crazy man." I reached forward to tap my finger on 20 my story and proceeded to rant and rave as only a crazy man could. "I did *not* make this stuff up," I insisted. "I'm *from* the ghetto." I went through the characters, one by one, citing various relatives on whom they were based, and I mentioned that, just the week before, my younger brother had been shot in the back while in McDonald's. I told him I had another brother who was in and out of prison, a heroin-addict sister-in-law, that I had once been arrested for car theft (falsely, but that was beside the point), and that many, many of my friends were presently still living in the miserable community in which I'd been raised. "You misread my story," I said in conclusion, "and you misread *me.*" I leaned back and folded my arms across my chest, waiting for his apology. Instead, I watched as he sprang from his chair and hurried from the room. He turned left into the hall, and a moment later he passed going right, with Frank Conroy calling after him, and then they passed left again, now with Connie Brothers, the program's administrator, in tow, and after two more passes this awful parade came to an end somewhere out of view. Now Connie stood before me, looking as nauseous as I felt. "Jim is the kindest soul on this earth," she said quietly. "Why, why would you insult him?"

For an instant, I saw myself at twelve, looking at a closed front door, behind which was my first love, who had just dumped me and left me standing on her porch trying, unsuccessfully, not to cry.

Connie magically produced a tissue and handed it to me. She rubbed my shoulders while I rambled incoherently, something about sleep deprivation and McPherson being my father. "It's okay, sweetie," Connie said. "I'll talk to him."

McPherson returned momentarily. I apologized. He told me it was okay, that workshops can make people uptight and sensitive. It had been difficult for him, too, he explained, when he was a student there in the seventies. There was a lull in the conversation before he said, "So, where're your people from?"

He still doesn't believe me, I thought. I mumbled, "Chicago."

"No, no. That's where they *are*. Where are they *from?*"

"Oh, sorry. Arkansas."

"Mine are from Georgia," he said. He smiled and added, "That place is a *motherfucker.*"

The essence of black America was conveyed in that response, a toughness of spirit, humor laced with tragedy, but at that moment all I saw was the man who had rejected my vision. Defeated, I thanked him for agreeing to meet with me as I rose to leave. He stood and shook my hand. As I was walking out the door, he called my name. I turned to face him.

"Stereotypes are valuable," he said. "But *only* if you use them to your advantage. They present your readers with something they'll recognize, and it pulls them into what appears to be familiar territory, a comfort zone. But once they're in, you have to move them beyond the stereotype. You have to show them what's real."

51

"What's real?" I asked.   30

Without hesitation, he said, "You."

It was one of those things that you instantly recognize as profound, and then, because you don't quite understand it, try to forget as quickly as you can. It was also one of those things that you cannot forget. And so it roamed freely in my subconscious, occasionally coming into sharp focus to remind me of its presence, but I allowed myself to be consumed by it no more than I would a housefly. For about a year. And then I went to see him again.

"I was wondering," I said, "if you wouldn't mind supervising an independent project."

"That depends," he responded, "on what you'd like to study."

"Me," I said. "I want to study me."   35

We started with black folklore and history. Next we moved on to blues and jazz, and then we covered a broad range of black literature and culture. We studied black intellectuals and philosophers, sociologists, anthropologists, activists, filmmakers, and ex-cons. For four years, we dissected nearly every aspect of black life and thought, and, in the process, a theme emerged that had been there all along: *life* is a motherfucker; living it anyway, and sometimes laughing in the process, is where humanity is won.

And this is what I learned about me: I had become my own stereotype, a character in one of my short stories who insisted on seeing himself primarily as a repository of pain and defeat, despite overwhelming evidence to the contrary. The very people with whom I had been raised and had dedicated myself to rendering in prose had become victims of my myopia. My stories showed people being affected by drug addiction, racism, poverty, murder, crime, violence, but they said nothing about the spirit that, despite being confronted with what often amounted to certain defeat, would continue to struggle and aspire for something better. That old slave song, "We Shall Overcome," pretty much says it all.

The coursework I conducted with McPherson ultimately contributed to a doctorate in Interdisciplinary Studies. McPherson served as my dissertation chair. I knew, when I started my academic career, that I owed him a debt to teach black literature in a certain way. "Less time needs to be spent on the dragons," he told me once, "and more on our ability to forge swords for battle, and the skill with which we've used them."

The man at the Christmas party, of course, would rather that I talk about the dragons. And at first, when students take my class, they are surprised, even a bit disappointed, to see the course will not head in that direction. But by the end of the semester, they have been invariably uplifted by the heroic nature of African Americans, in part, perhaps, because it is the nature found in us all. Sometimes, students thank me for this approach. On occasion, they ask me where I got the idea. I tell them I got it from my father.

STUDY QUESTIONS

1. How does Walker surprise and challenge the white man he meets at the party? How is Walker himself surprised and challenged by Professor McPherson? How does McPherson become his SYMBOLIC "father"?

2. How does Walker's younger self DEFINE himself? How do you know? How does his older self, the one relating the story, define himself? Refer to specific passages in your RESPONSE.

3. Who do you think is Walker's AUDIENCE? How can you tell?

4. *For Writing.* Consider the STEREOTYPES or labels that a stranger or a casual acquaintance might attach to you. Which of these labels are "dragons"— ideas that, once you've internalized them, can undermine an authentic and positive self-concept? In a PERSONAL ESSAY, explore how you would "slay" these dragons.

BELL HOOKS $\Big\{$ *Talking Back*

BELL HOOKS (b. 1952) was born Gloria Jean Watkins in Hopkinsville, Kentucky, one of six siblings. Her father worked as a janitor, while her mother stayed home to care for the children. After attending segregated schools for her early education, hooks graduated from the integrated Hopkinsville High School before leaving Kentucky for California. She then graduated from Stanford University with a BA in English in 1973, earned an MA in English from the University of Wisconsin–Madison in 1976, and completed her PhD dissertation on Toni Morrison at the University of California–Santa Cruz in 1983. An academic, hooks has taught at Yale University, Oberlin College, the City College of New York, and Berea College, where she currently serves as Distinguished Professor in Residence. She writes on the intersection of race, class, and gender, taking care to emphasize the "folk," whose perspective she sees as missing from white feminist scholarship. Her books include *Ain't I a Woman? Black Women and Feminism* (1981), *Feminist Theory: From Margin to Center* (1984), the children's picture book *Happy to Be Nappy* (1999), and *Yearning: Race, Gender, and Cultural Politics* (1990).

This essay comes from hooks's 1989 book *Talking Back: Thinking Feminist, Thinking Black.* It explicates her need for her voice to be heard within black culture, a culture that tends to ignore the experiences of black women, according to hooks. As you read, consider hooks's discussions of talking and of being heard. Watch for ways the author defines "talking back," "right speech," and "silence."

IN THE WORLD OF THE southern black community I grew up in, "back talk" and "talking back," meant speaking as an equal to an authority figure. It meant daring to disagree and sometimes it just meant having an opinion. In the "old school," children were meant to be seen and not heard. My great-grandparents, grandparents, and parents were all from the old school. To make yourself heard if you were a child was to invite punishment, the back-hand lick, the slap across the face that would catch you unaware, or the feel of switches stinging your arms and legs.

To speak then when one was not spoken to was a courageous act—an act of risk and daring. And yet it was hard not to speak in warm rooms where heated discussions began at the crack of dawn, women's voices filling the air, giving orders, making threats, fussing. Black men may have excelled in the art of poetic preaching in the male-dominated church, but in the church of the home, where the everyday rules of how to live and how to act were established, it was black women who preached. There, black women spoke in a language so rich, so poetic, that it felt to me like being shut off from life, smothered to death if one were not allowed to participate.

It was in that world of woman talk (the men were often silent, often absent) that was born in me the craving to speak, to have a voice, and not just any voice but one that could be identified as belonging to me. To make my voice, I had to speak, to hear myself talk—and talk I did—darting in and out of grown folks' conversations and dialogues, answering questions that were not directed at me, endlessly asking questions, making speeches. Needless to say, the punishments for these acts of speech seemed endless. They were intended to silence me—the child—and more particularly the girl child. Had I been a boy, they might have encouraged me to speak believing that I might some-day be called to preach. There was no "calling" for talking girls, no legitimized rewarded speech. The punishments I received for "talk-ing back" were intended to suppress all possibility that I would create my own speech. That speech was to be suppressed so that the "right speech of womanhood" would emerge.

Within feminist circles, silence is often seen as the sexist "right speech of womanhood"—the sign of woman's submission to patriar-chal authority. This emphasis on woman's silence may be an accurate remembering of what has taken place in the households of women from WASP backgrounds in the United States, but in black communities (and diverse ethnic communities), women have not been silent. Their voices can be heard. Certainly for black women, our struggle has not been to emerge from silence into speech but to change the nature and direction of our speech, to make a speech that compels listeners, one that is heard.

Our speech, "the right speech of womanhood," was often the solilo- 5 quy, the talking into thin air, the talking to ears that do not hear you— the talk that is simply not listened to. Unlike the black male preacher whose speech was to be heard, who was to be listened to, whose words were to be remembered, the voices of black women—giving orders, making threats, fussing—could be tuned out, could become a kind of background music, audible but not acknowledged as significant speech. Dialogue—the sharing of speech and recognition—took place not between mother and child or mother and male authority figure but among black women. I can remember watching fascinated as our mother talked with her mother, sisters, and women friends. The intimacy and intensity of their speech—the satisfaction they received from talking to one another, the pleasure, the joy. It was in this world of woman speech, loud talk, angry words, women with tongues quick and sharp, tender sweet tongues, touching our world with their words, that I made speech my birthright—and the right to voice, to author- ship, a privilege I would not be denied. It was in that world and because of it that I came to dream of writing, to write.

Writing was a way to capture speech, to hold onto it, keep it close. And so I wrote down bits and pieces of conversations, confessing in cheap diaries that soon fell apart from too much handling, expressing the intensity of my sorrow, the anguish of speech—for I was always saying the wrong thing, asking the wrong questions. I could not confine my speech to the necessary corners and concerns of life. I hid these writings under my bed, in pillow stuffings, among faded underwear. When my sisters found and read them, they ridiculed and mocked me—poking fun. I felt violated, ashamed, as if the secret parts of my self had been exposed, brought into the open, and hung like newly clean laundry, out in the air for everyone to see. The fear of exposure, the fear that one's deepest emotions and innermost thoughts will be dismissed as mere nonsense, felt by so many young girls keeping diaries, holding and hiding speech, seems to me now one of the barriers that women have always needed and still need to destroy so that we are no longer pushed into secrecy or silence.

Despite my feelings of violation, of exposure, I continued to speak and write, choosing my hiding places well, learning to destroy work when no safe place could be found. I was never taught absolute silence, I was taught that it was important to speak but to talk a talk that was in itself a silence. Taught to speak and yet beware of the betrayal of too much heard speech, I experienced intense confusion and deep anxiety in my efforts to speak and write. Reciting poems at Sunday afternoon church service might be rewarded. Writing a poem (when one's time could be "better" spent sweeping, ironing, learning to cook) was luxurious activity, indulged in at the expense of others. Questioning authority, raising issues that were not deemed appropriate subjects brought pain, punishments—like telling mama I wanted to die before her because I could not live without her—that was crazy talk, crazy speech, the kind that would lead you to end up in a mental institution. "Little girl," I would be told, "if you don't stop all this crazy talk and crazy acting you are going to end up right out there at Western State."[1]

Madness, not just physical abuse, was the punishment for too much talk if you were female. Yet even as this fear of madness haunted me, hanging over my writing like a monstrous shadow, I could not stop the words, making thought, writing speech. For this terrible madness which I feared, which I was sure was the destiny of daring women born to intense speech (after all, the authorities emphasized this point daily), was not as threatening as imposed silence, as suppressed speech.

Safety and sanity were to be sacrificed if I was to experience defiant speech. Though I risked them both, deep-seated fears and anxieties characterized my childhood days. I would speak but I would not ride a bike, play hardball, or hold the gray kitten. Writing about the ways

---

[1]Western State Hospital, opened in 1854, is a mental health facility in Hopkinsville, Kentucky, where the author grew up.

we are traumatized in our growing-up years, psychoanalyst Alice Miller makes the point in *For Your Own Good* that it is not clear why childhood wounds become for some folk an opportunity to grow, to move forward rather than backward in the process of self-realization. Certainly, when I reflect on the trials of my growing-up years, the many punishments, I can see now that in resistance I learned to be vigilant in the nourishment of my spirit, to be tough, to courageously protect that spirit from forces that would break it.

While punishing me, my parents often spoke about the necessity of 10 breaking my spirit. Now when I ponder the silences, the voices that are not heard, the voices of those wounded and/or oppressed individuals who do not speak or write, I contemplate the acts of persecution, torture—the terrorism that breaks spirits, that makes creativity impossible. I write these words to bear witness to the primacy of resistance struggle in any situation of domination (even within family life); to the strength and power that emerges from sustained resistance and the profound conviction that these forces can be healing, can protect us from dehumanization and despair.

These early trials, wherein I learned to stand my ground, to keep my spirit intact, came vividly to mind after I published *Ain't I A Woman* and the book was sharply and harshly criticized. While I had expected a climate of critical dialogue, I was not expecting a critical avalanche that had the power in its intensity to crush the spirit, to push one into silence. Since that time, I have heard stories about black women, about women of color, who write and publish (even when the work is quite successful) having nervous breakdowns, being made mad because they cannot bear the harsh responses of family, friends, and unknown critics, or becoming silent, unproductive. Surely, the absence of a humane critical response has tremendous impact on the writer from any oppressed, colonized group who endeavors to speak. For us, true speaking is not solely an expression of creative power; it is an act of resistance, a political gesture that challenges politics of domination that would render us nameless and voiceless. As such, it is a courageous act—as such, it represents a threat. To those who wield oppressive power, that which is threatening must necessarily be wiped out, annihilated, silenced.

Recently, efforts by black women writers to call attention to our work serve to highlight both our presence and absence. Whenever I peruse women's bookstores; I am struck not by the rapidly growing body of feminist writing by black women, but by the paucity of available published material. Those of us who write and are published remain few in number. The context of silence is varied and multi-dimensional. Most obvious are the ways racism, sexism, and class exploitation act to suppress and silence. Less obvious are the inner struggles, the efforts made to gain the necessary confidence to write, to re-write, to fully develop craft and skill—and the extent to which such efforts fail.

Although I have wanted writing to be my life-work since childhood, it has been difficult for me to claim "writer" as part of that which identifies and shapes my everyday reality. Even after publishing books, I would often speak of wanting to be a writer as though these works did not exist. And though I would be told, "you are a writer," I was not yet ready to fully affirm this truth. Part of myself was still held captive by domineering forces of history, of familial life that had charted a map of silence, of right speech. I had not completely let go of the fear of saying the wrong thing, of being punished. Somewhere in the deep recesses of my mind, I believed I could avoid both responsibility and punishment if I did not declare myself a writer.

One of the many reasons I chose to write using the pseudonym bell hooks, a family name (mother to Sarah Oldham, grandmother to Rosa Bell Oldham, great-grandmother to me), was to construct a writer-identity that would challenge and subdue all impulses leading me away from speech into silence. I was a young girl buying bubble gum at the corner store when I first really heard the full name bell hooks. I had just "talked back" to a grown person. Even now I can recall the surprised look, the mocking tones that informed me I must be kin to bell hooks— a sharp-tongued woman, a woman who spoke her mind, a woman who was not afraid to talk back. I claimed this legacy of defiance, of will, of courage, affirming my link to female ancestors who were bold and daring in their speech. Unlike my bold and daring mother and grandmother, who were not supportive of talking back, even though they were assertive and powerful in their speech, bell hooks as I discovered, claimed, and invented her was my ally, my support.

That initial act of talking back outside the home was empowering.   15
It was the first of many acts of defiant speech that would make it possible for me to emerge as an independent thinker and writer. In retro-
spect, "talking back" became for me a rite of initiation, testing my
courage, strengthening my commitment, preparing me for the days
ahead—the days when writing, rejection notices, periods of silence,
publication, ongoing development seem impossible but necessary.

Moving from silence into speech is for the oppressed, the colonized, the exploited, and those who stand and struggle side by side
a gesture of defiance that heals, that makes new life and new growth
possible. It is that act of speech, of "talking back," that is no mere
gesture of empty words, that is the expression of our movement from
object to subject—the liberated voice.

STUDY QUESTIONS

1. What distinction does hooks make between silence for "women from WASP backgrounds" and silence for women from "black communities"? How did hooks get her pseudonym, and how does it connect to those silences?

2. Find examples of hooks's use of the strategy of COMPARISON AND CONTRAST. How does she use the device to strengthen and develop her essay?

3. Hooks ANALYZES THE PROCESS of black women using their voices effectively. How did she learn to "talk back"? What obstacles did she encounter, and how did she surmount them?

4. *For Writing.* Hooks demonstrates that the process of *claiming* and *using* both one's speaking and one's writing voice is informed by "silence." In an essay, explore the various kinds of silences that hooks experiences. How do they function to limit black women's voices? What, according to hooks, must a black woman do to challenge them? Be sure to discuss concrete examples from the text.

JUNOT DIAZ { *Fiesta, 1980*

JUNOT DIAZ (b. 1968) was born in Santo Domingo, Dominican
Republic, the middle child of five. While his father lived and worked in
New Jersey, Diaz lived with his mother, grandparents, and siblings. Diaz
immigrated to the United States in 1974. He holds a bachelor's degree
from Rutgers University and a master of fine arts in creative writing from
Cornell University. He currently teaches at the Massachusetts Institute
of Technology. His work includes the novel *The Brief Wondrous Life of
Oscar Wao* (2007), for which he won the Pulitzer Prize for fiction, and
the story collections *This Is How You Lose Her* (2012) and *Drown*
(1996), from which the following selection is taken.

"Fiesta, 1980" provides a glimpse into the life of an immigrant family
through the eyes of Yunior (Junior). As the family prepares to attend a
party at a relative's house, Yunior and his mother worry about the fact
that the boy gets carsick in his father's van. This anxiety about the
motion sickness and the father's reaction to it pervades the story,
providing a framework for examining relationships, cultural identity,
and coming of age. Speculate on whether you think there might be a
psychological reason for Yunior's illness.

───────────

MAMI'S YOUNGEST SISTER—MY TÍA Yrma—finally made it to the
United States that year. She and tío Miguel got themselves an apartment in the Bronx, off the Grand Concourse and everybody decided
that we should have a party. Actually, my pops decided, but everybody—
meaning Mami, tía Yrma, tío Miguel and their neighbors—thought it
a dope idea. On the afternoon of the party Papi came back from work

around six. Right on time. We were all dressed by then, which was a smart move on our part. If Papi had walked in and caught us lounging around in our underwear, he would have kicked our asses something serious.

He didn't say nothing to nobody, not even my moms. He just pushed past her, held up his hand when she tried to talk to him and headed right into the shower. Rafa gave me the look and I gave it back to him; we both knew Papi had been with that Puerto Rican woman he was seeing and wanted to wash off the evidence quick.

Mami looked really nice that day. The United States had finally put some meat on her; she was no longer the same flaca[1] who had arrived here three years before. She had cut her hair short and was wearing tons of cheap-ass jewelry which on her didn't look too lousy. She smelled like herself, like the wind through a tree. She always waited until the last possible minute to put on her perfume because she said it was a waste to spray it on early and then have to spray it on again once you got to the party.

We—meaning me, my brother, my little sister and Mami—waited for Papi to finish his shower. Mami seemed anxious, in her usual dispassionate way. Her hands adjusted the buckle of her belt over and over again. That morning, when she had gotten us up for school, Mami told us that she wanted to have a good time at the party. I want to dance, she said, but now, with the sun sliding out of the sky like spit off a wall, she seemed ready just to get this over with.

Rafa didn't much want to go to no party either, and me, I never 5 wanted to go anywhere with my family. There was a baseball game in the parking lot outside and we could hear our friends, yelling, Hey, and, Cabrón,[2] to one another. We heard the pop of a ball as it sailed over the cars, the clatter of an aluminum bat dropping to the concrete. Not that me or Rafa loved baseball; we just liked playing with the local kids, thrashing them at anything they were doing. By the sounds of the shouting, we both knew the game was close, either of us could have

[1]Skinny woman (Spanish).
[2]Literally, male goat (Spanish). A term of insult.

made a difference. Rafa frowned and when I frowned back, he put up his fist. Don't you mirror me, he said.

Don't you mirror me, I said.

He punched me—I would have hit him back but Papi marched into the living room with his towel around his waist, looking a lot smaller than he did when he was dressed. He had a few strands of hair around his nipples and a surly closed-mouth expression, like maybe he'd scalded his tongue or something.

Have they eaten? he asked Mami.

She nodded. I made you something.

You didn't let him eat, did you?   10

Ay, Dios mío,[3] she said, letting her arms fall to her side.

Ay, Dios mío is right, Papi said.

I was never supposed to eat before our car trips, but earlier, when she had put out our dinner of rice, beans and sweet platanos, guess who had been the first one to clean his plate? You couldn't blame Mami really, she had been busy—cooking, getting ready, dressing my sister Madai. I should have reminded her not to feed me but I wasn't that sort of son.

Papi turned to me. Coño, muchacho,[4] why did you eat?

Rafa had already started inching away from me. I'd once told him I   15 considered him a low-down chicken-shit for moving out of the way every time Papi was going to smack me.

Collateral damage, Rafa had said. Ever heard of it?

No.

Look it up.

Chickenshit or not, I didn't dare glance at him. Papi was old-fashioned; he expected your undivided attention when you were getting your ass whupped. You couldn't look him in the eye either—that wasn't allowed. Better to stare at his belly button, which was perfectly round and immaculate. Papi pulled me to my feet by my ear.

If you throw up—   20

I won't, I cried, tears in my eyes, more out of reflex than pain.

[3]Oh, my God (Spanish).
[4]Loosely translates to "What the hell, boy?" (Spanish).

Ya, Ramón, ya. It's not his fault, Mami said.

They've known about this party forever. How did they think we were going to get there? Fly?

He finally let go of my ear and I sat back down. Madai was too scared to open her eyes. Being around Papi all her life had turned her into a major-league wuss. Anytime Papi raised his voice her lip would start trembling, like some specialized tuning fork. Rafa pretended that he had knuckles to crack and when I shoved him, he gave me a *Don't start* look. But even that little bit of recognition made me feel better.

I was the one who was always in trouble with my dad. It was like my 25 God-given duty to piss him off, to do everything the way he hated. Our fights didn't bother me too much. I still wanted him to love me, something that never seemed strange or contradictory until years later, when he was out of our lives.

By the time my ear stopped stinging Papi was dressed and Mami was crossing each one of us, solemnly, like we were heading off to war. We said, in turn, Bendición,[5] Mami, and she poked us in our five cardinal spots while saying, Que Dios te bendiga.

This was how all our trips began, the words that followed me every time I left the house.

None of us spoke until we were inside Papi's Volkswagen van. Brand-new, lime-green and bought to impress. Oh, we were impressed, but me, every time I was in that VW and Papi went above twenty miles an hour, I vomited. I'd never had trouble with cars before—that van was like my curse. Mami suspected it was the upholstery. In her mind, American things—appliances, mouthwash, funny-looking upholstery— all seemed to have an intrinsic badness about them. Papi was careful about taking me anywhere in the VW, but when he had to, I rode up front in Mami's usual seat so I could throw up out a window.

¿Cómo te sientes?[6] Mami asked over my shoulder when Papi pulled onto the turnpike. She had her hand on the base of my neck. One thing about Mami, her palms never sweated.

---

[5]Both *bendición* and *Que Dios te bendiga* are blessings in Spanish on the children. The five cardinal spots refer to the places a Latino Catholic would touch in making the sign of the cross: forehead, chest, both shoulders, and lips.

[6]How are you feeling? (Spanish).

I'm OK, I said, keeping my eyes straight ahead. I definitely didn't 30
want to trade glances with Papi. He had this one look, furious and
sharp, that always left me feeling bruised.

Toma.[7] Mami handed me four mentas. She had thrown three out
her window at the beginning of our trip, an offering to Eshú; the rest
were for me.

I took one and sucked it slowly, my tongue knocking it up against my
teeth. We passed Newark Airport without any incident. If Madai had
been awake she would have cried because the planes flew so close to
the cars.

How's he feeling? Papi asked.

Fine, I said. I glanced back at Rafa and he pretended like he didn't
see me. That was the way he was, at school and at home. When I was
in trouble, he didn't know me. Madai was solidly asleep, but even with
her face all wrinkled up and drooling she looked cute, her hair all
separated into twists.

I turned around and concentrated on the candy. Papi even started to 35
joke that we might not have to scrub the van out tonight. He was beginning to loosen up, not checking his watch too much. Maybe he was
thinking about that Puerto Rican woman or maybe he was just happy
that we were all together. I could never tell. At the toll, he was feeling
positive enough to actually get out of the van and search around under
the basket for dropped coins. It was something he had once done to
amuse Madai, but now it was habit. Cars behind us honked their horns
and I slid down in my seat. Rafa didn't care; he grinned back at the
other cars and waved. His actual job was to make sure no cops were
coming. Mami shook Madai awake and as soon as she saw Papi stoop-
ing for a couple of quarters she let out this screech of delight that
almost took off the top of my head.

That was the end of the good times. Just outside the Washington
Bridge, I started feeling woozy. The smell of the upholstery got all up
inside my head and I found myself with a mouthful of saliva. Mami's

[7]Take this (Spanish). *Mentas*: mints. *Eshú*: a Yoruban god who served, in part, as protec-
tor of travelers.

hand tensed on my shoulder and when I caught Papi's eye, he was like, No way. Don't do it.

The first time I got sick in the van Papi was taking me to the library. Rafa was with us and he couldn't believe I threw up. I was famous for my steel-lined stomach. A third-world childhood could give you that. Papi was worried enough that just as quick as Rafa could drop off the books we were on our way home. Mami fixed me one of her honey-and-onion concoctions and that made my stomach feel better. A week later we tried the library again and on this go-around I couldn't get the window open in time. When Papi got me home, he went and cleaned out the van himself, an expression of askho[8] on his face. This was a big deal, since Papi almost never cleaned anything himself. He came back inside and found me sitting on the couch feeling like hell.

It's the car, he said to Mami. It's making him sick.

This time the damage was pretty minimal, nothing Papi couldn't wash off the door with a blast of the hose. He was pissed, though; he jammed his finger into my cheek, a nice solid thrust. That was the way he was with his punishments: imaginative. Earlier that year I'd written an essay in school called "My Father the Torturer," but the teacher made me write a new one. She thought I was kidding.

We drove the rest of the way to the Bronx in silence. We only stopped 40 once, so I could brush my teeth. Mami had brought along my tooth-brush and a tube of toothpaste and while every car known to man sped by us she stood outside with me so I wouldn't feel alone.

Tío Miguel was about seven feet tall and had his hair combed up and out, into a demi-fro. He gave me and Rafa big spleen-crushing hugs and then kissed Mami and finally ended up with Madai on his shoulder. The last time I'd seen Tío was at the airport, his first day in the United States. I remembered how he hadn't seemed all that troubled to be in another country.

[8]Meaning unclear.

He looked down at me. Carajo,[9] Yunior, you look horrible!

He threw up, my brother explained.

I pushed Rafa. Thanks a lot, ass-face.

Hey, he said. Tío asked.   45

Tío clapped a bricklayer's hand on my shoulder. Everybody gets sick sometimes, he said. You should have seen me on the plane over here. Dios mio! He rolled his Asian-looking eyes for emphasis. I thought we were all going to die.

Everybody could tell he was lying. I smiled like he was making me feel better.

Do you want me to get you a drink? Tío asked. We got beer and rum.

Miguel, Mami said. He's young.

Young? Back in Santo Domingo, he'd be getting laid by now.   50

Mami thinned her lips, which took some doing.

Well, it's true, Tío said.

So, Mami, I said. When do I get to go visit the D.R.[1]?

That's enough, Yunior.

It's the only pussy you'll ever get, Rafa said to me in English.   55

Not counting your girlfriend, of course.

Rafa smiled. He had to give me that one.

Papi came in from parking the van. He and Miguel gave each other the sort of handshakes that would have turned my fingers into Wonder bread.

Coño, compa'i, ¿cómo va todo?[2] they said to each other.

Tía came out then, with an apron on and maybe the longest Lee Press-   60
On Nails I've ever seen in my life. There was this one guru motherfucker in the *Guinness Book of World Records* who had longer nails, but I tell you, it was close. She gave everybody kisses, told me and Rafa how guapo we were—Rafa, of course, believed her—told Madai how bella she was, but when she got to Papi, she froze a little, like maybe she'd seen a wasp on the tip of his nose, but then kissed him all the same.

---

[9]Vulgar word for penis (Spanish), used as an expletive.

[1]Dominican Republic.

[2]A casual greeting: Damn, Friend, how's everything going?

Mami told us to join the other kids in the living room. Tío said, Wait a minute, I want to show you the apartment. I was glad Tía said, Hold on, because from what I'd seen so far, the place had been furnished in Contemporary Dominican Tacky. The less I saw, the better. I mean, I liked plastic sofa covers but damn, Tío and Tía had taken it to another level. They had a disco ball hanging in the living room and the type of stucco ceilings that looked like stalactite heaven. The sofas all had golden tassels dangling from their edges. Tía came out of the kitchen with some people I didn't know and by the time she got done introducing everybody, only Papi and Mami were given the guided tour of the four-room third-floor apartment. Me and Rafa joined the kids in the living room. They'd already started eating. We were hungry, one of the girls explained, a pastelito[3] in hand. The boy was about three years younger than me but the girl who'd spoken, Leti, was my age. She and another girl were on the sofa together and they were cute as hell.

Leti introduced them: the boy was her brother Wilquins and the other girl was her neighbor Mari. Leti had some serious tetas and I could tell that my brother was going to gun for her. His taste in girls was predictable. He sat down right between Leti and Mari and by the way they were smiling at him I knew he'd do fine. Neither of the girls gave me more than a cursory one-two, which didn't bother me. Sure, I liked girls but I was always too terrified to speak to them unless we were arguing or I was calling them stupidos, which was one of my favorite words that year. I turned to Wilquins and asked him what there was to do around here. Mari, who had the lowest voice I'd ever heard, said, He can't speak.

What does that mean?

He's mute.

I looked at Wilquins incredulously. He smiled and nodded, as if he'd   65
won a prize or something.

Does he understand? I asked.

Of course he understands, Rafa said. He's not dumb.

[3]Cuban puff pastry, filled sometimes with cheese or fruit, others with meat.

I could tell Rafa had said that just to score points with the girls. Both of them nodded. Low-voice Mari said, He's the best student in his grade.

I thought, Not bad for a mute. I sat next to Wilquins. After about two seconds of TV Wilquins whipped out a bag of dominos and motioned to me. Did I want to play? Sure. Me and him played Rafa and Leti and we whupped their collective asses twice, which put Rafa in a real bad mood. He looked at me like maybe he wanted to take a swing, just one to make him feel better. Leti kept whispering into Rafa's ear, telling him it was OK.

In the kitchen I could hear my parents slipping into their usual modes. Papi's voice was loud and argumentative; you didn't have to be anywhere near him to catch his drift. And Mami, you had to put cups to your ears to hear hers. I went into the kitchen a few times—once so the tíos could show off how much bullshit I'd been able to cram in my head the last few years; another time for a bucket-sized cup of soda. Mami and Tía were frying tostones[4] and the last of the pastelitos. She appeared happier now and the way her hands worked on our dinner you would think she had a life somewhere else making rare and precious things. She nudged Tía every now and then, shit they must have been doing all their lives. As soon as Mami saw me though, she gave me the eye. Don't stay long, that eye said. Don't piss your old man off.

Papi was too busy arguing about Elvis to notice me. Then somebody mentioned María Montez[5] and Papi barked, María Montez? Let me tell *you* about María Montez, compa'i.

Maybe I was used to him. His voice—louder than most adults'—didn't bother me none, though the other kids shifted uneasily in their seats. Wilquins was about to raise the volume on the TV, but Rafa said, I wouldn't do that. Muteboy had balls, though. He did it anyway and then sat down. Wilquins's pop came into the living room a second later, a bottle of Presidente in hand. That dude must have had Spider-senses or something. Did you raise that? he asked Wilquins and Wilquins nodded.

[4]Fried plantains.
[5]Dominican actress (1912–51) known for her exotic beauty.

Is this your house? his pops asked. He looked ready to beat Wilquins silly but he lowered the volume instead.

See, Rafa said. You nearly got your ass *kicked*.

I met the Puerto Rican woman right after Papi had gotten the van.   75
He was taking me on short trips, trying to cure me of my vomiting. It wasn't really working but I looked forward to our trips, even though at the end of each one I'd be sick. These were the only times me and Papi did anything together. When we were alone he treated me much better, like maybe I was his son or something.

Before each drive Mami would cross me.

Bendición, Mami, I'd say.

She'd kiss my forehead. Que Dios te bendiga. And then she would give me a handful of mentas because she wanted me to be OK. Mami didn't think these excursions would cure anything, but the one time she had brought it up to Papi he had told her to shut up, what did she know about anything anyway?

Me and Papi didn't talk much. We just drove around our neighborhood. Occasionally he'd ask, How is it?

And I'd nod, no matter how I felt.   80

One day I was sick outside of Perth Amboy. Instead of taking me home he went the other way on Industrial Avenue, stopping a few minutes later in front of a light blue house I didn't recognize. It reminded me of the Easter eggs we colored at school, the ones we threw out the bus windows at other cars.

The Puerto Rican woman was there and she helped me clean up. She had dry papery hands and when she rubbed the towel on my chest, she did it hard, like I was a bumper she was waxing. She was very thin and had a cloud of brown hair rising above her narrow face and the sharpest blackest eyes you've ever seen.

He's cute, she said to Papi.

Not when he's throwing up, Papi said.

What's your name? she asked me. Are you Rafa?   85

I shook my head.

Then it's Yunior, right?

I nodded.

You're the smart one, she said, suddenly happy with herself. Maybe you want to see my books?

They weren't hers. I recognized them as ones my father must have 90 left in her house. Papi was a voracious reader, couldn't even go cheating without a paperback in his pocket.

Why don't you go watch TV? Papi suggested. He was looking at her like she was the last piece of chicken on earth.

We got plenty of channels, she said. Use the remote if you want.

The two of them went upstairs and I was too scared of what was happening to poke around. I just sat there, ashamed, expecting something big and fiery to crash down on our heads. I watched a whole hour of the news before Papi came downstairs and said, Let's go.

About two hours later the women laid out the food and like always nobody but the kids thanked them. It must be some Dominican tradition or something. There was everything I liked—chicharrones,[6] fried chicken, tostones, sancocho, rice, fried cheese, yuca, avocado, potato salad, a meteor-sized hunk of pernil, even a tossed salad which I could do without—but when I joined the other kids around the serving table, Papi said, Oh no you don't, and took the paper plate out of my hand. His fingers weren't gentle.

What's wrong now? Tía asked, handing me another plate. 95

He ain't eating, Papi said. Mami pretended to help Rafa with the pernil.

Why can't he eat?

Because I said so.

The adults who didn't know us made like they hadn't heard a thing and Tío just smiled sheepishly and told everybody to go ahead and eat. All the kids—about ten of them now—trooped back into the living room with their plates a-heaping and all the adults ducked into the kitchen and the dining room, where the radio was playing loud-ass bachatas.[7] I was

[6]Pork rinds. *Sancocho:* a national dish of the Dominican Republic, usually made with rice, red beans, and one or more meats. *Pernil:* a pork dish.

[7]*Bachata* is a genre of music native to the Dominican Republic. Songs are typically romantic tales of heartbreak.

the only one without a plate. Papi stopped me before I could get away from him. He kept his voice nice and low so nobody else could hear him.

If you eat anything, I'm going to beat you. ¿Entiendes?[8]   100

I nodded.

And if your brother gives you any food, I'll beat him too. Right here in front of everybody. ¿Entiendes?

I nodded again. I wanted to kill him and he must have sensed it because he gave my head a little shove.

All the kids watched me come in and sit down in front of the TV.

What's wrong with your dad? Leti asked.   105

He's a dick, I said.

Rafa shook his head. Don't say that shit in front of people.

Easy for you to be nice when you're eating, I said.

Hey, if I was a pukey little baby, I wouldn't get no food either.

I almost said something back but I concentrated on the TV. I wasn't   110
going to start it. No fucking way. So I watched Bruce Lee beat Chuck Norris into the floor of the Colosseum and tried to pretend that there was no food anywhere in the house. It was Tía who finally saved me. She came into the living room and said, Since you ain't eating, Yunior, you can at least help me get some ice.

I didn't want to, but she mistook my reluctance for something else.

I already asked your father.

She held my hand while we walked; Tía didn't have any kids but I could tell she wanted them. She was the sort of relative who always remembered your birthday but who you only went to visit because you had to. We didn't get past the first-floor landing before she opened her pocketbook and handed me the first of three pastelitos she had smuggled out of the apartment.

Go ahead, she said. And as soon as you get inside make sure you brush your teeth.

Thanks a lot, Tía, I said.   115

Those pastelitos didn't stand a chance.

She sat next to me on the stairs and smoked her cigarette. All the way down on the first floor and we could still hear the music and the

[8]Do you understand? (Spanish)

adults and the television. Tía looked a ton like Mami; the two of them were both short and light-skinned. Tía smiled a lot and that was what set them apart the most.

How is it at home, Yunior?

What do you mean?

How's it going in the apartment? Are you kids OK? 120

I knew an interrogation when I heard one, no matter how sugar-coated it was. I didn't say anything. Don't get me wrong, I loved my tía, but something told me to keep my mouth shut. Maybe it was family loyalty, maybe I just wanted to protect Mami or I was afraid that Papi would find out—it could have been anything really.

Is your mom all right?

I shrugged.

Have there been lots of fights?

None, I said. Too many shrugs would have been just as bad as an 125 answer. Papi's at work too much.

Work, Tía said, like it was somebody's name she didn't like.

Me and Rafa, we didn't talk much about the Puerto Rican woman. When we ate dinner at her house, the few times Papi had taken us over there, we still acted like nothing was out of the ordinary. Pass the ketchup, man. No sweat, bro. The affair was like a hole in our living room floor, one we'd gotten so used to circumnavigating that we sometimes forgot it was there.

By midnight all the adults were crazy dancing. I was sitting outside Tía's bedroom—where Madai was sleeping—trying not to attract attention. Rafa had me guarding the door; he and Leti were in there too, with some of the other kids, getting busy no doubt. Wilquins had gone across the hall to bed so I had me and the roaches to mess around with.

Whenever I peered into the main room I saw about twenty moms and dads dancing and drinking beers. Every now and then somebody yelled, ¡Quisqueya![9] And then everybody else would yell and stomp

[9]Mother of all lands (Taino). Another name for the Dominican Republic.

their feet. From what I could see my parents seemed to be enjoying themselves.

Mami and Tía spent a lot of time side by side, whispering, and I kept 130
expecting something to come of this, a brawl maybe. I'd never once
been out with my family when it hadn't turned to shit. We weren't even
theatrical or straight crazy like other families. We fought like sixth-
graders, without any real dignity. I guess the whole night I'd been waiting for a blowup, something between Papi and Mami. This was how I
always figured Papi would be exposed, out in public, where everybody
would know.

You're a cheater!

But everything was calmer than usual. And Mami didn't look like she
was about to say anything to Papi. The two of them danced every now
and then but they never lasted more than a song before Mami joined
Tía again in whatever conversation they were having.

I tried to imagine Mami before Papi. Maybe I was tired, or just sad,
thinking about the way my family was. Maybe I already knew how it
would all end up in a few years, Mami without Papi, and that was why
I did it. Picturing her alone wasn't easy. It seemed like Papi had always
been with her, even when we were waiting in Santo Domingo for him
to send for us.

The only photograph our family had of Mami as a young woman,
before she married Papi, was the one that somebody took of her at an
election party that I found one day while rummaging for money to go
to the arcade. Mami had it tucked into her immigration papers. In the
photo, she's surrounded by laughing cousins I will never meet, who
are all shiny from dancing, whose clothes are rumpled and loose. You
can tell it's night and hot and that the mosquitos have been biting. She
sits straight and even in a crowd she stands out, smiling quietly like
maybe she's the one everybody's celebrating. You can't see her hands
but I imagined they're knotting a straw or a bit of thread. This was the
woman my father met a year later on the Malecón,[1] the woman Mami
thought she'd always be.

---

[1] A boardwalk in Havana, Cuba.

Mami must have caught me studying her because she stopped what   135
she was doing and gave me a smile, maybe her first one of the night.
Suddenly I wanted to go over and hug her, for no other reason than I
loved her, but there were about eleven fat jiggling bodies between us.
So I sat down on the tiled floor and waited.

I must have fallen asleep because the next thing I knew Rafa was
kicking me and saying, Let's go. He looked like he'd been hitting those
girls off; he was all smiles. I got to my feet in time to kiss Tía and Tío
good-bye. Mami was holding the serving dish she had brought with
her.

Where's Papi? I asked.

He's downstairs, bringing the van around. Mami leaned down to
kiss me.

You were good today, she said.

And then Papi burst in and told us to get the hell downstairs before   140
some pendejo[2] cop gave him a ticket. More kisses, more handshakes
and then we were gone.

I don't remember being out of sorts after I met the Puerto Rican woman,
but I must have been because Mami only asked me questions when she
thought something was wrong in my life. It took her about ten passes
but finally she cornered me one afternoon when we were alone in the
apartment. Our upstairs neighbors were beating the crap out of their
kids, and me and her had been listening to it all afternoon. She put her
hand on mine and said, Is everything OK, Yunior? Have you been
fighting with your brother?

Me and Rafa had already talked. We'd been in the basement, where
our parents couldn't hear us. He told me that yeah, he knew about her.

Papi's taken me there twice now, he said.

Why didn't you tell me? I asked.

What the hell was I going to say? *Hey, Yunior, guess what happened*   145
yesterday? I met Papi's sucia[3]!

[2]Literally, pubic hair (Spanish). Loosely translated to dumbass or jerk.
[3]Dirty woman (Spanish).

I didn't say anything to Mami either. She watched me, very very closely. Later I would think, maybe if I had told her, she would have confronted him, would have done something, but who can know these things? I said I'd been having trouble in school and like that everything was back to normal between us. She put her hand on my shoulder and squeezed and that was that.

We were on the turnpike, just past Exit 11, when I started feeling it again. I sat up from leaning against Rafa. His fingers smelled and he'd gone to sleep almost as soon as he got into the van. Madai was out too but at least she wasn't snoring.

In the darkness, I saw that Papi had a hand on Mami's knee and that the two of them were quiet and still. They weren't slumped back or anything; they were both wide awake, bolted into their seats. I couldn't see either of their faces and no matter how hard I tried I could not imagine their expressions. Neither of them moved. Every now and then the van was filled with the bright rush of somebody else's headlights. Finally I said, Mami, and they both looked back, already knowing what was happening.

STUDY QUESTIONS

1. Why won't Yunior's father let him eat at the party?

2. How would you characterize Yunior's relationship with his father? How does it differ from his relationship with his mother? What EVIDENCE can you find in the text to support your characterization?

3. What are the SETTINGS of this story? How does each setting seem to make Yunior feel? Why?

4. *For Writing* Write a story or an essay about a time when you got attention from your family for a negative action, like Yunior's motion sickness. How did it make you feel? Is any attention better than none? Why or why not?

WILLIAM M. CHACE { *A Question of Honor*

WILLIAM M. CHACE (b. 1938) is an American university scholar and
administrator. He received his BA from Haverford College in 1961, and his
MA (1963) and PhD (1968) from the University of California at Berkeley.
He served as Professor of English at Stanford University from 1968 to
1988, as president of Wesleyan University from 1988 to 1994, and finally
as president of Emory University from 1995 to 2003. In addition to his
scholarly work on literature, Chace has written extensively on university
politics and culture, and is the author of *One Hundred Semesters: My
Adventures as Student, Professor, and University President, and What
I Learned Along the Way* (2006).

   This essay appeared in *The American Scholar* in 2012. Chace begins by
describing what he sees as an American higher education system in decline.
Next, he argues that one thing colleges and universities can do to reverse
that downward trend is to recommit themselves to principles of academic
integrity, including taking a stronger stand against plagiarism. He argues
that developing a sense of "moral awareness" can be an effective method for
preventing plagiarism. As you read, pay attention to how Chace describes
what he sees as common attitudes toward plagiarism in the academy and
why he feels they need to be challenged.

ONE OF THE GLOOMIEST RECENT reports about the nation's colleges
and universities reinforces the suspicion that students are studying
less, reading less, and learning less all the time: "American higher
education is characterized," sociologists Richard Arum and Josipa
Roksa said last year, "by limited or no learning for a large proportion

of students." Their book, *Academically Adrift,* joins a widening, and often negative, reassessment of what universities contribute to American life. Even President Obama has gotten into the act, turning one problem with higher education into an applause line in his latest State of the Union address. "So let me put colleges and universities on notice," he said: "If you can't stop tuition from going up, the funding you get from taxpayers will go down. Higher education can't be a luxury—it is an economic imperative that every family in America should be able to afford."

Where should we lay the blame for the worsening state of one of the foundations of American civilization, one that has long filled us with justifiable pride? The big public universities are already bogged down by diminishing financial support from the states; private education is imperiled by tuition costs that discourage hundreds of thousands of middle-class and poorer students from applying. Some schools have made heroic attempts to diversify their student bodies, but too little financial aid is available to make access possible for all the applicants with academic promise.

What is happening inside the classroom for those who do get in? Who is teaching the students? Less and less often it is a member of an institution's permanent faculty, and rarer still one of its distinguished professors. More and more of the teaching has been parceled out to part-time instructors who have no hope of landing a full-time position. Because of this, their loyalty to the school that hired them, and to the students they will probably meet in just one course and never again, has diminished.

Amid such melancholy reports from the front, campus amusements that have nothing to do with education—intercollegiate athletics leads the festivities—sop up money, keep coaches in the headlines, and divert public attention from the essential mission of education: to strengthen the minds of young people and to prepare them to cope with the demands of life.

Perhaps that is why, when the public is asked about colleges and 5 universities, the response is increasingly negative with each passing year. According to the Pew Research Center, most American citizens (57 percent) say that higher education "fails to provide good value for the money students and their families spend." Within the innermost sanctum of the academy the view is almost the same: "About four in ten college presidents say the system is headed in the wrong direction," according to Pew. If university presidents, who by profession and temperament routinely find every glass more than half-full, are so disconsolate, the public can't be expected to be optimistic.

Were this situation to get any worse, it could legitimately be called a crisis. But American colleges and universities are not going under anytime soon. Despite their problems, they employ hundreds of thousands of people, keep towns and even cities financially afloat, and offer cultural resources and, yes, athletic and other entertainments. They adorn the nation with their well-kept campuses. The research done on those campuses makes us safer, improves our health, and inspires our nobler human impulses. Along the way, colleges and universities provide multiyear habitat for millions of postadolescents who, more often than not, are bewilderingly short of ideas about what to do after leaving secondary school. And they continue to offer a haven to those who finish their undergraduate years and do not or cannot enter the present bleak job market. Most of these students are happy to find themselves—for four, five, or even six years—with other people their age, with whom they can develop social skills while entertaining each other and themselves and exposing their minds to selected academic topics. For all these reasons, the college experience in this country long ago became one of its most acceptable rites of passage. The schools are there because they serve a variety of needs. The challenge is to make them better.

But now they are up against a spectrum of problems whose magnitude they have never faced before. What can they do—amid financial pressures, dwindling public esteem, pre-professional anxieties on the part of their students, and eroded faculty loyalty—to recover the prestige they once enjoyed?

One answer, I believe, rests in what they can do, and must do, about a large and ugly presence on almost every campus: academic dishonesty. Cheating now hurts American higher education; it might well be cheating that can begin to save it.

• ○ •

IN COLLEGE AND UNIVERSITY classrooms across the country, every student sooner or later faces the apparently simple task of writing an essay. The essay might focus on a philosophical topic (the argumentative structure of John Stuart Mill's[1] *On Liberty,* for example), or the student's interpretation of a play (Harold Pinter's[2] *The Homecoming,* say), or a political issue (the likely shape of demographic changes in the United States in the next 20 years). The topics are endless, but the ground rules are not: be clear, employ the rules of logic, and most pointedly, be original.

The last requirement is where the system gets confused. No teacher   10 really expects any student essay to revolutionize our understanding of the world, to be so original that the firmament begins to wobble. The opportunity to be truly original has gotten rarer through the eons. As Mark Twain[3] put it, "What a good thing Adam had. When he said a good thing he knew nobody had said it before." No, originality means something more modest: that the student, after much reflection and weighing of the assembled evidence, has written in a way that reflects the particular contours of his or her thinking. The turns and twists of the prose, the things emphasized and the things neglected, the way the essay opens and closes, and how errors, some small and some large, inevitably infiltrate the prose—these features, constituting the essay's fingerprint, are evidence that the student has written something original. But truth to tell, it's not working that way. Today, lots of students cheat. They use the work of others. They buy essays. They plagiarize. Still, even though the Web makes cheating easier than ever before, and thus more prevalent, the phenomenon of cheating is nothing new. Students have been at it for a long time.

Eighty years ago, Dean Clarence W. Mendell of Yale University declared that the problem of cheating at his school was widespread

---

[1] British philosopher and political scientist (1806–1873).

[2] British playwright (1930–2008), winner of the 2005 Nobel Prize in Literature.

[3] American humorist, essayist, and novelist (1835–1910), author of *The Adventures of Tom Sawyer* (1876) and *The Adventures of Huckleberry Finn* (1885).

enough to require instant reform: "It is altogether imperative that the growing disregard of this traditional standard on the part of many unthinking undergraduates should be wiped out." He sternly added, "the faculty has but one attitude toward cheating, an attitude shared, we believe, by the undergraduate body." But 45 years later, in 1976, another Yale dean, Eva Balogh, described cheating at the school as "rampant." New Haven hadn't changed much, and Yale was no isolated case. That same year, on the other side of the country, the student newspaper at the University of Southern California reported that as many as 40 percent of students there were plagiarizing their written work.

The first comprehensive study of cheating at colleges and universities (5,000 students at almost 100 institutions) was completed in 1964. It found that 75 percent of the students had engaged in one form or another of academic dishonesty. A generation later, in 2001, an authoritative survey conducted by Donald L. McCabe of Rutgers and his colleagues concluded that cheating was now "prevalent" across the country and that "some forms of cheating have increased dramatically in the last 30 years."

Indeed, every study over the decades has concluded that cheating at American colleges and universities is rampant. Despite Dean Mendell's desire long ago to wipe it out, grim admonitions from college presidents year after year, and any number of cheating eruptions around the nation, dishonesty, indigenous to almost every campus, flourishes. A recent survey by the online journal *Inside Higher Ed* of more than a thousand chief academic officers at schools nationwide revealed that more than two-thirds of them believe that cheating has become a much worse problem than it once was. But, interestingly enough, fewer than a quarter of them thought it was on the rise on their own campuses.

Students cheat for many reasons, some of them even doing so without malign intent, either because they don't understand the rules of academic honesty or are confused about the assignment. Some students cheat because of pressures to succeed in a competitive world. Some cheat because they are lazy, tired, or indifferent. Some, overwhelmed by the oceanic wash of information pouring in upon them as they open their computers to the Web, conclude that there is nothing new to say. And some cheat because they look at all academic tasks as exciting opportunities to fool the system as well as the teacher.

They learn early. The Josephson Institute of Ethics sampled more than 40,000 public and private high school students and found that three-fifths of them admitted to having cheated on a test. Nearly half of these were honors students; a third had cheated twice or more in the previous year. In high school, every applicant to college is given an open invitation to cheat—the personal essay that college admissions offices require. How many students write these essays without help? How many parents write them? How many friends, counselors, and commercial agencies write them? No one knows, but the pressure to get such help must be precisely as strong as the pressure to write the kind of essay that will win respect from an admissions dean. The temptation to cross the line shows up early in a young person's life.

As with any transgressive cultural activity both scorned and widespread (running red lights, using recreational drugs, evading taxes), some cheaters are exposed while others go untouched. For every cheating student who is nabbed, another slips under the radar. Nor is the radar kept in good working order. Some teachers know when a student's work is fraudulent but elect to do nothing. It takes time, and time is expensive; bringing a student before a campus judicial council is also labor intensive, and the outcome is unpredictable; students or their parents can retain attorneys to fight the charges and endlessly complicate the procedure; administrators cannot be counted on to back up professors making accusations. Professors like the elevation of teaching but not the grubby business of prosecuting. For the increasing number of adjunct instructors, vigilance about cheating could put their professional futures at risk. They could earn an unappealing tag: "high maintenance." And some teachers have concluded that the only person hurt by cheating is the cheater, and so they wash their hands of the entire business.

On many campuses, dishonesty is simply accepted as an unwelcome but ubiquitous feature of teaching and learning, the equivalent of friction in the pedagogical machine. Reflect on what Dean Mendell said, but perhaps only dimly understood, all those decades ago. The "unthinking undergraduates" at Yale who were cheating made up part of the undergraduate body at Yale as a whole that presumably shared the faculty's revulsion toward cheating. Denouncing a wrong does not necessarily mean being innocent of committing it. Most students know that cheating surrounds them, but few see ways to do anything about it, even when they hold it in contempt. Some of those who cheat are morally offended by others who cheat, but they too are, for obvious reasons, disinclined to complain. In every cultural domain, we grow accustomed to breaches that, with time and repetition, we wind up believing are normal.

But how does cheating become tolerated, assimilated, and ultimately absorbed into our understanding of normality? The answer partly resides in the peculiar kind of wrong it is. Compared with the violation of copyright, a crime punishable in a court of law, cheating at school is "only" a moral and ethical wrong. Plagiarism, one of the most common forms of cheating, often leaves behind no apparent victim; the author from whose body of work the plagiarist extracts a useful portion might never know anything has happened; and the work, despite the theft, remains in the author's possession (lawyers call this "usufruct"). The downloading without attribution of finished essays from the Internet, another immensely popular way of completing classroom assignments, harms no honest author, as copying them for publication would. And if several students conspire to compose an essay in the name of one, who is the exploited party? Any outrage can seem tolerable if it looks victimless.

Consider, moreover, with what emollients any feeling of guilt about cheating can be soothed in a student's mind. To begin, the culture outside the campus gates seems long ago to have accepted dishonesty when it comes to the writings of certain important people. Just how much of *Profiles in Courage* did John F. Kennedy write and how much did Theodore Sorensen write? How strongly do we care? What should we say about the Rev. Martin Luther King Jr.'s doctoral dissertation at Boston University, once we know that it is filled with the writings of others, copied down paragraph after paragraph, in vast profusion? Think also of Roger Clemens, Barry Bonds, and almost everyone involved in international cycling—sports figures about whom allegations of cheating are now featured in every newspaper in the land. What of the plagiarism of prize-winning historians Doris Kearns Goodwin and Stephen E. Ambrose, not to mention the elaborate transfer, generations ago, of the ideas of German philosophers into the "philosophy" of Samuel Taylor Coleridge? Don't we just note such derelictions and then generously move on to matters more pressing?

The much-quoted aphorism by T. S. Eliot[4] that "immature poets   20 imitate; mature poets steal" can give license enough to a student faced with the chore of writing an original senior thesis on, say, Eliot himself. That immature student, emboldened by fantasies, can think himself into maturity by doing no more than what Eliot said the great customarily do: steal.

•   ◦   •

YET ANOTHER SOCIAL REALITY erodes the moral offensiveness of cheating, a reality that universities and colleges find themselves ill equipped to cope with. Given that so much professional life—the legal and medical systems, entrepreneurial capitalism, the operations of established companies and the public sector, the very working life that many college graduates will enter—is based on the pooling of ideas and the energy of teamwork, how is it that the academic world can demand wholly independent work and originality? Indeed, students can wonder why colleges observe the principles of solitary labor when they will soon work in offices where ideas are meant to be merged and where the inspiration of one person achieves value only when coupled with the inspiration of many others.

Nowhere is this tension between the ethical code of the campus and that of the working world more awkwardly felt than in the discipline of computer science. On campuses, students taking courses in this fertile area of study are urged to work independently to develop their skills, but if they are fortunate enough upon graduation to get a job with a firm making use of such skills, they will join highly ambitious teams of men and women who, to succeed, will merge their talent and

---

[4] Thomas Stearns Eliot (1888–1965), Anglo-American poet and literary critic; winner of the 1948 Nobel Prize in Literature.

their scientific knowledge to create something—a new piece of money-making software, for instance—that not one of them, working alone, could have come up with.

On campus, solitary independence; off campus, collective energy. The contradiction between these two methods partially explains why the greatest incidence of cheating at high-powered universities like Stanford and others occurs among students enrolled in computer science courses. Those students must hold in their minds that a wrong in one place is highly prized in another. Nor is it irrelevant, as one imagines the incentives to cheat, to consider the attractive beginning salaries offered to successful computer-science graduates of schools such as Stanford. The urge to succeed can yield to the temptation to cheat if a good job awaits just beyond the campus gates.

Few students are ignorant of the prevailing ethical standards of their home institutions. Should those standards be strong and consistently enforced, and should those institutions provide example after example of moral courage, students who cheat do so with the knowledge that they are violating a code of honor that has substance. But if the institutions themselves exhibit questionable ethical standards—leaving a trail of shoddy compromise, corner cutting, and breaches of trust—those students come to understand that honor is only a word and not a practice. Since nothing more quickly leaps into a young person's mind than the recognition of hypocrisy, cheating becomes easier once institutional duplicity is detected.

In colleges and universities, then, where primary teaching duties 25 are given over to part-time instructors so that well-paid professors can devote themselves to research projects; where tuition is very high but certain classes are large and crowded; where extra tutorial help is lavishly provided to students on athletic scholarships (many of whom never would be admitted on academic grounds) and only rarely to students who play no intercollegiate sports; where the values seem to be corporate rather than academic; where, as at Claremont McKenna College, an administrator submits false SAT scores to publications like *U.S. News & World Report* in order to boost the school's "selective" reputation; and where, as a consequence, campus morale is low, some students can and will respond as one would to any organization proclaiming one set of values while practicing another. Students entering colleges and universities are told that these places are, and have been, "special." When they turn out to be commonplace, commonplace standards will triumph.

Students are under personal, parental, and pre-professional pressures that have never been more intense. Getting into the right school, and achieving in such a way that one can then proceed to the next right station in life, makes the college experience for many young people more a matter of getting ahead—acquiring the proper credential—than undergoing a unique ritual devoted to self-knowledge and intellectual growth. If resources beyond oneself are needed to get ahead—even illicit resources such as the writings of others, all easily acquired by a few keyboard strokes in the privacy of one's room, and all gained with no apparent sense of injury to anyone else—so be it. Nothing seems lost; forward motion has been sustained.

The most appalling aspect of the rise of cheating on campus in recent times is that some professors themselves have offered sophisticated defenses of plagiarism. An ambitious student can now turn to the writings of teachers who have made ingenious theoretical defenses for the very cheating practices proscribed by the universities at which they teach. If a student faces the accusation that his work is not original, that student can respond: Don't you know that the idea of "originality" has been hammered into nothingness by thinkers such as Michel Foucault?[5] After all, he proclaimed four decades ago that the very idea of an author, any author, is dead, and hence there is no one around to claim originality. Instead, wrote Foucault, in *What Is an Author?*, we should welcome a new world in which the inhibiting codes of authorship have been cast to the winds:

> All discourses, whatever their status, form, value, and whatever the treatment to which they will be subjected, would then develop in the anonymity of a murmur. We would no longer hear the questions that have been rehashed for so long: Who really spoke? Is it really he and not someone else? With what authenticity or originality? . . .

[5] French philosopher and historian (1926–1984).

And behind all these questions, we would hear hardly anything but the stirring of an indifference: What difference does it make who is speaking?

Once a student adopts, under so impressive an aegis as Foucault, an indifference about authorship, the coast is clear and all noisome ethical restrictions can be jettisoned. *Perspectives on Plagiarism* (1999), edited by Lise Buranen and Alice Myers Roy, brings together essays demonstrating the problem. Gilbert Larochelle, who teaches political philosophy at the University of Quebec and who is a professorial devotee of the celebrated philosopher, puts it this way: "Can plagiarism still exist in an intellectual universe where it has become impossible to differentiate the representation from the referent, the copy from the original, and the copyist from the author?" Another teacher, Debora Halbert of Otterbein College, inspired by both Foucault and feminism, ups the ante and provides students who might be thinking of plagiarizing with dreams of anti-establishment revolution: "Appropriation or plagiarism are acts of sedition against an already established mode of knowing, a way of knowing indebted to male creation and property rights. . . . No concept of intellectual property should exist in a feminist future." Yet another professor, Marilyn Randall of the University of Western Ontario, writes that "later critical discourse whole-heartedly adopts the notion of plagiarism as an intentional political act" and, perhaps sensitive to the unattractive connotations of the word itself, repackages plagiarism as "discursive repetition." Buoyed up by such sophisticated arguments, and keen to be part of a bright new future, students might well be ashamed if they did *not* cheat.

A less theoretical defense of cheating comes by way of something called "patchwriting." It combines low-level Foucauldian thinking ("no such thing as originality") with American confessionalism ("folks, let's be honest, everybody cheats all the time"). It argues that whatever we write is no more than proof that we are forever standing on the shoulders of giants. We're fooling ourselves if we believe that we are writing something that has not, in so many words, been written before. Human beings can't be original. As a species, we endlessly use and reuse what has been used and reused before, forever recycling the logic, the words, the turns of phrase, and all the rest. So why not, says a chief apologist for patchwriting, go easy on the students? Teach them, says Rebecca Moore Howard of Syracuse University, that it's okay to download essays from the Internet, to pluck useful phrases or even paragraphs from Wikipedia, and to cobble whatever seems to fit together into the semblance of an essay ready for grading. "[Patch-writing] is a form of verbal sculpture, molding new shapes from pre-existing materials," Howard writes. "It is something that all academic writers do. Patchwriting belongs not in a category with cheating on exams and purchasing term papers but in a category with the ancient tradition of learning through apprenticeship and mimicry." It's really how we all write anyway, if only we had the courage as patchwriters to say so.

What explains this peculiar defense of plagiarism? Pedagogical   30 and professional anxiety may be one cause: if we go after cheaters, pursuing them all the way to the judicial councils, we will have done nothing, say the defenders, but reinforce the barriers between teach-ers and students, the invidious social hierarchies separating those possessing the standards (even if they are ill-paid teachers of composi-tion) and those supplying the tuition (even if they are freshmen and sophomores). In the interests of both candor and classroom egalitari-anism, why not let everyone in on the secret about writing: plagiarism is at the heart of prose; it's how it gets done. Once that forbidden truth is out in the open, genuine teaching can begin. Neither students nor teacher will feel inferior any longer. They will hold in common the abiding truth of writing: it's all patched together.

And yet. As I have written these words, one by one, knowing all the while that none of them is original with me, all of them (except "usu-fruct") drawn from the common well of English diction, and recog-nizing that neither my sentence construction nor my way of organizing paragraphs is unique to me, and while I have gone to many sources to find the information I've needed to write, I believe this essay is mine, mine alone, and would not exist had I not written it. I don't believe I have patched, or that I've plagiarized. As it is with me, so it has always been with writers, and so it will always be. The arguments protecting or even championing plagiarism fall before the palpable evidence of originality, modest and grand, ephemeral and enduring, as it has existed in writing everywhere.

• ○ •

ALMOST EVERY READER OF this essay began, I assume, with the presumption that plagiarism is a serious wrong. Most readers will find its assorted defenders more ridiculous than credible, whether they are disciples of postmodern theory or teachers warning students away from the allegedly phony attractions of originality. Such readers can find kinship, then, with the students who do not cheat. To them we must turn our attention. Both groups have a stake in a clean system. For the students, it means grades honestly earned; for the readers, it means the hope that this country's educational enterprise is ethically sound. Together the two groups can find much to respect in what another kind of composition teacher, Augustus M. Kolich, expressed a generation ago:

> [P]lagiarism cuts deeply into the integrity and morality of what I teach my students, and it sullies my notions about the sanctity of my relationship to students. It is a lie, and although lies are often private matters between two people, plagiarism is never merely private because it breaches a code of behavior that encompasses my classroom, my teaching, my university, and my society.

Here, then, is the situation: abundant evidence that something is wrong, coupled with an abiding sense that the wrong is pernicious and widespread, and highly resistant to remedies. So, to quote Vladimir Lenin's famous pamphlet (whose title was plagiarized from a novel by Nikolai Chernyshevsky): *What Is to Be Done?*

Assuming that something should be done, one response could be to stiffen the apparatus of policing. Internet sites such as "Turnitin," to which students and teachers can submit student work to see if it contains material from essays already on electronic file, could be employed by more and more teachers to track down those who misuse the material. Penalties could be increased; the pursuers could try to become more clever than the pursued; teaching could take on an even more suspicious and hostile attitude. But this plan of attack might well underestimate the resourceful talents of young people—versed as they are in every aspect of the digital world—to outwit even vigilant professorial hawks.

But another strategy already exists. Some institutions, rare but 35 sturdily resolute in spirit, have fought the infection of cheating for decades. Many of them, but hardly all, are small liberal arts colleges. They have had history and tradition at their back. All of them have expended both time and social capital in encouraging honesty and trust. Instead of a campus culture in which adversarial tensions between administrators and students are a given and where cheating is presumed, these institutions convey to the students themselves the authority to monitor the ethical behavior of their classmates. Every student on these campuses is informed, directly and formally, what honor means and why it is important. Every student is presumed to want every classmate to observe the principles of honor. This puts everyone at the same moral starting line. Then students are expected to act as if the work of one is in fact the responsibility of all. Nothing about this is perfunctory. Indeed, at these schools, academic honor is a dominating concern.

Which are these colleges and universities, few in number and proud of their traditions? Washington and Lee, Haverford, Rice, Cal Tech, and the University of Virginia are among them. At some of them, the students themselves hear cases of alleged honor violations and render the judgments with no members of the faculty joining them. Professors note the violation; students then take charge. At such schools, when students cheat, students mete out the justice, which can be swift and uncompromising. At a few of these schools, there exists what is called the "single sanction": any violation of the honor code means permanent expulsion. At all these places, honor has been enshrined as fundamental to the history and the life of the institution. Known to every student who enrolls, the code of honor is already in practice while they matriculate; it is remembered with respect after they graduate. By maintaining such systems, these campuses are less likely to be collections of individuals than, at their best, small societies of truthful men and women. They see the dangers of cheating for what they are: practices in which many students can be hurt by the dishonesty of a few. And not just students but, in the words of Professor Kolich, the university as a whole, and the larger society beyond the gates.

Can the number of such campuses increase? More than 100 American campuses have some form of honor code already, even if many of them give only lip service to the concept. What would it take to transform classrooms throughout the United States into arenas of moral practice? How would American higher education look then? Might it have in hand one small but powerful argument to turn aside the criticisms hurled against it by those who think that it has lost its ethical bearings and who see it as given over to misplaced values such as pre-professional practicalities or simple-minded political correctness? Such critics—noisy and passionate—might be brought to attention with the news that moral instruction, at the foundation of some of the nation's best schools, had been given a central position at other schools across the country.

If such a reconsideration of one of the essential purposes of higher education were to take place, things on American campuses could begin to seem quite different. Instead of training a suspicious eye on students, professors could turn to them with an understanding of how much they have at stake, and how much they fear they can lose, as long as cheating thrives. In those students who do not cheat resides a core of strength, a habit of mind and morality, thus far employed at too few schools. Those schools should remind themselves of one central fact: at their best, students are dedicated to learning. Students who cheat undermine who they are. At its core, cheating is self-destructive.

The lesson is about students and what they alone can do, not about schools and what they have failed to do. The institutions, after all, can always find ways to walk away from the problem. Although no school welcomes negative publicity about academic dishonesty, administrators can always point the finger downward at those who break the rules. And professors can always distance themselves in the same way. So it is the students who stand at the center of this drama.

Doubters might say that what works at small schools couldn't work   40
at larger ones. Big universities, sprawling with students, promote anonymity, and with anonymity comes blamelessness. At such places, no
one is responsible for anything and honor codes are bound to fail. But
even big places are composed of individual classes, each taught by one
teacher, often in small rooms where, once again, principles of individual honor and personal responsibility can be secured and, once
again, those with the most to lose can act to bring honesty to bear.
Keep in mind that though universities might be large or small, the
average student-teacher ratio today is excellent, according to a 2010
survey by *U.S. News & World Report:* slightly less than 15-to-one,
with liberal arts colleges averaging 12.2 students per faculty member,
and national universities averaging 15.5 students per faculty member.
The numbers are small enough to permit, if not to encourage, local
and intimate moral responsibility.

To do nothing is not an answer. Once the emptiness of such a
response to so serious a problem is recognized, a form of education
beneficial to all can come. To encourage moral awareness is to appreciate what rests at the heart of what it means to teach. In the end, it
also rests at the heart of what it means to learn.

Should such a pattern of student responsibility spread more widely
across the nation, classroom after classroom will benefit. Students
will more fully understand how legitimate societies are established
and how they survive—by a consensual agreement that they will gov-
ern themselves by rule, by mutual respect, and by vigilance. At that
point, universities and colleges will be able to recover some of the
trust and respect they have lost. They will be able to say, with authority, that the essential virtue of honorable behavior is both promoted
and protected on campus.

STUDY QUESTIONS

1. According to Chace, what are some of the most pressing challenges that colleges and universities in America face?

2. What are some of the words that Chace uses to describe scholars whom he sees as defenders of plagiarism? What TONE do those words create in the essay?

3. What types of EVIDENCE does Chace present to support his claims, and which did you find most effective?

4. *For Writing.* In a short essay, reflect on your own feelings on academic honesty. How important is it for students to do their own original work, and why? What can schools do to increase academic honesty?

JAMES BARSZCZ { *Can You Be Educated from a Distance?*

JAMES BARSZCZ (b. 1955) has worked in the Internet industry since 1995. After earning both his BA and his PhD in English literature from Rutgers University and his MA from Indiana University, he taught a variety of courses in literature and composition at Rutgers. Barszcz has since moved on to the telecommunications field, but he continues to publish essays on literary topics and is the founding editor of the *College Hill Review*, an online quarterly magazine.

Barszcz's essay "Can You Be Educated from a Distance?" was first printed in 2003, as online courses began to establish themselves in higher education. Barszcz considers some common arguments for "distance learning" and offers his own argument in favor of on-site education. While online classes can indeed provide a student with information, he says, a "true education" is about much more than simply acquiring information. As you read, ask yourself what you consider to be the most important features of your education and what your education really *educes*, or "draws out," from you.

BY ALMOST ANY MEASURE, THERE is a boom in Internet-based instruction. In just a few years, 34 percent of American colleges and universities have begun offering some form of what's called "distance learning" (DL), and among the larger schools, it's closer to 90 percent. If you doubt the popularity of the trend, you probably haven't heard of the University of Phoenix. It grants degrees entirely on the basis of online instruction. It enrolls 90,000 students, a statistic used to support its claim to be the largest private university in the country.

While the kinds of instruction offered in these programs will differ, DL usually signifies a course in which the instructors post syllabi, reading assignments, and schedules on Web sites, and students send in their written assignments by e-mail. Other forms of communication often come into play, such as threaded messaging, which allows for posting questions and comments that are publicly viewable, as a bulletin board would, as well as chat rooms for real-time interchanges. Generally speaking, face-to-face communication with an instructor is minimized or eliminated altogether.

The attraction for students might at first seem obvious. Primarily, there's the convenience promised by courses on the Net: you can do the work, as they say, in your pajamas. But figures indicate that the reduced effort results in a reduced commitment to the course. While attrition rates for all freshmen at American universities is around 20 percent, the rate for online students is 35 percent. Students themselves seem to understand the weaknesses inherent in the setup. In a survey conducted for eCornell, the DL division of Cornell University, less than a third of the respondents expected the quality of the online course to be as good as the classroom course.

Clearly, from the schools' perspective, there's a lot of money to be saved. Although some of the more ambitious programs require new investments in servers and networks to support collaborative software, most DL courses can run on existing or minimally upgraded systems. The more students who enroll in a course but don't come to campus, the more the school saves on keeping the lights on in the classrooms, paying custodians, and maintaining parking lots. And, while there's evidence that instructors must work harder to run a DL course for a variety of reasons, they won't be paid any more, and might well be paid less.

But as a rule, those who champion distance learning don't base 5 their arguments on convenience or cost savings. More often, they claim DL signals an advance in the effectiveness of education. Consider the vigorous case made by Fairleigh Dickinson University (FDU), in Madison, New Jersey, where students—regardless of their expectations or desires—are now required to take one DL course per year. By setting this requirement, they say, FDU recognizes the Internet as "a premier learning tool" of the current technological age. Skill in using online resources "prepares our students, more than others, for life-long learning—for their jobs, their careers, and their personal growth." Moreover, Internet-based courses will connect FDU students to a "global virtual faculty," a group of "world-class scholars, experts, artists, politicians, and business leaders around the world."

Sounds pretty good. But do the claims make much sense? First, it should be noted that students today and in the future might well use the Internet with at least as much facility as the faculty. It's not at all clear that they need to be taught such skills. More to the point, how much time and effort do you suppose "world-class scholars" (much less politicians and business leaders) will expend for the benefit of students they never meet or even see? Probably a lot less than they're devoting to the books, journal articles, and position papers that are already available to anyone with access to a library.

Another justification comes from those who see distance learning as the next step in society's progress toward meritocracy. A recent article in *Forbes* magazine cites Professor Roger Schank of Northwestern University, who predicts that soon "students will be able to shop around, taking a course from any institution that offers a good one. . . . Quality education will be available to all. Students will learn what they want to learn rather than what some faculty committee decided was the best practical compromise." In sum, says Professor Schank, who is also chairman of a distance-learning enterprise called CognitiveArts, "Education will be measured by what you know rather than by whose name appears on your diploma."

Statements like these assume education consists in acquiring information ("what you know"). Accept that and it's hard to disagree with the conclusions. After all, what does it matter how, or through what medium, you get the information? But few truly educated people hold such a mechanistic view. Indeed, traditionally, education was aimed at cultivating intellectual and moral values, and the "information" you picked up was decidedly secondary. It was commonplace for those giving commencement speeches to note that, based on etymology, education is a drawing out, not a putting in. That is, a true education *educes,* or draws out, from within a person qualities of intellect and character that would otherwise have remained hidden or dormant.

Exactly how this kind of educing happens is hard to pin down. Only in part does it come from watching professors in the classroom present material and respond to student questions, the elements of education that can be translated to the Net with reasonable fidelity. Other educational experiences include things like watching how professors joke with each other (or not!) in the hallways, seeing what kinds of pictures are framed in a professor's office, or going out for coffee after class with people in your dorm. Such experiences, and countless others, are sometimes labeled (and dismissed) as "social life on campus." But they also contribute invaluably to education. Through them, you learn a style, in the noblest sense of that term, a way of regarding the information you acquire and the society you find yourself in. This is what the philosopher Alfred North Whitehead meant when he called style the ultimate acquisition of a cultivated mind. And it's the mysterious ways of cultivating that style that the poet Robert Frost meant when he said that all that a college education requires is that you "hang around until you catch on." Hanging around, that is, on campus, not lurking on the Net.

STUDY QUESTIONS

1. What unusual requirement must students at Fairleigh Dickinson University fulfill?

2. How does Barszcz DEFINE a "true education"? Why is this definition important to his ARGUMENT?

3. What arguments does Barszcz cite for distance learning? How does he refute these arguments? What is the main REASON he is against distance learning?

4. *For Writing.* Consider how and where you learn as you receive your education. Drawing on your own experience, write an argument in which you take a POSITION on distance learning. You may argue for it, against it, or for some combination of the two (you might be for certain aspects of it but against others, for instance).

T. ALLEN CULPEPPER { *The Myth of Inferiority*

T. ALLEN CULPEPPER (b. 1962) is an American professor and poet. He was born and raised in Alabama and earned a BA in English from the University of Alabama (1985), an MA in English from the University of West Florida (1993), and a PhD in English from the University of Tulsa (1998). In addition to his work as an academic and poet, Culpepper worked as a journalist for several years in the 1980s and early 1990s. He has taught at a number of colleges and universities in the United States, and is currently an assistant professor of English at Tulsa Community College.

"The Myth of Inferiority" was published in *The Chronicle of Higher Education*, a journal written for professors and others who work at colleges and universities, in 2006. In the essay, Culpepper challenges the idea that community-college students are less academically capable than their counterparts at four-year colleges and universities. He goes on to argue that the way in which teachers think about their students (and teaching in general) can have a major impact on their instructional practices. As you read, take special note of what Culpepper describes as the opinions that many teachers and administrators hold regarding community-college students and what he describes as the reality at both community colleges and four-year colleges and universities.

A CANDIDATE FOR A FACULTY position at a community college usually faces some version of the question "Why are you particularly well suited to working with the kinds of students who come here?" Having been interviewed for a number of such positions and having served on

"The Myth of Inferiority" by T. Allen Culpepper from *The Chronicle of Higher Education*, October 27, 2006. Used by permission of T. Allen Culpepper, formerly of State College of Florida, now teaches English at Tulsa Community College in Oklahoma.

several search committees charged with filling them, I speak from experience. At least superficially straightforward and appropriate, the question seldom surprises job candidates who have even casually attempted to prepare for their interviews. But that the question arises at all reflects widely held misconceptions of community-college students that job candidates, and even interviewers—who should know better—may have unconsciously internalized. For the incautious candidate, answering that unsurprising, but sometimes surprisingly loaded, question can be perilous.

As a novice job candidate myself, I simply (and perhaps naïvely) took the question at face value, accepting that community-college students differ significantly from students at other kinds of institutions. I genuinely wanted to teach at a community college. Having dutifully done my research and formulated my "statement of teaching philosophy," I began my first interview by stating my familiarity with the particular challenges that many community-college students face: being a first-generation college student, coping with economic hardship and lack of intellectual confidence, balancing academic responsibilities with competing obligations to employers and families. After emphasizing my desire to work with exactly those kinds of students, I declared my commitment to "student-centered learning." I emphasized my ability to help students succeed in the face of their challenges and to recognize the myriad "learning styles" that students bring to the classroom. I spoke of my ability to use various teaching methods to engage students, always being mindful of the need to stress the subject matter's "real-world connections" and "workplace value."

That kind of answer works well enough, if you make it with conviction and avoid any hint of irony when speaking the buzzwords. It is true that candidates must convey a clear understanding of the allegedly unique characteristics of community-college students, along with a sincere desire to teach such students. But at the same time, it is essential to steer clear of even the slightest suggestion that one considers community colleges or their students in any way inferior to four-year institutions or students who attend them. That is especially important if the interviewer's tone or framing of the question implies that he or she might hold that view.

Even early in my first job search, the question made me uneasy, mainly because of the subtle implication that teaching at a community college amounts to settling for second- or third-rate students. Merely asking the question somehow suggests, however faintly and unintentionally, that there is something wrong with students who choose to attend community colleges.

In later phases of job hunting, with more experience as an interviewee and as a teacher at various kinds of institutions (a private research university, a large land-grant university, two community colleges, and an institution in transition from two-year college to regional university), I gently challenged the question's underlying assumption that one finds totally different students at community colleges than at universities. In my experience, first- and second-year students, regardless of the type of institution they attend, are more alike than different. At every institution where I have taught, including the private research university, I have found poorly prepared first-generation students with few economic, academic, or social resources. And at every institution, including the community colleges, I have worked with well-prepared, intellectually gifted students with friends in all the right places and money to burn.

In four years at the same community college, I have watched the ebb and flow of students through several semesters, during some of which I have raved to anyone who would listen about how wonderful my students are, and during others of which I have whined incessantly, whether anyone listened or not, about how shockingly clueless my students are. While it is probably true that there were more high-caliber students in my honors classes at the private university than there are in my standard classes at the similarly sized community college where I teach now, only the proportions—not the types—of students have varied.

Although I have not conducted formal research in this area, I suspect that if one looked at essays from a representative sampling of students in freshman-composition classes at a university and at a community college, one would find it difficult to determine which essays came from which institution. In writing classes at both community colleges and universities, I have encountered intellectually gifted students who can write deeply analytical essays in eloquent prose, brilliant students who cannot write a shopping list that makes sense, students who write beautifully but fail to say anything of substance, and students who can hardly read, much less write clearly or think critically. At both kinds of institutions, I have also found students who manage to complete a full load of classes successfully while working three jobs, rearing multiple children alone, caring for elderly relatives, and coping with chronic illness or disability, as well as students who take a relatively light load of courses and don't do much else (except illicit drugs) but still manage to fail all their classes, despite considerable intelligence and ability.

Students are students, wherever they are.

The danger is that the perception of difference between the two groups of students can lead to low expectations of community-college students and an institutional culture that enables them to live down to those expectations. Unfortunately, the false belief persists among the general public, students themselves, and even some faculty members that students choose to attend community colleges because they couldn't survive academically at a university. That might be true for some, but many students choose community colleges for a variety of good reasons, such as cost, location, emphasis on teaching, and flexible class schedules.

Regardless of why students come to community colleges, we wel- 10 come them with open arms and make every accommodation we can to help them succeed. We want them, of course, to become well-adjusted, well-informed, clear-thinking citizens who can contribute productively and ethically to our society. We also want the enrollment figures that bring in revenue, the graduation and retention rates that impress accreditation teams, and the glowing evaluations of our teaching that earn us promotions and tenure. If we even unconsciously assume our students' inferiority while pursuing those goals, however, we risk lowering our standards rather than teaching our students how to meet them.

In seeking to satisfy our students while enhancing our own performance ratings, we might also yield too easily to educational fads of dubious value, as when we embrace and carry out the advice of the alleged pedagogical experts, who, as far as I can tell, denounce the lecture style of teaching while insisting that students learn most when they teach themselves and insist that hands-on learning is best (provided of course that people never touch each other), that teaching cannot occur without at least one computer in the room, and that, because every student has a different "learning style," professors must cater to the whims of all their students individually but simultaneously.

Do not misunderstand: Teachers should be willing to do whatever it takes, within reason, to engage students with the course material—to "meet students where they are." And it is true that the one thing worse than a bad lecture is a bad lecture with PowerPoint slides. But I am skeptical that there even is such a thing as "learning styles," for example. In my view, teachers will achieve better results by determining their own strengths and using them effectively than by attempting to use pedagogical methods that make them feel incompetent or uncomfortable because some expert says that is the "right" thing to do. In my experience, most students respond favorably to professors who teach well and respond negatively to professors who teach badly, regardless of the teaching methods employed.

If current and potential community-college faculty members allow ourselves, or even worse, our students, to accept the myth of community-college students' inherent inferiority, we may be, despite all our efforts to "retain" them as successful students, enabling them to fail. The means would be our own failure to uphold high performance standards and our willingness to make allowances for shoddy work, plagiarism, missed deadlines, chronic absence, and other academic sins because so many of our students have hard lives.

Let us again consider the question "Why are you particularly well suited to working with the kinds of students who come here?" Regardless of where "here" is and what kind of students it is known for, the best answer might be "I have learned to maintain high standards, expect students to meet them, and do whatever I can to help students meet those expectations." To lower our standards is to accept the false assumption that students "here" are inferior to students "there."

STUDY QUESTIONS

1. According to the essay, what are the *perceived* challenges that community-college students and teachers face? What does Culpepper say is the reality?

2. This piece was primarily written for a professional AUDIENCE—in this case, educators. How does Culpepper acknowledge what he sees as the common attitudes of his audience toward community-college students, and how does he challenge those attitudes?

3. As he moves away from discussing community-college students, what broader CLAIMS does Culpepper make about education, and how does he support them?

4. *For Writing.* Think about what Culpepper says about teaching and learning styles. Write a short essay in which you agree or disagree with Carr, citing your own educational experience—what are the best, most effective educational experiences you have had, and what made them the best?

SEAMUS HEANEY { *Mid-Term Break*

SEAMUS HEANEY (b. 1939) was born in Northern Ireland, the eldest of nine children. At twelve, he enrolled in St. Columb's College, a Catholic boarding school located in Derry, on scholarship. He graduated from Queens University of Belfast in 1961 with a degree in English language and literature. During his first position as a teacher he began to publish poetry with the encouragement of his headmaster, the writer Michael McLaverty. He has achieved great critical and commercial success as a poet, lecturer, and translator, culminating in the Nobel Prize in Literature in 1995. Heaney often draws on his rural and working-class roots (his father was a farmer; his mother's family were linen millworkers) for his body of work, which includes *Death of a Naturalist* (1967), *Wintering Out* (1973), and *The Haw Lantern* (1987). He has taught at Harvard University and the University of Oxford. His lyrical translation of *Beowulf* (2000) brought the Anglo-Saxon epic to a contemporary audience, as Heaney melded modern language with Old English form.

"Mid-Term Break" is based on a true event: the death of Heaney's four-year-old brother while the poet was away at St. Columb's. Composed from the distance of time, the poem engages with memory as it addresses the speaker's process of gradually coming to terms with what has happened. How does memory act as a filter as well as a clear lens through which to view this sad occasion?

I sat all morning in the college sick bay
Counting bells knelling classes to a close.
At two o'clock our neighbours drove me home.

In the porch I met my father crying—
He had always taken funerals in his stride—   5
And Big Jim Evans saying it was a hard blow.

The baby cooed and laughed and rocked the pram
When I came in, and I was embarrassed
By old men standing up to shake my hand

And tell me they were "sorry for my trouble."   10
Whispers informed strangers I was the eldest,
Away at school, as my mother held my hand

In hers and coughed out angry tearless sighs.
At ten o'clock the ambulance arrived
With the corpse, stanched and bandaged by the nurses.   15

Next morning I went up into the room. Snowdrops
And candles soothed the bedside; I saw him
For the first time in six weeks. Paler now,

Wearing a poppy bruise on his left temple,
He lay in the four foot box as in his cot.   20
No gaudy scars, the bumper knocked him clear.

A four foot box, a foot for every year.

STUDY QUESTIONS

1. What is the occasion for this poem?

2. Consider the language in this poem. For instance, how does the title "Mid-Term Break" function on a literal and on a SYMBOLIC level? Choose two to three other examples and explore their multiple meanings. What do the different readings bring to the poem?

3. How does Heaney employ "memory" to help his speaker ANALYZE THE PROCESS of coming to terms with a death in the family? What is the effect?

4. How does Heaney use—and not use—emotion in this poem? How does Heaney employ both emotion and neutrality? What is the effect? Be sure to cite concrete language from the poem to support your points.

5. *For Writing.* Write a poem or an essay about a significant, highly emotional event in your life. Carefully choose the TONE that you feel will best convey your reaction to the event. Describe the event using details that appeal to the senses.

TOM WAYMAN ⎱ *Did I Miss Anything?*

TOM WAYMAN (b. 1945) is a Canadian poet and critic. Born in Ontario and raised from age seven in British Columbia, Wayman received a BA in English from the University of British Columbia and holds an MFA in English and writing from the University of California at Irvine. He has worked as a professor of English and creative writing at a number of colleges in the United States and in Canada, and is the author of seventeen books of poetry, including *Waiting for Wayman* (1973), *In a Small House on the Outskirts of Heaven* (1989), *Did I Miss Anything? New and Selected Poems 1973–1993* (1993), and *The Astonishing Weight of the Dead* (1994), in addition to three volumes of fiction and three books of criticism.

In the poem "Did I Miss Anything?" Wayman gives a number of humorous responses to a question that students frequently ask their teachers after an absence—"Did I miss anything?" The narrator's responses fall into two categories: "Nothing" and "Everything." "Nothing" implies that the class either had no content or it just could not happen without the student's presence. "Everything" implies that the class was extremely valuable, and by missing a single meeting, the student has missed out entirely. Although both are exaggerations, "nothing" and "everything" correspond to different ways of looking at the value of the class. As you read, think about what each response says about the class— and what the teacher and students think about it.

―――――――――――

Question frequently asked by
students after missing a class

"Did I Miss Anything?" by Tom Wayman from *Did I Miss Anything: Selected Poems 1973–1993*, Harbour Publishing, 1993, www.harbourpublishing.com.

Nothing. When we realized you weren't here
we sat with our hands folded on our desks
in silence, for the full two hours

> Everything. I gave an exam worth
> 40 per cent of the grade for this term   5
> and assigned some reading due today
> on which I'm about to hand out a quiz
> worth 50 per cent

Nothing. None of the content of this course
has value or meaning   10
Take as many days off as you like:
any activities we undertake as a class
I assure you will not matter either to you or me
and are without purpose

> Everything. A few minutes after we began last time   15
> a shaft of light descended and an angel
> or other heavenly being appeared
> and revealed to us what each woman or man must do
> to attain divine wisdom in this life and
> the hereafter   20
> This is the last time the class will meet
> before we disperse to bring this good news to all people on earth

Nothing. When you are not present
how could something significant occur?

> Everything. Contained in this classroom   25
> is a microcosm of human existence
> assembled for you to query and examine and ponder
> This is not the only place such an opportunity has been gathered

but it was one place

And you weren't here   30

113

STUDY QUESTIONS

1. What opinions about the class do "nothing" and "everything" seem to represent?

2. Who do you think the AUDIENCE is for this poem—students who ask what they missed or teachers who are asked the question?

3. Both "nothing" and "everything" are examples of HYPERBOLE— exaggeration for rhetorical effect. Which of the two did you find most effective, and why?

4. *For Writing.* The poem's epigraph reads "Question asked frequently by students who have missed class." In a short essay, consider another question you think teachers receive frequently, as well as some exaggerated responses that it might receive.

TRIP GABRIEL { *Plagiarism Lines Blur for*
Students in Digital Age

TRIP GABRIEL (b. 1955) is a reporter for the *New York Times*, where
he writes on issues related to education and politics. He holds a bachelor's degree in philosophy from Middlebury College in Vermont and
has worked as a reporter and editor for the *Times* since 1986. From 1998
to 2010, he served as editor for the paper's "Styles" section, and his work
has appeared in a number of other national publications, including
Rolling Stone, *GQ*, and *Sports Illustrated*.

In this article, published in the *New York Times* in 2010, Gabriel
describes how attitudes toward intellectual property and plagiarism
seem to be changing among college students. He begins by giving several
examples of students who have been caught plagiarizing using Internet
sources. Then he moves on to discuss a potential cause of the problem
by citing several experts who argue that these changes are part of a
generational shift; as students grow up in a world in which they have
ready access to information through digital sources, they are less likely
to see using that information without attribution as inappropriate. As
you read, note the variety of arguments that Gabriel's sources give
regarding plagiarism and how they believe attitudes toward plagiarism
have changed over time.

AT RHODE ISLAND COLLEGE, A freshman copied and pasted from a
Web site's frequently asked questions page about homelessness—and

did not think he needed to credit a source in his assignment because the page did not include author information.

At DePaul University, the tip-off to one student's copying was the purple shade of several paragraphs he had lifted from the Web; when confronted by a writing tutor his professor had sent him to, he was not defensive—he just wanted to know how to change purple text to black.

And at the University of Maryland, a student reprimanded for copying from Wikipedia in a paper on the Great Depression said he thought its entries—unsigned and collectively written—did not need to be credited since they counted, essentially, as common knowledge.

Professors used to deal with plagiarism by admonishing students to give credit to others and to follow the style guide for citations, and pretty much left it at that.

But these cases—typical ones, according to writing tutors and offi-   5
cials responsible for discipline at the three schools who described the plagiarism—suggest that many students simply do not grasp that using words they did not write is a serious misdeed.

It is a disconnect that is growing in the Internet age as concepts of intellectual property, copyright and originality are under assault in the unbridled exchange of online information, say educators who study plagiarism.

Digital technology makes copying and pasting easy, of course. But that is the least of it. The Internet may also be redefining how students—who came of age with music file-sharing, Wikipedia and Web-linking—understand the concept of authorship and the singularity of any text or image.

"Now we have a whole generation of students who've grown up with information that just seems to be hanging out there in cyberspace and doesn't seem to have an author," said Teresa Fishman, director of the Center for Academic Integrity at Clemson University. "It's possible to believe this information is just out there for anyone to take."

Professors who have studied plagiarism do not try to excuse it— many are champions of academic honesty on their campuses—but rather try to understand why it is so widespread.

In surveys from 2006 to 2010 by Donald L. McCabe, a co-founder   10
of the Center for Academic Integrity and a business professor at

Rutgers University, about 40 percent of 14,000 undergraduates admitted to copying a few sentences in written assignments.

Perhaps more significant, the number who believed that copying from the Web constitutes "serious cheating" is declining—to 29 percent on average in recent surveys from 34 percent earlier in the decade.

Sarah Brookover, a senior at the Rutgers campus in Camden, N.J., said many of her classmates blithely cut and paste without attribution.

"This generation has always existed in a world where media and intellectual property don't have the same gravity," said Ms. Brookover, who at 31 is older than most undergraduates. "When you're sitting at your computer, it's the same machine you've downloaded music with, possibly illegally, the same machine you streamed videos for free that showed on HBO last night."

Ms. Brookover, who works at the campus library, has pondered the differences between researching in the stacks and online. "Because you're not walking into a library, you're not physically holding the article, which takes you closer to 'this doesn't belong to me,'" she said. Online, "everything can belong to you really easily."

A University of Notre Dame anthropologist, Susan D. Blum, disturbed by the high rates of reported plagiarism, set out to understand how students view authorship and the written word, or "texts" in Ms. Blum's academic language. 15

She conducted her ethnographic research among 234 Notre Dame undergraduates. "Today's students stand at the crossroads of a new way of conceiving texts and the people who create them and who quote them," she wrote last year in the book *My Word!: Plagiarism and College Culture,* published by Cornell University Press.

Ms. Blum argued that student writing exhibits some of the same qualities of pastiche that drive other creative endeavors today—TV shows that constantly reference other shows or rap music that samples from earlier songs.

In an interview, she said the idea of an author whose singular effort creates an original work is rooted in Enlightenment ideas of the individual. It is buttressed by the Western concept of intellectual property rights as secured by copyright law. But both traditions are being challenged.

"Our notion of authorship and originality was born, it flourished, and it may be waning," Ms. Blum said.

She contends that undergraduates are less interested in cultivat- 20 ing a unique and authentic identity—as their 1960s counterparts were—than in trying on many different personas, which the Web enables with social networking.

"If you are not so worried about presenting yourself as absolutely unique, then it's O.K. if you say other people's words, it's O.K. if you say things you don't believe, it's O.K. if you write papers you couldn't care less about because they accomplish the task, which is turning something in and getting a grade," Ms. Blum said, voicing student attitudes. "And it's O.K. if you put words out there without getting any credit."

The notion that there might be a new model young person, who freely borrows from the vortex of information to mash up a new creative work, fueled a brief brouhaha earlier this year with Helene Hegemann, a German teenager whose best-selling novel about Berlin club life turned out to include passages lifted from others.

Instead of offering an abject apology, Ms. Hegemann insisted, "There's no such thing as originality anyway, just authenticity." A few critics rose to her defense, and the book remained a finalist for a fiction prize (but did not win).

That theory does not wash with Sarah Wilensky, a senior at Indiana University, who said that relaxing plagiarism standards "does not foster creativity, it fosters laziness."

"You're not coming up with new ideas if you're grabbing and mix- 25 ing and matching," said Ms. Wilensky, who took aim at Ms. Hegemann in a column in her student newspaper headlined "Generation Plagiarism."

"It may be increasingly accepted, but there are still plenty of creative people—authors and artists and scholars—who are doing original work," Ms. Wilensky said in an interview. "It's kind of an insult that that ideal is gone, and now we're left only to make collages of the work of previous generations."

In the view of Ms. Wilensky, whose writing skills earned her the role of informal editor of other students' papers in her freshman dorm, plagiarism has nothing to do with trendy academic theories.

The main reason it occurs, she said, is because students leave high school unprepared for the intellectual rigors of college writing.

"If you're taught how to closely read sources and synthesize them into your own original argument in middle and high school, you're not going to be tempted to plagiarize in college, and you certainly won't do so unknowingly," she said.

At the University of California, Davis, of the 196 plagiarism cases 30 referred to the disciplinary office last year, a majority did not involve students ignorant of the need to credit the writing of others.

Many times, said Donald J. Dudley, who oversees the discipline office on the campus of 32,000, it was students who intentionally copied—knowing it was wrong—who were "unwilling to engage the writing process."

"Writing is difficult, and doing it well takes time and practice," he said.

And then there was a case that had nothing to do with a younger generation's evolving view of authorship. A student accused of plagiarism came to Mr. Dudley's office with her parents, and the father admitted that he was the one responsible for the plagiarism. The wife assured Mr. Dudley that it would not happen again.

STUDY QUESTIONS

1. According to Trip Gabriel, what STANCES do students have about plagiarism while using digital sources?

2. What EVIDENCE do Gabriel and his sources present to show readers how plagiarism and students' attitudes toward it are changing on college campuses? What evidence shows that things might not be that different after all?

3. Several of the experts Gabriel quotes CLAIM that changes in digital technology have altered the way that students think about intellectual honesty. What are some of the reasons they give for this claim, and do you find them convincing?

4. *For Writing.* Think about your own experience with digital materials. Do you think that traditional rules of intellectual property and plagiarism should apply to them in the same way that the rules apply to "traditional" media? For instance, should a website be treated in the same way as a book? Why or why not?

ANNE PERRIN { *Stop Blaming Teachers*

ANNE PERRIN (b. 1948) received her BA from the University of Houston, her MA from Sam Houston State University, and her PhD from the University of Houston. She has taught at the University of Houston, at Lone Star College, North Harris, and at two public high schools. She also served as a department chair for a private high school. Co-editor of *Chican@s in the Conversations* (2007), Perrin has had essays published in *Hands Across Borders: A Reader for Writers* (2003), *Contemporary Issues* and *Decisions: Reading, Writing, and Thinking in Today's World* (2006), and *Diverse Issues, Diverse Answers: Reading, Writing, and Thinking about Social Issues* (2006).

In "Stop Blaming Teachers," Perrin argues that the No Child Left Behind (NCLB) law, particularly its emphasis on teacher performance, is damaging public education. According to Perrin, NCLB has replaced real teaching with a regime of standardized testing, to the detriment of student learning and teacher satisfaction. She insists that parents, school administrators, government officials, and students all need to accept responsibility for the problems plaguing education—and accept responsibility for fixing them.

I AM WRITING THIS ARTICLE dog-tired and frustrated. I have worked ten hours today, mostly on my feet, dealt with lesson plans, students, and a mediocre technology system slower than government reform, and ended the day with an 80-minute session on the latest security measures for the upcoming round of Texas Assessment of Knowledge and Skills tests, commonly known in the state as TAKS. Teachers hate this test, actually HATE it at their genetic core, not because of the oaths, security training, or even the ridiculous budget-gouging costs of TAKS supplies, but because the test actually has nothing to do with teaching. TAKS has everything to do with teacher accountability. In short, whatever happens on the TAKS test is, ultimately, the teacher's fault. Driven by a manic desire to appease the No Child Left Behind[1] gods and reap the rewards of millions in federal dollars, Texas, along with many other states, has developed educational tunnel vision. In some weird, myopic way, the nation has recognized its dismal educational woes and decided to put a bull's-eye on the only one standing in the classroom, the teacher. The time has come for teachers to sit down and let the real culprits in this matter stand up and take the heat: government officials, administrators, parents, and especially the students.

The minute many readers finish that last sentence, I'm sure reactions bordering on accusations of child abuse will start festering. However, if you want to see the ridiculousness of the situation teachers face daily, imagine a child of sixteen getting a minor infection. The parent/guardian takes the teenager to the doctor, who provides a thorough and correct diagnosis, writes a prescription, and sends the patient home. However, that night the teenager is not made to take all the medicine as directed, and, instead of being made to rest, is permitted to play video games and watch TV and even keep up with her/his part-time job and social fun. Now imagine the parent blaming the doctor for the child's failure to get well, and you have only part of the situation teachers work in every day. Picture the doctor getting a call from the parent wanting a conference to explain why the doctor failed to cure the teenager and the doctor's local medical board wanting to investigate every procedure the doctor performed to make sure she/he was not at fault. In addition, the child's failure to get well is added to the doctor's "failure-to-cure rate," which cannot exceed 15 percent. Before you laugh, you might want to ask a local teacher what the "failure rate" is in her/his school. I personally have taught in a school district that imposed a 10 percent failure rate on teachers; go over the 10 percent mark, and you risk being "intervened," a educational, bureau-

---

[1] That is, the No Child Left Behind Act of 2001, a law passed by Congress with the goal of requiring greater accountability in public schools; in practice, the law has led to a greater emphasis on standardized testing of student progress.

cratic term for intensive monitoring, humiliation, and intimidation. I have also been told that any—*any*—failure in my room is my fault. At times the administrative intimidation has been so heavy that experienced teachers have confided to me that they are afraid to fail students.

If the doctor metaphor above seems hard to take in, the reason may be the enormous firewalls of protection that now surround the students of America. Pick up any recent article on the disappointing performance of the American educational system in relation to the global classroom, and nowhere will you see anyone looking at the person sitting in the classroom desk. Instead, the articles randomly point to any number of accomplices to educational failure, starting at the top with the federal level and working their way down through a myriad of state and local entities, all inevitably settling on the teacher like granite boulders. Granted, the educational situation of America in relation to the rest of the world is not something to brag about. Amanda Paulson points out that in 2007 the United States "ranked 29th" in science "behind countries like Croatia, the Czech Republic, and Liechtenstein" (1). As for math, the best critique that analysts such as Paul Farhi of the *Washington Post* can offer is a milquetoast description of the United States as landing "roughly in the middle of the pack" of foreign countries, ranking about 12th for elementary students and 14th for middle schoolers (B2). In reading, our scores on the Progress in International Reading Literacy Study (PIRLS) place American fourth graders seventh out of 39 countries, behind Russia, Hong Kong, and Singapore, and the scores have not changed since 2001 (Manzo 1). On a national level for history, we fare no better: the scores for history on the National Assessment of Educational Progress for 2006 showed that more than half of American twelfth graders demonstrated a "poor command of basic facts" in American history (Dillon 2).

What surprises me in looking at all those figures is that the students, parents, administrators, states, and even the federal government assume that the person who stands up in a classroom every day, all day, assists students, provides lessons tailored to individual learning styles, deals with discipline problems that at times are insulting and possibly downright dangerous, is underpaid and overworked can be the scapegoat for our nation's educational ills. Imagine the federal government working as much as a teacher: there would not be one bill left to vote on within a month. Instead, according to OMB Watch, a public research group that scrutinizes the federal Office of Management and Budget, what the country got was a do-nothing Congress that worked "on average . . . 152 days per session" for the last 20 years and only 125 days in 2006 (1).

The great contribution of this lazy effort at government is the No   5 Child Left Behind (NCLB) law passed in 2001. As Andrew Ferguson explains, what NCLB does is require that all instructors will "be 'highly qualified' and that every student will be 'proficient' in reading and math by the 2013–14 school year" (5). The marker for judging such competency: federal testing of "every student in every public school" in America. The horror attached to such testing: federal dollars for grades. The nightmare result: as Ferguson points out, approximately 40 percent of schools have reduced instruction in history, civics, and government to focus on reading and math (2). And this is only the tip of the proverbial iceberg. In its own nearsighted fashion, the federal government has divided students in every school into categories; some sections are based on "race and ethnicity" and others on language abilities and family finances. If a school fails to score well in any of these sections, the school risks not only losing what little monies the federal government portions out but also runs the risk of federal intervention in the school itself: a nightmare takeover scenario reminiscent of the film *Night of the Living Dead* (5).

In a paradoxical way, the loss of federal dollars, so coveted by school districts nationwide, would not be the nuclear hot spot envisioned by bleary-eyed school administrators. Myron Lieberman, in his book *The Educational Morass: Overcoming the Stalemate in American Education,* points out the lack of "correlation" between federal monies and student success (qtd. in Ferguson 8). Thank goodness for Lieberman's findings because the federal government has been so lax in funding NCLB that Texas, Michigan, and Vermont joined together recently and won a federal lawsuit that found fault with the federal government for failing to provide a fair explanation of "financial liabilities" tied to federal dollars. The lawsuit has been sent back to the lower courts for further deliberation (Dillon 2).

What is so pathetic about the whole federal funding testing debacle is the fact that standardized testing has attached itself to the federal mindset like the monster creatures in *Alien,* infiltrating its host and hiding while it festers and grows, only to reemerge in a horrifying scene of carnage. Currently, there are two relevant educational bills before Congress. One is sponsored by Senator Christopher J. Dodd of Connecticut (D) and Rep. Vernon J. Ehlers of Michigan (R), who want to give states federal monies for embracing on a "voluntary" basis the federal standards in mathematics and science: the payoff—$4 million per state (Olson 1–2). The other one, proposed by Senator Edward Kennedy of Massachusetts (D), "encourage(s)" each state to align its standards to those of the National Assessment of Educational Progress (NAEP) (Olson 1). The initial payoff here goes not to the classroom but to the committees set up to *study* the situation: $200 million for state grants to form "councils" to study the proposal and $75 million for a state "consortia" (Olson 4). What I don't understand is how the federal government can send to the president a bill offering $46 billion in "one-time business tax breaks" and a bailout for Fannie Mae ("For Many Students" 2, 7) and, quicker than a scantron can grade a test, suggest $275 million in committees to study proposals, but states have to sue just to get the government to help our nation's educational staff and students. It's a shame there wasn't a No Government Left Behind law passed in its place.

Before you get all dewy-eyed about the states' championing teachers in a Herculean battle with the federal demigods, you might want to consider life in a Texas school. Texas teachers live under a double cloud of scrutiny. Not only do our students have to meet federal standards, they have to meet state standards as well. I long for the 125-day work year that Congress has! A recent article in *American Teacher* notes that federal and state demands in Texas classrooms result in as many as 130 days a year aimed at some activity related to testing ("Can We Teach" 1). I, personally, have taught in a district that instructed its teachers to put aside the curriculum and teach the test. The great fear for administrators in this district is the loss of what monies there are to be had and the fear of federal intervention. The great sadness for teachers is that students are missing out on a planned curriculum that would have provided them with a broader cultural and analytical background—to say nothing of losing much of the joy in learning.

And Texas is not alone in its difficulties. For example, according to Jason Song, the Los Angeles Unified School District will lose $36 million from its budget this year and up to $500 million next year (1). The target: teacher wages (Song 3). But the great hidden secret about state testing in Texas is that testing is a cash cow for the state. I find a rather twisted humor in the fact that Texas sued the federal government for failure to fund properly, then turned around and now sells its own booklets for whopping amounts to its school districts, thus draining enormous amounts of school tax dollars away from schools and into the state budget. Try going to the Texas Education Agency Web site for its district offices and shopping the Web site for TAKS preparation materials for state-mandated tests. The Texas *TAKS Reading Preparation Series,* teacher edition, is $50 and each student edition is $12. The *TAKS Reading Preparation Posters and Graphic Organizers* are $25 each (region 41). Just be careful in ordering to check if you can copy the materials for your students without breaking the copyright laws; you may have to spend a lot more than you originally thought out of your meager department budget.

But the educational buck does not stop with the state. School 10 districts are now locked between the proverbial rock of desperately needed federal funds and the hard place of schools that do not meet federal or, in Texas's case, state standards. What amuses me as I write these comments are the ways school districts deflect responsibility away from themselves. The solution is to avoid the inner sanctum of the school board meeting room and/or superintendent's office and look elsewhere for the solution.

The *Christian Science Monitor*'s article "Math Teacher Says She Was Fired for Failing Students" takes a typical approach: tie the teacher to the student-failure rate. The article describes the firing of Adele Jones for failing too many math students: her rate had actually dropped from 42 percent in 1990–91 to 27 percent in 1991–92 (1).

The school board claimed "incompetent" teaching but the issue of negative grades was brought up at her hearing. According to Jones, an Algebra II teacher, her instructions were to "evaluate her students' level and teach 'Algebra 1-1/2'" (2).

I, personally, think a gigantic wall-size mirror should be put in every administrator's office so each can at look at him-/herself and practice saying "It's all your fault" before going out and telling that to a teacher who just spent her or his entire weekend grading. I have been a department chairperson four times in my life, once for history and three times for English, and it is a rare, let me assure you, *rare* event to find an incompetent teacher. You may have a new, inexperienced one, but you will have to look long and hard to find one who does not work overtime; come in early and/or stay late for tutoring; keep up with staff development and technology hours; call and e-mail parents; and devise lesson plans to satisfy student needs, parent concerns, administrators' expectations, state standards, and the federal government. Add to that the sponsorship of clubs, sports, athletic events, band, choir, and a host of other related activities. Furthermore, I am sick of the frivolous potshots often taken at teachers' instructional decisions. For example, the *English Journal* recently ran an article by Kevin R. St. Jarre blaming teachers for low reading scores because they gave "sexist" and "feminine" materials to boys (2). At the time I was teaching fiction analysis, and my students voluntary chose their stories to analyze. I asked the male students about St. Jarre's article: they thought it was ridiculous since many of them had chosen exactly what the article termed a poor choice for males. When I asked them about analyzing *Field & Stream* magazine (St. Jarre 2), one of the article's suggestions, they laughed and, quite frankly, were insulted. And people wonder why teachers leave the profession in droves. I'm surprised that any stay.

If you have kept a scorecard on this Blame Game, you'll note that not once has the issue of student responsibility entered the picture. Overcrowding of our schools has put student discipline problems in a pressure cooker. I teach in a suburban school, and my students tell me that they are often afraid of other students who intimidate them in the halls or restrooms. Often a classroom may have students just out of juvenile detention sitting next to a struggling student and causing trouble.

From a different perspective, students are pros at "working" the system of counselors and parents to get transferred to easier classes. They often just don't read. Remember, this is the Barney generation that grew up glued to a TV screen and now are glued to a computer screen. They are glued! Want to calm a class down? Turn on the projector: it's a narcotic! Furthermore, they will often and frankly admit that they just didn't do their homework. But be careful in your grading: if your failure rate is too high, you risk intervention, and the students are quite aware of that fact. If a student knows she/he can make up an assignment four weeks late, why rush? Would you? The only problem is that the hardworking students feel cheated, and they are. These are the silent, invisible victims of a system designed to pass at least 80 percent.

The most disturbing point I have discovered about student responsibility is the amount of time my students work after school. Most students have seven classes, and I find it frightening that a great many work anywhere from 4–8 hours after school and on weekends, many just to afford luxuries that their parents/guardians refuse to buy. When parents are brought into the failure/pass equation by the analysts, it is usually for what an article in the *Washington Post* terms the "dysfunctional family" situations ranging from abuse to neglect. ("For the Record" 2) What is often left out of the family equation are the passive problems: allowing high schoolers to work on school nights or all weekend, placing too much family responsibility on older siblings for younger ones, or worse, establishing a pattern of parents intimidating teachers to raise student grades. Now throw into the equation the fact that the student hates the state test, has devoted so many hours to testing that the teacher is directed by his/her administrator to tell the student specifically that the test given by the state is "the actual test" and not another practice test, then you have a major problem, and it does not involve the person standing at the front of the room.

In closing, I would like you to consider yourself as a Texas teacher 15 for a few moments. Your class size is 30–35, six times a day, and may include mainstreamed special education students; now, be sure to keep up with all the different learning styles and needs of each student, every period of every day. It starts with the exhausted student who worked six hours after school the day before, only partially did his/her homework, and who has baseball or band practice after school. Be sure when you give that lesson that you tailor its presentation to fit all 30–35 of your students and that you keep them focused on a state test they have seen so much that they need bribing just to attempt it. Then pray that your scores are high enough.

WORKS CITED

"Can We Teach, Please?" *American Teacher* 92.4 (Dec. 2007/Jan. 2008): 8+. *ProQuest*. Lone Star Coll. Lib. 13 Feb. 2008 <http://proquest.umi.com>.

Dillon, Sam. "Court Revives Lawsuit Against Federal Education Law." *New York Times* 8 Jan 2008: A 18. *ProQuest*. Lone Star Coll. Lib. 12 Feb. 2008 <http://proquest.umi.com>.

———. "Students Gain Only Marginally on Test of U.S. History." *New York Times*. 17 May 2007: A19. *ProQuest*. Lone Star Coll. Lib. 12 Feb. 2008 <http://proquest.umi.com>.

Farhi, Paul. "Five Myths About U.S. Kids Outclassed by the Rest of the World." *Washington Post* 21 Jan. 2007: B2.

Ferguson, Andrew. "No Child Left Alone." *The Weekly Standard* 13.2 (24 Sept. 2007): 30+. *ProQuest*. Lone Star Coll. Lib. 11 Feb. 2008 <http://proquest.umi.com>.

"For Many Students, the Hardest Tests Are at Home." *The Washington Post* 5 Oct. 2006: T5. *ProQuest*. Lone Star Coll. Lib. 11 Feb. 2008 <http://proquest.umi.com>.

"For the Record Here's How So . . ." *The Washington Post* 10 Feb. 2008: T13. *ProQuest*. Lone Star Coll. Lib. 12 Feb. 2008 <http://proquest. umi.com>.

Hu, Winnie, and David W. Chen. "New Jersey Suburbs Fear a Drop in Special Education Aid." *New York Times*. 8 Dec. 2007: B1. *ProQuest*. Lone Star Coll. Lib. 12 Feb. 2008 <http://proquest.umi.com>.

Manzo, Kathleen Kennedy. "America Idles on International Reading Test." *Education Week* 2.14 (5 Dec. 2007): 11. *ProQuest*. Lone Star Coll. Lib. 12 Feb. 2008 <http://proquest.umi.com>.

"Math Teacher Says She Was Fired for Failing Students." *The Christian Science Monitor* 12 Aug. 1993. *ProQuest*. Lone Star Coll. Lib. 12 Feb. 2008 <http://proquest.umi.com>.

Olson, Lynn. "Standards Get Boost on the Hill." *Education Week* 26.19 (17 Jan. 2007): 1+. *ProQuest.* Lone Star Coll. Lib. 12 Feb. 2008 <http://proquest.umi.com>.

OMB Watch. "Congress to Have Short Year; Appropriations Work Likely to Suffer." 7 Feb. 2006. 27 Feb. 2008 <http://www.ombwatch.org/article/articleprint/3272/-1/{category_id}>.

Paulson, Amanda. "New Report Ranks U.S. Teens 29th in Science Worldwide." *The Christian Science Monitor* 5 Dec. 2007: 2. *ProQuest.* Lone Star Coll. Lib. 12 Feb. 2008 <http://proquest.umi.com>.

Reeder, Scott. "Teacher Failures." *Investigative Reporters and Editors, Inc.: the IRE Journal* 29.2 (Mar./Apr. 2006): 18+. *ProQuest.* Lone Star Coll. Lib. 11 Feb. 2008 <http://proquest.umi.com>.

region4 Educational Solutions. "TAKS Reading/Language Arts." 24 Feb. 2008 <http://www.esc4.net>.

St. Jarre, Kevin R. "Don't Blame the Boys: We're Giving Them Girly Books" *English Journal* 97.3 (Jan. 2008): 15+. *ProQuest.* Lone Star Coll. Lib. 12 Feb. 2008 <http://proquest.umi.com>.

Song, Jason, and Howard Blume. "The State Budget Crisis/Education; L. A. Unified Cuts Could Hurt Reforms; The District Might Have to Trim $36 million Now and $500 million Next Year. It's Unacceptable, Board President Says." *Los Angeles Times* 11 Jan. 2008: A18. *ProQuest.* Lone Star Coll. Lib. 12 Feb. 2008 <http://proquest.umi.com>.

STUDY QUESTIONS

1. Explain the analogy that Perrin makes between teachers and doctors. How effective do you find it, and why?

2. Identify the THESIS of this essay. What EVIDENCE does Perrin use to support that thesis? How effective do you find her evidence, and why? Do you think she's correct that student responsibility never "enters the picture"?

3. Humor is often an effective way to approach an issue and take the edge off a negative critique. Select several examples of Perrin's humor and explain why she has used humor and why it is (or isn't) effective in each case. Could she more effectively make her points by taking a more sober approach? Explain.

4. *For Writing.* REFLECT on your own high-school experiences and the teachers you had. Did No Child Left Behind affect the teaching or learning in your classes? If so, how? Were you aware of administrative intervention into the curriculum at any time? Did your school mandate standardized testing as a requirement for graduation? If you think NCLB didn't affect your school, why not? If you finished school before the law was passed, how do you think your education differs from those who went to school under the law? Write a PERSONAL ESSAY in response to Perrin's article, agreeing or disagreeing with her according to your own experiences.

NATALIE ANGIER { *Men, Women, Sex*
and Darwin

NATALIE ANGIER (b. 1958) has built a career writing books and articles
that explain the intricacies of science to the nonscientist. Born and raised in
New York City, Angier graduated from Barnard College, where she studied
physics, astronomy, and English. She began working as a science writer for
Discovery magazine in 1980, and in 1990 she joined the staff of the *New York
Times*, where she won a Pulitzer Prize for beat reporting in 1991. She has
published four books, all of them bestsellers: *Natural Obsessions* (1988),
The Beauty of the Beastly (1995), *Woman: An Intimate Geography* (2000),
and *The Canon: A Whirligig Tour of the Beautiful Basics of Science* (2007).

In "Men, Women, Sex and Darwin," published in the *New York Times* in
1999, Angier examines the most common theories proposed by evolutionary psychologists to explain male and female sexual behavior—for instance,
that men are naturally more promiscuous than women and that women are
naturally more interested in marriage than men. Drawing on empirical evidence and the work of psychologists, anthropologists, and primatologists,
Angier finds reason to doubt these theories and offers alternative explanations of her own. As you read, notice how Angier summarizes and synthe-
sizes information from many different sources.

LIFE IS SHORT BUT JINGLES are forever. None more so, it seems, than
the familiar ditty, variously attributed to William James, Ogden Nash
and Dorothy Parker: "Hoggamus, higgamus,/Men are polygamous,/Higgamus, hoggamus,/Women monogamous."

Lately the pith of that jingle has found new fodder and new fans, through the explosive growth of a field known as evolutionary psychology. Evolutionary psychology professes to have discovered the fundamental modules of human nature, most notably the essential nature of man and of woman. It makes sense to be curious about the evolutionary roots of human behavior. It's reasonable to try to understand our impulses and actions by applying Darwinian logic to the problem. We're animals. We're not above the rude little prods and jests of natural and sexual selection. But evolutionary psychology as it has been disseminated across mainstream consciousness is a cranky and despotic Cyclops, its single eye glaring through an overwhelmingly masculinist lens. I say "masculinist" rather than "male" because the view of male behavior promulgated by hard-core evolutionary psychologists is as narrow and inflexible as their view of womanhood is.

I'm not interested in explaining to men what they really want or how they should behave. If a fellow chooses to tell himself that his yen for the fetching young assistant in his office and his concomitant disgruntlement with his aging wife make perfect Darwinian sense, who am I to argue with him? I'm only proposing here that the hard-core evolutionary psychologists have got a lot about women wrong—about some of us, anyway—and that women want more and deserve better than the cartoon Olive Oyl[1] handed down for popular consumption.

The cardinal premises of evolutionary psychology of interest to this discussion are as follows: 1. Men are more promiscuous and less sexually reserved than women are. 2. Women are inherently more interested in a stable relationship than men are. 3. Women are naturally attracted to high-status men with resources. 4. Men are naturally attracted to youth and beauty. 5. Humankind's core preferences and desires were hammered out long, long ago, a hundred thousand years or more, in the legendary Environment of Evolutionary Adaptation, or E.E.A., also known as the ancestral environment, also known as the Stone Age, and they have not changed appreciably since then, nor are they likely to change in the future.

---

[1]Popeye's long-suffering sweetheart in the *Popeye* comic strip and animations, first created by cartoonist Elzie Crisler Segar in 1929.

In sum: Higgamus, hoggamus, Pygmalionus, *Playboy* magazine, 5
eternitas. Amen.

Hard-core evolutionary psychology types go to extremes to argue in
favor of the yawning chasm that separates the innate desires of women
and men. They declare ringing confirmation for their theories even in
the face of feeble and amusingly contradictory data. For example:
Among the cardinal principles of the evo-psycho set is that men are by
nature more polygamous than women are, and much more accepting
of casual, even anonymous, sex. Men can't help themselves, they say:
they are always hungry for sex, bodies, novelty and nubility. Granted,
men needn't act on such desires, but the drive to sow seed is there
nonetheless, satyric and relentless, and women cannot fully understand its force. David Buss, a professor of psychology at the University
of Texas at Austin and one of the most outspoken of the evolutionary
psychologists, says that asking a man not to lust after a pretty young
woman is like telling a carnivore not to like meat.

At the same time, they recognize that the overwhelming majority of
men and women get married, and so their theories must extend to different innate mate preferences among men and women. Men look for
the hallmarks of youth, like smooth skin, full lips and perky breasts;
they want a mate who has a long childbearing career ahead of her. Men
also want women who are virginal and who seem as though they'll be
faithful and not make cuckolds of them. The sexy, vampy types are fine
for a Saturday romp, but when it comes to choosing a marital partner,
men want modesty and fidelity.

Women want a provider, the theory goes. They want a man who
seems rich, stable and ambitious. They want to know that they and
their children will be cared for. They want a man who can take charge,
maybe dominate them just a little, enough to reassure them that the
man is genotypically, phenotypically, eternally, a king. Women's innate
preference for a well-to-do man continues to this day, the evolutionary
psychologists insist, even among financially independent and profes-
sionally successful women who don't need a man as a provider. It was
adaptive in the past to look for the most resourceful man, they say, and
adaptations can't be willed away in a generation or two of putative cultural change.

And what is the evidence for these male-female verities? For the difference in promiscuity quotas, the hard-cores love to raise the example of the differences between gay men and lesbians. Homosexuals are seen as a revealing population because they supposedly can behave according to the innermost impulses of their sex, untempered by the need to adjust to the demands and wishes of the opposite sex, as heterosexuals theoretically are. What do we see in this ideal study group? Just look at how gay men carry on! They are perfectly happy to have hundreds, thousands, of sexual partners, to have sex in bathhouses, in bathrooms, in Central Park. By contrast, lesbians are sexually sedate. They don't cruise sex clubs. They couple up and stay coupled, and they like cuddling and hugging more than they do serious, genitally based sex.

In the hard-core rendering of inherent male-female discrepancies in 10 promiscuity, gay men are offered up as true men, real men, men set free to be men, while lesbians are real women, ultrawomen, acting out every woman's fantasy of love and commitment. Interestingly, though, in many neurobiology studies gay men are said to have somewhat feminized brains, with hypothalamic nuclei that are closer in size to a woman's than to a straight man's, and spatial-reasoning skills that are modest and ladylike rather than manfully robust. For their part, lesbians are posited to have somewhat masculinized brains and skills—to be sportier, more mechanically inclined, less likely to have played with dolls or tea sets when young—all as an ostensible result of exposure to prenatal androgens. And so gay men are sissy boys in some contexts and Stone Age manly men in others, while lesbians are battering rams one day and flower into the softest and most sexually divested girlish girls the next.

On the question of mate preferences, evo-psychos rely on surveys, most of them compiled by David Buss. His surveys are celebrated by some, derided by others, but in any event they are ambitious—performed in thirty-seven countries, he says, on six continents. His surveys, and others emulating them, consistently find that men rate youth and beauty as important traits in a mate, while women give comparatively greater weight to ambition and financial success. Surveys show that surveys never lie. Lest you think that women's mate preferences change with their own mounting economic clout, surveys assure us that they do not. Surveys of female medical students, according to John Marshall Townsend, of Syracuse University, indicate that they hope to marry men with an earning power and social status at least equal to and preferably greater than their own.

Perhaps all this means is that men can earn a living wage better, even now, than women can. Men make up about half the world's population, but they still own the vast majority of the world's wealth—the currency, the minerals, the timber, the gold, the stocks, the amber fields of grain. In her superb book *Why So Slow?* Virginia Valian, a professor of psychology at Hunter College, lays out the extent of lingering economic discrepancies between men and women in the United States. In 1978 there were two women heading Fortune 1000 companies; in 1994, there were still two; in 1996, the number had jumped all the way to four. In 1985, 2 percent of the Fortune 1000's senior-level executives were women; by 1992, that number had hardly budged, to 3 percent. A 1990 salary and compensation survey of 799 major companies showed that of the highest-paid officers and directors, less than one-half of 1 percent were women. Ask, and he shall receive. In the United States the possession of a bachelor's degree adds $28,000 to a man's salary but only $9,000 to a woman's. A degree from a high-prestige school contributes $11,500 to a man's income but subtracts $2,400 from a woman's. If women continue to worry that they need a man's money, because the playing field remains about as level as the surface of Mars, then we can't conclude anything about innate preferences. If women continue to suffer from bag-lady syndrome even as they become prosperous, if they still see their wealth as provisional and capsizable, and if they still hope to find a man with a dependable income to supplement their own, then we can credit women with intelligence and acumen, for inequities abound.

There's another reason that smart, professional women might respond on surveys that they'd like a mate of their socioeconomic status or better. Smart, professional women are smart enough to know that men can be tender of ego—is it genetic?—and that it hurts a man to earn less money than his wife, and that resentment is a noxious chemical in a marriage and best avoided at any price. "A woman who is more successful than her mate threatens his position in the male hierarchy," Elizabeth Cashdan, of the University of Utah, has written. If women could be persuaded that men didn't mind their being high achievers, were in fact pleased and proud to be affiliated with them, we might predict that the women would stop caring about the particulars of their mates' income. The anthropologist Sarah Blaffer Hrdy writes that "when female status and access to resources do not depend on her mate's status, women will likely use a range of criteria, not primarily or even necessarily prestige and wealth, for mate selection." She cites a 1996 *New York Times* story about women from a wide range of professions—bankers, judges, teachers, journalists—who marry male convicts. The allure of such men is not their income, for you can't earn much when you make license plates for a living. Instead, it is the men's gratitude that proves irresistible. The women also like the fact that their husbands' fidelity is guaranteed. "Peculiar as it is," Hrdy writes, "this vignette of sex-reversed claustration[2] makes a serious point about just how little we know about female choice in breeding systems where male interests are not paramount and patrilines[3] are not making the rules."

Do women love older men? Do women find gray hair and wrinkles attractive on men—as attractive, that is, as a fine, full head of pigmented hair and a vigorous, firm complexion? The evolutionary psychologists suggest yes. They believe that women look for the signs of maturity in men because a mature man is likely to be a comparatively wealthy and resourceful man. That should logically include baldness, which generally comes with age and the higher status that it often confers. Yet, as Desmond Morris points out, a thinning hairline is not considered a particularly attractive state.

Assuming that women find older men attractive, is it the men's alpha   15
status? Or could it be something less complimentary to the male, something like the following—that an older man is appealing not because he is powerful but because in his maturity he has lost some of his power, has become less marketable and desirable and potentially

[2]Cloistering, enclosing.
[3]Groups of patrilineages, or lines of descent from a male ancestor.

more grateful and gracious, more likely to make a younger woman feel that there is a balance of power in the relationship? The rude little calculation is simple: He is male, I am female—advantage, man. He is older, I am younger—advantage, woman. By the same token, a woman may place little value on a man's appearance because she values something else far more: room to breathe. Who can breathe in the presence of a handsome young man, whose ego, if expressed as a vapor, would fill Biosphere II? Not even, I'm afraid, a beautiful young woman.

In the end, what is important to question, and to hold to the fire of alternative interpretation, is the immutability and adaptive logic of the discrepancy, its basis in our genome rather than in the ecological circumstances in which a genome manages to express itself. Evolutionary psychologists insist on the essential discordance between the strength of the sex drive in males and females. They admit that many nonhuman female primates gallivant about rather more than we might have predicted before primatologists began observing their behavior in the field—more, far more, than is necessary for the sake of reproduction. Nonetheless, the credo of the coy female persists. It is garlanded with qualifications and is admitted to be an imperfect portrayal of female mating strategies, but then, that little matter of etiquette attended to, the credo is stated once again.

"Amid the great variety of social structure in these species, the basic theme . . . stands out, at least in minimal form: males seem very eager for sex and work hard to find it; females work less hard," Robert Wright says in *The Moral Animal*. "This isn't to say the females don't like sex. They love it, and may initiate it. And, intriguingly, the females of the species most closely related to humans—chimpanzees and bonobos—seem particularly amenable to a wild sex life, including a variety of partners. Still, female apes don't do what male apes do: search high and low, risking life and limb, to find sex, and to find as much of it, with as many different partners, as possible; it has a way of finding them." In fact female chimpanzees do search high and low and take great risks to find sex with partners other than the partners who have a way of finding them. DNA studies of chimpanzees in West Africa show that half the offspring in a group of closely scrutinized chimpanzees turned out not to be the offspring of the resident males.

The females of the group didn't rely on sex "finding" its way to them; they proactively left the local environs, under such conditions of secrecy that not even their vigilant human observers knew they had gone, and became impregnated by outside males. They did so even at the risk of life and limb—their own and those of their offspring. Male chimpanzees try to control the movements of fertile females. They'll scream at them and hit them if they think the females aren't listening. They may even kill an infant they think is not their own. We don't know why the females take such risks to philander, but they do, and to say that female chimpanzees "work less hard" than males do at finding sex does not appear to be supported by the data.

Evo-psychos pull us back and forth until we might want to sue for whiplash. On the one hand we are told that women have a lower sex drive than men do. On the other hand we are told that the madonna-whore dichotomy is a universal stereotype. In every culture, there is a tendency among both men and women to adjudge women as either chaste or trampy. The chaste ones are accorded esteem. The trampy ones are consigned to the basement, a notch or two below goats in social status. A woman can't sleep around without risking terrible retribution, to her reputation, to her prospects, to her life. "Can anyone find a single culture in which women with unrestrained sexual appetites aren't viewed as more aberrant than comparably libidinous men?" Wright asks rhetorically.

Women are said to have lower sex drives than men, yet they are universally punished if they display evidence to the contrary—if they disobey their "natural" inclination toward a stifled libido. Women supposedly have a lower sex drive than men do, yet it is not low enough. There is still just enough of a lingering female infidelity impulse that cultures everywhere have had to gird against it by articulating a rigid dichotomy with menacing implications for those who fall on the wrong side of it. There is still enough lingering female infidelity to justify infibulation, purdah, claustration. Men have the naturally higher sex drive, yet all the laws, customs, punishments, shame, strictures, mystiques and antimystiques are aimed with full hominid fury at that tepid, sleepy, hypoactive creature, the female libido.

"It seems premature . . . to attribute the relative lack of female inter- 20

139

est in sexual variety to women's biological nature alone in the face
of overwhelming evidence that women are consistently beaten for
promiscuity and adultery," the primatologist Barbara Smuts has written. "If female sexuality is muted compared to that of men, then
why must men the world over go to extreme lengths to control and
contain it?"

Why indeed? Consider a brief evolutionary apologia for President
Clinton's adulteries written by Steven Pinker, of the Massachusetts
Institute of Technology. "Most human drives have ancient Darwinian
rationales," he wrote. "A prehistoric man who slept with fifty women
could have sired fifty children, and would have been more likely to
have descendants who inherited his tastes. A woman who slept with
fifty men would have no more descendants than a woman who slept
with one. Thus, men should seek quantity in sexual partners; women,
quality." And isn't it so, he says, everywhere and always so? "In our
society," he continues, "most young men tell researchers that they
would like eight sexual partners in the next two years; most women say
that they would like one." Yet would a man find the prospect of a string
of partners so appealing if the following rules were applied: that no
matter how much he may like a particular woman and be pleased by
her performance and want to sleep with her again, he will have no say
in the matter and will be dependent on her mood and good graces for
all future contact; that each act of casual sex will cheapen his status and
make him increasingly less attractive to other women; and that society
will not wink at his randiness but rather sneer at him and think him
pathetic, sullied, smaller than life? Until men are subjected to the same
severe standards and threat of censure as women are, and until they are
given the lower hand in a so-called casual encounter from the start, it
is hard to insist with such self-satisfaction that, hey, it's natural, men
like a lot of sex with a lot of people and women don't.

Reflect for a moment on Pinker's philandering caveman who slept
with fifty women. Just how good a reproductive strategy is this chronic,
random shooting of the gun? A woman is fertile only five or six days a
month. Her ovulation is concealed. The man doesn't know when she's
fertile. She might be in the early stages of pregnancy when he gets to
her; she might still be lactating and thus not ovulating. Moreover, even

if our hypothetical Don Juan hits a day on which a woman is ovulating, the chances are around 65 percent that his sperm will fail to fertilize her egg; human reproduction is complicated, and most eggs and sperm are not up to the demands of proper fusion. Even if conception occurs, the resulting embryo has about a 30 percent chance of miscarrying at some point in gestation. In sum, each episode of fleeting sex has a remarkably small probability of yielding a baby—no more than 1 or 2 percent at best.

And because the man is trysting and running, he isn't able to prevent any of his casual contacts from turning around and mating with other men. The poor fellow. He has to mate with many scores of women for his wham-bam strategy to pay off. And where are all these women to be found, anyway? Population densities during that purportedly all-powerful psyche shaper the "ancestral environment" were quite low, and long-distance travel was dangerous and difficult.

There are alternatives to wantonness, as a number of theorists have emphasized. If, for example, a man were to spend more time with one woman rather than dashing breathlessly from sheet to sheet, if he were to feel compelled to engage in what animal behaviorists call mate guarding, he might be better off, reproductively speaking, than the wild Lothario, both because the odds of impregnating the woman would increase and because he'd be monopolizing her energy and keeping her from the advances of other sperm bearers. It takes the average couple three to four months of regular sexual intercourse to become pregnant. That number of days is approximately equal to the number of partners our hypothetical libertine needs to sleep with to have one encounter result in a "fertility unit," that is, a baby. The two strategies, then, shake out about the same. A man can sleep with a lot of women—the quantitative approach—or he can sleep with one woman for months at a time, and be madly in love with her—the qualitative tactic.

It's possible that these two reproductive strategies are distributed in discrete packets among the male population, with a result that some men are born philanderers and can never attach, while others are born romantics and perpetually in love with love; but it's also possible that men teeter back and forth from one impulse to the other, suffering an internal struggle between the desire to bond and the desire to retreat, with the circuits of attachment ever there to be toyed with, and their needs and desires difficult to understand, paradoxical, fickle, treacherous and glorious. It is possible, then, and for perfectly good Darwinian reason, that casual sex for men is rarely as casual as it is billed.

It needn't be argued that men and women are exactly the same, or that humans are meta-evolutionary beings, removed from nature and slaves to culture, to reject the perpetually regurgitated model of the coy female and the ardent male. Conflicts of interest are always among us, and the outcomes of those conflicts are interesting, more interesting by far than what the ultra-evolutionary psychology line has handed us. Patricia Gowaty, of the University of Georgia, sees conflict between males and females as inevitable and pervasive. She calls it sexual dialectics. Her thesis is that females and males vie for control over the means of reproduction. Those means are the female body, for there is as yet no such beast as the parthenogenetic[4] man.

Women are under selective pressure to maintain control over their reproduction, to choose with whom they will mate and with whom they will not—to exercise female choice. Men are under selective pressure to make sure they're chosen or, barring that, to subvert female choice and coerce the female to mate against her will. "But once you have this basic dialectic set in motion, it's going to be a constant push-me, pull-you," Gowaty says. That dynamism cannot possibly result in a unitary response, the caricatured coy woman and ardent man. Instead there are going to be some coy, reluctantly mating males and some ardent females, and any number of variations in between.

"A female will choose to mate with a male whom she believes, consciously or otherwise, will confer some advantage on her and her offspring. If that's the case, then her decision is contingent on what she brings to the equation." For example, she says, "the 'good genes' model leads to oversimplified notions that there is a 'best male' out there, a top-of-the-line hunk whom all females would prefer to mate with if they had the wherewithal. But in the viability model, a female brings

[4]Created from an unfertilized egg.

her own genetic complement to the equation, with the result that what looks good genetically to one woman might be a clash of colors for another."

Maybe the man's immune system doesn't complement her own, for example, Gowaty proposes. There's evidence that the search for immune variation is one of the subtle factors driving mate selection, which may be why we care about how our lovers smell; immune molecules may be volatilized and released in sweat, hair, the oil on our skin. We are each of us a chemistry set, and each of us has a distinctive mix of reagents. "What pleases me might not please somebody else," Gowaty says. "There is no one-brand great male out there. We're not all programmed to look for the alpha male and only willing to mate with the little guy or the less aggressive guy because we can't do any better. But the propaganda gives us a picture of the right man and the ideal woman, and the effect of the propaganda is insidious. It becomes self-reinforcing. People who don't fit the model think, I'm weird, I'll have to change my behavior." It is this danger, that the ostensible "discoveries" of evolutionary psychology will be used as propaganda, that makes the enterprise so disturbing.

Variation and flexibility are the key themes that get set aside in the breathless dissemination of evolutionary psychology. "The variation is tremendous, and is rooted in biology," Barbara Smuts said to me. "Flexibility itself is the adaptation." Smuts has studied olive baboons, and she has seen males pursuing all sorts of mating strategies. "There are some whose primary strategy is dominating other males, and being able to gain access to more females because of their fighting ability," she says. "Then there is the type of male who avoids competition and cultivates long-term relationships with females and their infants. These are the nice, affiliative guys. There's a third type, who focuses on sexual relationships. He's the consorter. . . . And as far as we can tell, no one reproductive strategy has advantages over the others."

Women are said to need an investing male. We think we know the reason. Human babies are difficult and time consuming to raise. Stone Age mothers needed husbands to bring home the bison. Yet the age-old assumption that male parental investment lies at the heart of human evolution is now open to serious question. Men in traditional

30

foraging cultures do not necessarily invest resources in their offspring. Among the Hadza of Africa, for example, the men hunt, but they share the bounty of that hunting widely, politically, strategically. They don't deliver it straight to the mouths of their progeny. Women rely on their senior female kin to help feed their children. The women and their children in a gathering-hunting society clearly benefit from the meat that hunters bring back to the group. But they benefit as a group, not as a collection of nuclear family units, each beholden to the father's personal pound of wildeburger.

This is a startling revelation, which upends many of our presumptions about the origins of marriage and what women want from men and men from women. If the environment of evolutionary adaptation is not defined primarily by male parental investment, the bedrock of so much of evolutionary psychology's theories, then we can throw the door wide open and ask new questions, rather than endlessly repeating ditties and calling the female coy long after she has run her petticoats through the presidential paper shredder.

For example: Nicholas Blurton Jones, of the University of California at Los Angeles, and others have proposed that marriage developed as an extension of men's efforts at mate guarding. If the cost of philandering becomes ludicrously high, the man might be better off trying to claim rights to one woman at a time. Regular sex with a fertile woman is at least likely to yield offspring at comparatively little risk to his life, particularly if sexual access to the woman is formalized through a public ceremony—a wedding. Looked at from this perspective, one must wonder why an ancestral woman bothered to get married, particularly if she and her female relatives did most of the work of keeping the family fed from year to year. Perhaps, Blurton Jones suggests, to limit the degree to which she was harassed. The cost of chronic male harassment may be too high to bear. Better to agree to a ritualized bond with a male and to benefit from whatever hands-off policy that marriage may bring, than to spend all of her time locked in one sexual dialectic or another.

Thus marriage may have arisen as a multifaceted social pact: between man and woman, between male and male and between the couple and the tribe. It is a reasonable solution to a series of cultural challenges that arose in concert with the expansion of the human neocortex. But its roots may not be what we think they are, nor may our contemporary mating behaviors stem from the pressures of an ancestral environment as it is commonly portrayed, in which a woman needed a mate to help feed and clothe her young. Instead, our "deep" feelings about marriage may be more pragmatic, more contextual and, dare I say it, more egalitarian than we give them credit for being.

If marriage is a social compact, a mutual bid between man and woman to contrive a reasonably stable and agreeable microhabitat in a community of shrewd and well-armed members, then we can understand why, despite rhetoric to the contrary, men are as eager to marry as women are. A raft of epidemiological studies have shown that marriage adds more years to the life of a man than it does to that of a woman. Why should that be, if men are so "naturally" ill suited to matrimony? 35

What do women want? None of us can speak for all women, or for more than one woman, really, but we can hazard a mad guess that a desire for emotional parity is widespread and profound. It doesn't go away, although it often hibernates under duress, and it may be perverted by the restrictions of habitat or culture into something that looks like its opposite. The impulse for liberty is congenital. It is the ultimate manifestation of selfishness, which is why we can count on its endurance.

STUDY QUESTIONS

1. What theories of evolutionary psychology does Angier call into question? What alternative theories does she propose?

2. List the people Angier quotes or cites. How does each contribute to her essay? What is the rhetorical effect of using these sources? How would the essay be different if she hadn't used sources?

3. *For Writing.* Write an essay in which you explain, in your own words, a theory of evolutionary psychology that Angier discusses. Then DESCRIBE the behavior of at least two people you know and explain how that behavior supports or refutes that theory.

MARGARET ATWOOD { *The Female Body*

MARGARET ATWOOD (b. 1939), best known for her novels *The Edible Woman* (1970) and *The Handmaid's Tale* (1983), was born in Ottawa, Canada. She received her BA from Victoria College at the University of Toronto and her MA from Ratcliffe College. Atwood has served as writer in residence at several universities in Canada and the United States. She has published thirty-five volumes of poetry, fiction, and nonfiction, including *Moral Disorder* and *The Tent,* collections of short fiction that were both published in 2006, and the poetry collection *The Door* (2007).

This narrator takes the reader on a tour of the various uses of, problems with, meanings of, and attitudes toward the female body. She is critical of how society views women as objects, but she softens the critique with humor that is surprisingly generous toward men. As you read, consider how the scenes presented contribute to the development of the narrative.

> *. . . entirely devoted to the subject of 'The Female Body.'*
> *Knowing how well you have written on this topic . . . this*
> *capacious topic . . .*
> —LETTER FROM THE MICHIGAN QUARTERLY REVIEW

1

I AGREE, IT'S A HOT topic. But only one? Look around, there's a wide range. Take my own, for instance.

I get up in the morning. My topic feels like hell. I sprinkle it with water, brush parts of it, rub it with towels, powder it, add lubricant. I dump in the fuel and away goes my topic, my topical topic, my controversial topic, my capacious topic, my limping topic, my nearsighted topic, my topic with back problems, my badly behaved topic, my vulgar topic, my outrageous topic, my aging topic, my topic that is out of the question and anyway still can't spell, in its oversized coat and worn winter boots, scuttling along the sidewalk as if it were flesh and blood, hunting for what's out there, an avacado, an alderman, an adjective, hungry as ever.

2

The basic Female Body comes with the following accessories: garter belt, panty girdle, crinoline, camisole, bustle, brassiere, stomacher, chemise, virgin zone, spike heels, nose ring, veil, kid gloves, fishnet stockings, fichu, bandeau, Merry Widow, weepers, chokers, barrettes, bangles, beads, lorgnette, feather boa, basic black, compact, Lycra stretch one-piece with modesty panel, designer peignoir, flannel nightie, lace teddy, bed, head.

3

The Female Body is made of transparent plastic and lights up when you plug it in. You press a button to illuminate the different systems. The Circulatory System is red, for the heart and arteries, purple for the veins; the Respiratory System is blue, the Lymphatic System is yellow, the Digestive System is green, with liver and kidneys in aqua. The nerves are done in orange and the brain in pink. The skeleton, as you might expect, is white.

The Reproductive System is optional, and can be removed. It comes 5 with or without a miniature embryo. Parental judgment can thereby be exercised. We do not wish to frighten or offend.

4

He said, I won't have one of those things in the house. It gives a young girl a false notion of beauty, not to mention anatomy. If a real woman was built like that she'd fall on her face.

She said, if we don't let her have one like all the other girls she'll feel singled out. It'll become an issue. She'll long for one and she'll long to turn into one. Repression breeds sublimation. You know that.

He said, It's not just the pointy plastic tits, it's the wardrobes. The wardrobes and that stupid male doll, what's his name, the one with the underwear glued on.

She said, Better to get it over with when she's young. He said, All right but don't let me see it.

She came whizzing down the stairs, thrown like a dart. She was stark naked. Her hair had been chopped off, her head was turned back to front, she was missing some toes and she'd been tattooed all over her body with purple ink, in a scrollwork design. She hit the potted azalea, trembled there for a moment like a botched angel, and fell.

He said, I guess we're safe.

5

The Female Body has many uses. It's been used as a door knocker, a bottle-opener, as a clock with a ticking belly, as something to hold up lampshades, as a nutcracker, just squeeze the brass legs together and out comes your nut. It bears torches, lifts victorious wreaths, grows copper wings, and raises aloft a ring of neon stars; whole buildings rest on its marble heads.

It sells cars, beer, shaving lotion, cigarettes, hard liquor; it sells diet plans and diamonds, and desire in tiny crystal bottles. Is this the face that launched a thousand products? You bet it is, but don't get any funny big ideas, honey, that smile is a dime a dozen.

It does not merely sell, it is sold. Money flows into this country or that country, flies in, practically crawls in, suitful after suitful, lured by all those hairless preteen legs. Listen, you want to reduce the national debt, don't you? Aren't you patriotic? That's the spirit. That's my girl.

She's a natural resource, a renewable one luckily, because those things 15
wear out so quickly. They don't make 'em like they used to. Shoddy goods.

6

One and one equals another one. Pleasure in the female is not a requirement. Pair-bonding is stronger in geese. We're not talking about love, we're talking about biology. That's how we all got here, daughter.

Snails do it differently. They're hermaphrodites, and work in threes.

7

Each female body contains a female brain. Handy. Makes things work. Stick pins in it and you get amazing results. Old popular songs. Short circuits. Bad dreams.

Anyway: each of these brains has two halves. They're joined together by a thick cord; neural pathways flow from one to the other, sparkles of electric information washing to and fro. Like light on waves. Like a conversation. How does a woman know? She listens. She listens in.

The male brain, now, that's a different matter. Only a thin connection. Space over here, time over there, music and arithmetic in their own 20
sealed compartments. The right brain doesn't know what the left brain is doing. Good for aiming though, for hitting the target when you pull the trigger. What's the target? Who's the target? Who cares? What matters is hitting it. That's the male brain for you. Objective.

This is why men are so sad, why they feel so cut off, why they think of themselves as orphans cast adrift, footloose and stringless in the deep void. What void? she says. What are you talking about? The void of the Universe, he says, and she says Oh and looks out the window and tries to get a handle on it, but it's no use, there's too much going on, too many rustlings in the leaves, too many voices, so she says, Would you like a cheese sandwich, a piece of cake, a cup of tea? And he grinds his teeth because she doesn't understand, and wanders off, not just alone but Alone, lost in the dark, lost in the skull, searching for the other half, the twin who could complete him.

Then it comes to him: he's lost the Female Body! Look, it shines in the gloom, far ahead, a vision of wholeness, ripeness, like a giant melon, like an apple, like a metaphor for *breast* in a bad sex novel; it shines like a balloon, like a foggy noon, a watery moon, shimmering in its egg of light.

Catch it. Put it in a pumpkin, in a high tower, in a compound, in a chamber, in a house, in a room. Quick, stick a leash on it, a lock, a chain, some pain, settle it down, so it can never get away from you again.

STUDY QUESTIONS

1. Two unnamed people, referred to simply as "he" and "she," talk about an unnamed object for which "he" has a definite distaste. What is the TOPIC of this conversation? Why was the conversation ultimately pointless?

2. Atwood divides this text into sections. How does the selection maintain its unity? Would the text have been better constructed with traditional PLOT development? Explain.

3. The original copyright date of "The Female Body" is 1983. How do you think it was received some twenty-five years ago? What is your RESPONSE to it now? Is there anything to be learned from this piece today? What?

4. *For Writing.* Identify the different DESCRIPTIONS and DEFINITIONS that Atwood's NARRATOR provides.Using the text as a model, write, either independently or collaboratively, a piece about the male body. Consider using humor in the form of SATIRE and IRONY, as Atwood does.

NAOMI WOLF { *The Beauty Myth*

NAOMI WOLF (b. 1962) earned her undergraduate degree at Yale University and her graduate degree at Oxford University, where she was a Rhodes Scholar. She has published several books on women's issues, including her first book and bestseller, *The Beauty Myth: How Images of Beauty Are Used Against Women* (1991), and on American democracy. Her writing appears regularly in such diverse publications as the *New Republic*, the *Wall Street Journal*, *Glamour*, *Ms.*, *Esquire*, the *Guardian*, the *Washington Post*, and the *New York Times*. Wolf is also politically active: she is a cofounder and board member of the Woodhull Institute for Ethical Leadership, an organization that provides women with leadership training and professional development, and she is a cofounder of the American Freedom Campaign, a grassroots movement to restore checks and balances to American democracy.

This introductory chapter from *The Beauty Myth* argues that women must first recognize and understand the current "beauty myth" in order to resist it. As an example of what some term "third-wave" feminism, this chapter discusses the challenges faced by first-wave feminists (e.g., Lucy Stone) and second-wave feminists (e.g., Betty Friedan), and it urges that current challenges, while different, are still detrimental to gender equality.

━━━━━━━━━━

AT LAST, AFTER A LONG silence, women took to the streets. In the two decades of radical action that followed the rebirth of feminism in the early 1970s, Western women gained legal and reproductive rights, pursued higher education, entered the trades and the professions, and overturned ancient and revered beliefs about their social role. A generation on, do women feel free?

The affluent, educated, liberated women of the First World, who can enjoy freedoms unavailable to any women ever before, do not feel as free as they want to. And they can no longer restrict to the subconscious their sense that this lack of freedom has something to do with—with apparently frivolous issues, things that really should not matter. Many are ashamed to admit that such trivial concerns—to do with physical appearance, bodies, faces, hair, clothes—matter so much. But in spite of shame, guilt, and denial, more and more women are wondering if it isn't that they are entirely neurotic and alone but rather that something important is indeed at stake that has to do with the relationship between female liberation and female beauty.

The more legal and material hindrances women have broken through, the more strictly and heavily and cruelly images of female beauty have come to weigh upon us. Many women sense that women's collective progress has stalled; compared with the heady momentum of earlier days, there is a dispiriting climate of confusion, division, cynicism, and above all, exhaustion. After years of much struggle and little recognition, many older women feel burned out; after years of taking its light for granted, many younger women show little interest in touching new fire to the torch.

During the past decade, women breached the power structure; meanwhile, eating disorders rose exponentially and cosmetic surgery became the fastest-growing medical specialty.[1] During the past five years, consumer spending doubled, pornography became the main media category,[2] ahead of legitimate films and records combined, and thirty-three thousand American women told researchers that they

---

[1] *Standard and Poor's Industry Surveys* (New York: Standard and Poor's Corp., 1988). [Unless otherwise indicated, the notes included with this selection are those of the author.]

[2] See "Crackdown on Pornography: A No-Win Battle," *U.S. News and World Report,* June 4, 1984. The Association of Fashion and Image Consultants tripled its membership between 1984 and 1989 alone (Annetta Miller and Dody Tsiantar, *Newsweek,* May 22, 1989). During the five or six years prior to 1986, consumer spending rose from $300 billion to $600 billion.

would rather lose ten to fifteen pounds than achieve any other goal.[3] More women have more money and power and scope and legal recognition than we have ever had before; but in terms of how we feel about ourselves *physically,* we may actually be worse off than our unliberated grandmothers. Recent research consistently shows that inside the majority of the West's controlled, attractive, successful working women, there is a secret "underlife" poisoning our freedom; infused with notions of beauty, it is a dark vein of self-hatred, physical obsessions, terror of aging, and dread of lost control.[4]

It is no accident that so many potentially powerful women feel this 5 way. We are in the midst of a violent backlash against feminism that uses images of female beauty as a political weapon against women's advancement: the beauty myth. It is the modern version of a social reflex that has been in force since the Industrial Revolution. As women released themselves from the feminine mystique of domesticity, the beauty myth took over its lost ground, expanding as it waned to carry on its work of social control.

The contemporary backlash is so violent because the ideology of beauty is the last one remaining of the old feminine ideologies that still has the power to control those women whom second-wave feminism would have otherwise made relatively uncontrollable: It has grown stronger to take over the work of social coercion that myths about motherhood, domesticity, chastity, and passivity no longer can manage. It is seeking right now to undo psychologically and covertly all the good things that feminism did for women materially and overtly.

This counterforce is operating to checkmate the inheritance of

[3]University of Cincinnati College of Medicine, 1984: Wooley, S. C., and O. W. Wooley, "Obesity and Women: A Closer Look at the Facts," *Women's Studies International Quarterly,* vol. 2 (1979), pp. 69–79. Data reprinted in "33,000 Women Tell How They Really Feel About Their Bodies," *Glamour,* February 1984.
[4]See Dr. Thomas Cash, Diane Cash, and Jonathan Butters, "Mirror-Mirror on the Wall: Contrast Effects and Self-Evaluation of Physical Attractiveness," *Personality and Social Psychology Bulletin,* September 1983, vol. 9, no. 3. Dr. Cash's research shows very little connection between "how attractive women are" and "how attractive they feel themselves to be." All the women he treated were, in his terms, "extremely attractive," but his patients compare themselves only to models, not to other women.

feminism on every level in the lives of Western women. Feminism gave us laws against job discrimination based on gender; immediately case law evolved in Britain and the United States that institutionalized job discrimination based on women's appearances. Patriarchal religion declined; new religious dogma, using some of the mind-altering techniques of older cults and sects, arose around age and weight to functionally supplant traditional ritual. Feminists, inspired by Friedan,[5] broke the stranglehold on the women's popular press of advertisers for household products, who were promoting the feminine mystique; at once, the diet and skin care industries became the new cultural censors of women's intellectual space, and because of their pressure, the gaunt, youthful model supplanted the happy housewife as the arbiter of successful womanhood. The sexual revolution promoted the discovery of female sexuality; "beauty pornography"—which for the first time in women's history artificially links a commodified "beauty" directly and explicitly to sexuality—invaded the mainstream to undermine women's new and vulnerable sense of sexual self-worth. Reproductive rights gave Western women control over our own bodies; the weight of fashion models plummeted to 23 percent below that of ordinary women, eating disorders rose exponentially, and a mass neurosis was promoted that used food and weight to strip women of that sense of control. Women insisted on politicizing health; new technologies of invasive, potentially deadly "cosmetic" surgeries developed apace to re-exert old forms of medical control of women.

Every generation since about 1830 has had to fight its version of the beauty myth. "It is very little to me," said the suffragist Lucy Stone in 1855, "to have the right to vote, to own property, etcetera, if I may not keep my body, and its uses, in my absolute right."[6] Eighty years later, after women had won the vote, and the first wave of the organized women's movement had subsided, Virginia Woolf wrote that it would still be decades before women could tell the truth about their bodies. In 1962, Betty Friedan quoted a young woman trapped in the

---

[5]Betty Friedan (1921–2006), American feminist and author of the influential *The Feminine Mystique* (1963). [Ed.]

[6]Lucy Stone, 1855, quoted in Andrea Dworkin, *Pornography: Men Possessing Women* (New York: Putnam, 1981), p. 11.

Feminine Mystique: "Lately, I look in the mirror, and I'm so afraid I'm going to look like my mother." Eight years after that, heralding the cataclysmic second wave of feminism, Germaine Greer described "the Stereotype": "To her belongs all that is beautiful, even the very word beauty itself . . . she is a doll . . . I'm sick of the masquerade."[7] In spite of the great revolution of the second wave, we are not exempt. Now we can look out over ruined barricades: A revolution has come upon us and changed everything in its path, enough time has passed since then for babies to have grown into women, but there still remains a final right not fully claimed.

The beauty myth[8] tells a story: The quality called "beauty" objectively and universally exists. Women must want to embody it and men must want to possess women who embody it. This embodiment is an imperative for women and not for men, which situation is necessary and natural because it is biological, sexual, and evolutionary: Strong men battle for beautiful women, and beautiful women are more reproductively successful. Women's beauty must correlate to their fertility, and since this system is based on sexual selection, it is inevitable and changeless.

None of this is true. "Beauty" is a currency system like the gold 10 standard. Like any economy, it is determined by politics, and in the modern age in the West it is the last, best belief system that keeps male dominance intact. In assigning value to women in a vertical hierarchy according to a culturally imposed physical standard, it is an expression of power relations in which women must unnaturally compete for resources that men have appropriated for themselves.

"Beauty" is not universal or changeless, though the West pretends

---

[7]Germaine Greer, *The Female Eunuch* (London: Paladin Grafton Books, 1970), pp. 55, 60.
[8]See also Roland Barthes's definition: "It [myth] transforms history into nature. . . . Myth has the task of giving an historical intention a natural justification, and making contingency appear eternal." Roland Barthes, "Myth Today," *Mythologies* (New York: Hill and Wang, 1972), p. 129.

   Anthropologist Bronislaw Malinowski's definition of "a myth or origin" is relevant to the beauty myth: A myth of origin, writes Ann Oakley, "tends to be worked hardest in times of social strain, when the state of affairs portrayed in the myth are called into question." Ann Oakley, *Housewife: High Value/Low Cost* (London: Penguin Books, 1987), p. 163.

that all ideals of female beauty stem from one Platonic Ideal Woman;[9] the Maori admire a fat vulva, and the Padung, droopy breasts. Nor is "beauty" a function of evolution: its ideals change at a pace far more rapid than that of the evolution of species, and Charles Darwin was himself unconvinced by his own explanation that "beauty" resulted from a "sexual selection"[1] that deviated from the rule of natural selection; for women to compete with women through "beauty" is a reversal of the way in which natural selection affects all other mammals. Anthropology has overturned the notion that females must be "beautiful" to be selected to mate: Evelyn Reed, Elaine Morgan, and others have dismissed sociobiological assertions of innate male polygamy and female monogamy. Female higher primates are the sexual initiators; not only do they seek out and enjoy sex with many partners, but "every nonpregnant female takes her turn at being the most desirable of all her troop. And that cycle keeps turning as long as she lives."[2] The inflamed pink sexual organs of primates are often cited by male sociobiologists as analogous to human arrangements relating to female "beauty," when in fact that is a universal, non-hierarchical female primate characteristic.

[9]See Plato's discussion of Beauty in *Symposium*. For varying standards of beauty, see Ted Polhemus, *BodyStyles* (Luton, England: Lennard Publishing, 1988).

[1]See Cynthia Eagle Russett, "Hairy Men and Beautiful Women," *Sexual Science: The Victorian Construction of Womanhood* (Cambridge, Mass.: Harvard University Press, 1989), pp. 78–103.

On page 84 Russett quotes Darwin: "Man is more powerful in body and mind than woman, and in the savage state he keeps her in a much more abject state of bondage, than does the male of any other animal; therefore it is not surprising that he should have gained the power of selection. . . . As women have long been selected for beauty, it is not surprising that some of their successive variations should have been transmitted exclusively to the same sex; consequently that they should have transmitted beauty in a somewhat higher degree to their female than to their male offspring, and thus have become more beautiful, according to general opinion, than men." Darwin himself noticed the evolutionary inconsistency of this idea that, as Russett puts it, "a funny thing happened on the way up the ladder: among humans, the female no longer chose but was chosen." This theory "implied an awkward break in evolutionary continuity," she observes: "In Darwin's own terms it marked a rather startling reversal in the trend of evolution."

See also Natalie Angier, "Hard-to-Please Females May Be Neglected Evolutionary Force," *The New York Times*, May 8, 1990, and Natalie Angier, "Mating for Life? It's Not for the Birds or the Bees," *The New York Times*, August 21, 1990.

[2]See Evelyn Reed, *Woman's Evolution: From Matriarchal Clan to Patriarchal Family* (New York: Pathfinder Press, 1986); and Elaine Morgan, *The Descent of Woman* (New York: Bantam Books, 1979). See especially "the upper primate," p. 91.

Nor has the beauty myth always been this way. Though the pairing of the older rich men with young, "beautiful" women is taken to be somehow inevitable, in the matriarchal Goddess religions that dominated the Mediterranean from about 25,000 B.C.E. to about 700 B.C.E., the situation was reversed: "In every culture, the Goddess has many lovers. . . . The clear pattern is of an older woman with a beautiful but expendable youth—Ishtar and Tammuz, Venus and Adonis, Cybele and Attis, Isis and Osiris . . . their only function the service of the divine 'womb.' "[3] Nor is it something only women do and only men watch: Among the Nigerian Wodaabes, the women hold economic power and the tribe is obsessed with male beauty; Wodaabe men spend hours together in elaborate makeup sessions, and compete—provocatively painted and dressed, with swaying hips and seductive expressions—in beauty contests judged by women.[4] There is no legitimate historical or biological justification for the beauty myth; what it is doing to women today is a result of nothing more exalted than the need of today's power structure, economy, and culture to mount a counteroffensive against women.

If the beauty myth is not based on evolution, sex, gender, aesthetics, or God, on what is it based? It claims to be about intimacy and sex

[3]Rosalind Miles, *The Women's History of the World* (London: Paladin Grafton Books, 1988), p. 43. See also Merlin Stone, *When God Was a Woman* (San Diego: Harvest Books, 1976).

[4]Leslie Woodhead, "Desert Dandies," *The Guardian*, July 1988.

In the West African Fulani tribe young women choose their husbands on the basis of their beauty: "The contestants . . . take part in the yaake, a line-up in which they sing and dance, stand on tip-toe and make faces, rolling and crossing their eyes and grimacing to show off their teeth to the judges. They keep this up for hours, aided by the consumption of stimulating drugs beforehand. Throughout all this, old ladies in the crowd hurl criticisms at those who do not live up to the Fulani idea of beauty." [Polhemus, op. cit., p. 21]

See also Carol Beckwith and Marion van Offelen, *Nomads of Niger* (London: William Collins Sons & Co. Ltd., 1984), cited in Carol Beckwith, "Niger's Wodaabe: People of the Taboo," *National Geographic*, vol. 164, no. 4, October 1983, pp. 483–509.

Paleolithic excavations suggest that it has been human males rather than females to whom adornment was assigned in prehistoric societies; in modern tribal communities men generally adorn at least as much as women, and often hold "a virtual monopoly" over adornment. The Sudanese Nuba, the Australian Waligigi, and the Mount Hagen men of New Guinea also spend hours painting themselves and perfecting their hairstyles to attract the women, whose toilette takes only minutes. See Polhemus, op. cit., pp. 54–55.

and life, a celebration of women. It is actually composed of emotional
distance, politics, finance, and sexual repression. The beauty myth is
not about women at all. It is about men's institutions and institutional power.

The qualities that a given period calls beautiful in women are merely
symbols of the female behavior that that period considers desirable:
*The beauty myth is always actually prescribing behavior and not
appearance.* Competition between women has been made part of the
myth so that women will be divided from one another. Youth and (until
recently) virginity have been "beautiful" in women since they stand for
experiential and sexual ignorance. Aging in women is "unbeautiful"
since women grow more powerful with time, and since the links
between generations of women must always be newly broken: Older
women fear young ones, young women fear old, and the beauty myth
truncates for all the female life span. Most urgently, women's identity
must be premised upon our "beauty" so that we will remain vulnerable to outside approval, carrying the vital sensitive organ of self-esteem
exposed to the air.

Though there has, of course, been a beauty myth in some form for 15
as long as there has been patriarchy, the beauty myth in its modern
form is a fairly recent invention. The myth flourishes when material
constraints on women are dangerously loosened. Before the Industrial
Revolution, the average woman could not have had the same feelings
about "beauty" that modern women do who experience the myth as
continual comparison to a mass-disseminated physical ideal. Before
the development of technologies of mass production—daguerrotypes,
photographs, etc.—an ordinary woman was exposed to few such images
outside the Church.[5] Since the family was a productive unit and
women's work complemented men's, the value of women who were
not aristocrats or prostitutes lay in their work skills, economic shrewd-
ness, physical strength, and fertility. Physical attraction, obviously,
played its part; but "beauty" as we understand it was not, for ordinary

[5]See, for example, Beaumont Newhall, *The History of Photography from 1839 to the Present*
(London: Secker & Warburg, 1986), p. 31. Photograph *Academie,* c. 1845, photographer
unknown.

women, a serious issue in the marriage marketplace. The beauty myth in its modern form gained ground after the upheavals of industrialization, as the work unit of the family was destroyed, and urbanization and the emerging factory system demanded what social engineers of the time termed the "separate sphere" of domesticity, which supported the new labor category of the "breadwinner" who left home for the workplace during the day. The middle class expanded, the standards of living and of literacy rose, the size of families shrank; a new class of literate, idle women developed, on whose submission to enforced domesticity the evolving system of industrial capitalism depended. Most of our assumptions about the way women have always thought about "beauty" date from no earlier than the 1830s, when the cult of domesticity was first consolidated and the beauty index invented.

For the first time new technologies could reproduce—in fashion plates, daguerreotypes, tintypes, and rotogravures—images of how women should look. In the 1840s the first nude photographs of prostitutes were taken; advertisements using images of "beautiful" women first appeared in mid-century. Copies of classical artworks, postcards of society beauties and royal mistresses, Currier and Ives prints, and porcelain figurines flooded the separate sphere to which middle-class women were confined.

Since the Industrial Revolution, middle-class Western women have been controlled by ideals and stereotypes as much as by material constraints. This situation, unique to this group, means that analyses that trace "cultural conspiracies" are uniquely plausible in relation to them. The rise of the beauty myth was just one of several emerging social fictions that masqueraded as natural components of the feminine sphere, the better to enclose those women inside it. Other such fictions arose contemporaneously: a version of childhood that required continual maternal supervision; a concept of female biology that required middle-class women to act out the roles of hysterics and hypochondriacs; a conviction that respectable women were sexually anesthetic; and a definition of women's work that occupied them with repetitive, time-consuming, and painstaking tasks such as needlepoint and lacemaking. All such Victorian inventions as these served a double function—that is, though they were encouraged as a means to expend female energy and intelligence in harmless ways, women often used them to express genuine creativity and passion.

But in spite of middle-class women's creativity with fashion and embroidery and child rearing, and, a century later, with the role of the suburban housewife that devolved from these social fictions, the fictions' main purpose was served: During a century and a half of unprecedented feminist agitation, they effectively counteracted middle-class women's dangerous new leisure, literacy, and relative freedom from material constraints.

Though these time- and mind-consuming fictions about women's natural role adapted themselves to resurface in the post-war Feminine Mystique, when the second wave of the women's movement took apart what women's magazines had portrayed as the "romance," "science," and "adventure" of homemaking and suburban family life, they temporarily failed. The cloying domestic fiction of "togetherness" lost its meaning and middle-class women walked out of their front doors in masses.

So the fictions simply transformed themselves once more: Since the women's movement had successfully taken apart most other necessary fictions of femininity, all the work of social control once spread out over the whole network of these fictions had to be reassigned to the only strand left intact, which action consequently strengthened it a hundredfold. This reimposed onto liberated women's faces and bodies all the limitations, taboos, and punishments of the repressive laws, religious injunctions and reproductive enslavement that no longer carried sufficient force. Inexhaustible but ephemeral beauty work took over from inexhaustible but ephemeral housework. As the economy, law, religion, sexual mores, education, and culture were forcibly opened up to include women more fairly, a private reality colonized female consciousness. By using ideas about "beauty," it reconstructed an alternative female world with its own laws, economy, religion, sexuality, education, and culture, each element as repressive as any that had gone before.

Since middle-class Western women can best be weakened psychologically now that we are stronger materially, the beauty myth, as it has resurfaced in the last generation, has had to draw on more technological

20

sophistication and reactionary fervor than ever before. The modern arsenal of the myth is a dissemination of millions of images of the current ideal; although this barrage is generally seen as a collective sexual fantasy, there is in fact little that is sexual about it. It is summoned out of political fear on the part of male-dominated institutions threatened by women's freedom, and it exploits female guilt and apprehension about our own liberation—latent fears that we might be going too far. This frantic aggregation of imagery is a collective reactionary hallucination willed into being by both men and women stunned and disoriented by the rapidity with which gender relations have been transformed: a bulwark of reassurance against the flood of change. The mass depiction of the modern woman as a "beauty" is a contradiction: Where modern women are growing, moving, and expressing their individuality, as the myth has it, "beauty" is by definition inert, timeless, and generic. That this hallucination is necessary and deliberate is evident in the way "beauty" so directly contradicts women's real situation.

And the unconscious hallucination grows ever more influential and pervasive because of what is now conscious market manipulation: powerful industries[6]—the $33-billion-a-year diet industry,[7] the $20-billion cosmetics industry, the $300-million cosmetic surgery industry,[8] and the $7-billion pornography industry[9]—have arisen from the capital made out of unconscious anxieties, and are in turn able, through their influence on mass culture, to use, stimulate, and reinforce the hallucination in a rising economic spiral.

This is not a conspiracy theory; it doesn't have to be. Societies tell themselves necessary fictions in the same way that individuals and families do. Henrik Ibsen called them "vital lies,"[1] and psychologist Daniel

---

[6]Diet items are a $74-billion-a-year industry in the United States, totaling one third of the nation's annual food bill. See David Brand, "A Nation of Healthy Worrywarts?," *Time,* July 25, 1988.

[7]Molly O'Neill, "Congress Looking into the Diet Business," the *New York Times,* March 28, 1990.

[8]*Standard and Poor's Industry Surveys,* op. cit. 1988.

[9]"Crackdown on Pornography," op. cit.

[1]Daniel Goleman, *Vital Lies, Simple Truths: The Psychology of Self-Deception* (New York: Simon and Schuster, 1983), pp. 16–17, quoting Henrik Ibsen's phrase: "The vital lie continues unrevealed, sheltered by the family's silence, alibis, stark denial."

Goleman describes them working the same way on the social level that they do within families: "The collusion is maintained by directing attention away from the fearsome fact, or by repackaging its meaning in an acceptable format." The costs of these social blind spots, he writes, are destructive communal illusions. Possibilities for women have become so open-ended that they threaten to destabilize the institutions on which a male-dominated culture has depended, and a collective panic reaction on the part of both sexes has forced a demand for counterimages.

The resulting hallucination materializes, for women, as something all too real. No longer just an idea, it becomes three-dimensional, incorporating within itself how women live and how they do not live: It becomes the Iron Maiden. The original Iron Maiden was a medieval German instrument of torture, a body-shaped casket painted with the limbs and features of a lovely, smiling young woman. The unlucky victim was slowly enclosed inside her; the lid fell shut to immobilize the victim, who died either of starvation or, less cruelly, of the metal spikes embedded in her interior. The modern hallucination in which women are trapped or trap themselves is similarly rigid, cruel, and euphemistically painted. Contemporary culture directs attention to imagery of the Iron Maiden, while censoring real women's faces and bodies.

Why does the social order feel the need to defend itself by evading 25 the fact of real women, our faces and voices and bodies, and reducing the meaning of women to these formulaic and endlessly reproduced "beautiful" images? Though unconscious personal anxieties can be a powerful force in the creation of a vital lie, economic necessity practically guarantees it. An economy that depends on slavery needs to promote images of slaves that "justify" the institution of slavery. Western economies are absolutely dependent now on the continued underpayment of women. An ideology that makes women feel "worth less" was urgently needed to counteract the way feminism had begun to make us feel worth more. This does not require a conspiracy; merely an atmosphere. The contemporary economy depends right now on the representation of women within the beauty myth. Economist John Kenneth Galbraith offers an economic explanation for "the persistence of the view of homemaking as a 'higher calling' ":[2] the concept of women as naturally trapped within the Feminine Mystique, he feels, "has been forced on us by popular sociology, by magazines, and by fiction to disguise the fact that women in her role of consumer has been essential to the development of our industrial society. . . . Behavior that is essential for economic reasons is transformed into a social virtue." As soon as a woman's primary social value could no longer be defined as the attainment of virtuous domesticity, the beauty myth redefined it as the attainment of virtuous beauty. It did so to substitute both a new consumer imperative and a new justification for economic unfairness in the workplace where the old ones had lost their hold over newly liberated women.

Another hallucination arose to accompany that of the Iron Maiden: The caricature of the Ugly Feminist[3] was resurrected to dog the steps of the women's movement. The caricature is unoriginal; it was coined to ridicule the feminists of the nineteenth century. Lucy Stone herself, whom supporters saw as "a prototype of womanly grace . . . fresh and fair as the morning," was derided by detractors with "the usual report" about Victorian feminists: "a big masculine woman, wearing boots, smoking a cigar, swearing like a trooper."[4] As Betty Friedan put it presciently in 1960, even before the savage revamping of that old caricature: "The unpleasant image of feminists today resembles less the feminists themselves than the image fostered by the interests who so bitterly opposed the vote for women in state after state."[5] Thirty years on, her conclusion is more true than ever: That resurrected caricature, which sought to punish women for their public acts by going after their private sense of self, became the paradigm for new limits placed on aspiring women everywhere. After the success of the women's movement's second wave,

[2]John Kenneth Galbraith, quoted in Michael H. Minton with Jean Libman Block, *What Is a Wife Worth?* (New York: McGraw-Hill, 1984), pp. 134–135.

[3]Marcia Cohen, *The Sisterhood: The Inside Story of the Women's Movement and the Leaders Who Made It Happen* (New York: Ballantine Books, 1988), pp. 205, 206, 287, 290, 322, 332.

[4]Betty Friedan, *The Feminine Mystique* (London: Penguin Books, 1982), p. 79, quoting Elinor Rice Hays, *Morning Star: A Biography of Lucy Stone* (New York: Harcourt, 1961), p. 83.

[5]Friedan, op. cit., p. 87.

the beauty myth was perfected to checkmate power at every level in individual women's lives. The modern neuroses of life in the female body spread to woman after woman at epidemic rates. The myth is undermining—slowly, imperceptibly, without our being aware of the real forces of erosion—the ground women have gained through long, hard, honorable struggle.

The beauty myth of the present is more insidious than any mystique of femininity yet: A century ago, Nora slammed the door of the doll's house;[6] a generation ago, women turned their backs on the consumer heaven of the isolated multiapplianced home; but where women are trapped today, there is no door to slam. The contemporary ravages of the beauty backlash are destroying women physically and depleting us psychologically. If we are to free ourselves from the dead weight that has once again been made out of femaleness, it is not ballots or lobbyists or placards that women will need first; it is a new way to see.

---

[6]Nora is the protagonist of Norwegian dramatist Henrik Ibsen's *A Doll House* (1879), a play that critiques Victorian gender roles. [Ed.]

STUDY QUESTIONS

1. What is one category of popular culture that Wolf identifies as demonstrating part of the beauty myth?

2. At the beginning of paragraph 8 Wolf claims, "Every generation since about 1830 has had to fight its version of the beauty myth." What is your own generation's version of the beauty myth? What are its effects?

3. What PURPOSE is served by the beauty myth (see paragraph 14)? What, according to Wolf, has made it so long-lived?

4. *For Writing.* Near the end of this piece, Wolf DESCRIBES the caricature of the Ugly Feminist and how it is used. How prevalent do you find this caricature in recent media portrayals of women? Select a text (either visual or written) that portrays a woman, preferably a public figure, and ANALYZE how it does or does not match the caricature of Ugly Feminist. Write an essay in which you use this analysis as EVIDENCE for or against the existence of the caricature in contemporary life.

DAVE BARRY { *A GPS Helps a Guy Always*
              Know Where His Couch Is

DAVE BARRY (b. 1947), a humorist, was recognized for his talent early: he was named Class Clown in his senior year of high school. Barry earned an English degree at Haverford College in 1969; after graduating, he worked as a newspaper reporter for the *Daily Local News* of West Chester, Pennsylvania. He then took a job as a business-writing consultant, but eight years later, in 1983, he returned to print journalism when he joined the *Miami Herald* as a humor columnist. Barry received the Pulitzer Prize for Commentary in 1988, and his columns are now nationally syndicated. His books include *Dave Barry's Complete Guide to Guys* (1991), *Dave Barry Is from Mars AND Venus* (1998), and *Dave Barry's History of the Milennium (So Far)* (2007).

In "A GPS Helps a Guy Always Know Where His Couch Is," first published in the *Miami Herald,* Barry takes a look at electronic gadgetry by means of an old comedy standby: he compares and contrasts the attitudes of men with those of women. As you read, take note of how often Barry ostensibly asserts a position while simultaneously undercutting it with irony, the stuff of which so much humor is made.

———————

I'M A BIG FAN OF technology. Most guys are. This is why all important inventions were invented by guys.

For example, millions of years ago, there was no such thing as the wheel. One day, some primitive guys were watching their wives drag a dead mastodon to the food-preparation area. It was exhausting work; the guys were getting tired just WATCHING. Then they noticed some large, smooth, rounded boulders, and they had an idea: They could sit on the boulders and watch! This was the first in a series of break-throughs that ultimately led to television.

So we see that there are vital reasons why guys are interested in tech-nology, and why women should not give them a hard time about always wanting to have the "latest gadget." And when I say "women," I mean "my wife."

For example, as a guy, I feel I need a new computer every time a new model comes out, which is every 15 minutes. This baffles my wife, who has had the same computer since the Civil War and refuses to get a new one because—get THIS for an excuse—the one she has works fine. I try to explain that, when you get a new computer, you get exciting new features. My new computer has a truly fascinating feature: Whenever I try to turn it off, the following message, which I am not making up, appears on the screen:

"An exception 0E has occurred at 0028:F000F841 in VxD—. This 5 was called from 0028:C001D324 in VxD NDIS(01) + 00005AA0. It may be possible to continue normally."

Clearly, this message is not of human origin. Clearly, my new com-puter is receiving this message from space aliens. I don't understand all of it, but apparently there has been some kind of intergalactic problem that the aliens want to warn us about. What concerns me is the last sentence, because if the aliens are telling us that "it may be possible to continue normally," they are clearly implying that it may NOT be pos-sible to continue normally. In other words, the Earth may be doomed, and the aliens have chosen ME to receive this message. If I can figure out exactly what they're saying, I might be able to save humanity!

Unfortunately, I don't have time, because I'm busy using my new GPS device. This is an extremely important gadget that every guy in the world needs. It receives signals from orbiting satellites, and somehow—I suspect the "cosine" is involved—it figures out exactly where on the Earth you are. Let's say you're in the town of Arcola, Illinois, but for some reason you do not realize this. You turn on your GPS, and, after pondering for a few minutes, it informs you that you are in . . . Arcola, Illinois! My wife argues that it's easier to just ASK somebody, but of course you cannot do that, if you truly are a guy.

I became aware of how useful a GPS can be when I was on a plane trip with a literary rock band I belong to called the Rock Bottom Remainders, which has been hailed by critics as having one of the world's highest ratios of noise to talent. On this trip were two band members whom I will identify only as "Roger" and "Steve," so that you will not know that they are actually Roger McGuinn, legendary co-founder of the Byrds, and Stephen King, legendary legend.

We were flying from Chicago to Boston, and while everybody else was reading or sleeping, "Roger" and "Steve," who are both fully grown men, were staring at their GPS devices and periodically inform-ing each other how far we were from the Boston airport. "Roger" would say, "I'm showing 238 miles," and "Steve" would say, "I'm showing 241 miles." Then "Roger" would say, "Now I'm showing 236 miles," and "Steve" would come back with another figure, and so on. My wife, who was confident that the airplane pilot did not need help locating Boston, thought this was the silliest thing she had ever seen. Whereas I thought: I NEED one of those.

So I got a GPS for Christmas, and I spent the entire day sitting on a couch, putting it to good use. Like, I figured out exactly where our house is. My wife told me this was exciting news. I think she was being sarcastic, but I couldn't be sure, because I had to keep watching the GPS screen, in case our house moved. I also used my GPS to figure out exactly how far my couch is from LaGuardia Airport (1,103 miles). There is NO END to the usefulness of this device! If you're a guy, you need to get one NOW, so you can locate yourself on the planet. While we still have one.

STUDY QUESTIONS

1. According to Barry, why do men want the newest technology? Who does Barry say he means by "women"?

2. COMPARE AND CONTRAST Barry's depictions of men's and women's attitudes toward technology. Why does he call men "guys" but women "women" throughout the article? How seriously does he advocate one perspective over another?

3. *For Writing.* Consider the various electronic devices that you own. Compose an essay in which you REFLECT on how and how often you use them, perhaps comparing and contrasting your use of technology to that of a parent, a sibling, or someone else whose technological skills are markedly different from your own.

ANNA QUINDLEN { *Still Needing the F Word*

ANNA QUINDLEN (b. 1952) graduated from Barnard College in 1972 and joined the *New York Times* in 1977 as a general assignment reporter. In 1981 Quindlen began writing columns for the *Times*: "About New York," "Life in the 30's," and, in 1990, "Public and Private," which made her the third woman in the history of the *Times* to become a weekly columnist for its Op-Ed pages. She received a Pulitzer Prize for Commentary in 1992. Quindlen wrote a biweekly column for *Newsweek* on society, politics, and news from 1999 to 2009. She is the author of several best-selling novels, including *One True Thing* (1992), *Black and Blue* (1998), and *Blessings* (2002), as well as the nonfiction work *A Short Guide to a Happy Life* (2000).

In this column that both invokes and redefines "the F word," Quindlen argues that feminism is a necessary but often absent component in young women's lives. She rejects the claim that we live in a postfeminist era and calls on young women to reject the passive, "nice" model of femininity that many still follow. Do Quindlen's remarks ring true for you? Should young people embrace feminism?

LET'S USE THE F WORD here. People say it's inappropriate, offensive, that it puts people off. But it seems to me it's the best way to begin, when it's simultaneously devalued and invaluable.

Feminist. Feminist, feminist, feminist.

Conventional wisdom has it that we've moved on to a postfeminist era, which is meant to suggest that the issues have been settled, the inequities addressed, and all is right with the world. And then suddenly from out of the South like Hurricane Everywoman, a level '03 storm, comes something like the new study on the status of women at Duke University, and the notion that we're post-anything seems absurd. Time to use the F word again, no matter how uncomfortable people may find it.

Fem-i-nism *n. 1. Belief in the social, political and economic equality of the sexes.*

That wasn't so hard, was it? Certainly not as hard as being a female 5 undergraduate at Duke, where apparently the operative ruling principle is something described as "effortless perfection," in which young women report expending an enormous amount of effort on clothes, shoes, workout programs and diet. And here's a blast from the past: they're expected "to hide their intelligence in order to succeed with their male peers."

"Being 'cute' trumps being smart for women in the social environment," the report concludes.

That's not postfeminist. That's prefeminist. Betty Friedan wrote *The Feminine Mystique* exactly 40 years ago, and yet segments of the Duke report could have come right out of her book. One 17-year-old girl told Friedan, "I used to write poetry. The guidance office says I have this creative ability and I should be at the top of the class and have a great future. But things like that aren't what you need to be popular. The important thing for a girl is to be popular."

Of course, things have changed. Now young women find themselves facing not one but two societal, and self-imposed, straitjackets. Once they obsessed about being the perfect homemaker and meeting the standards of their male counterparts. Now they also obsess about being the perfect professional and meeting the standards of their male counterparts. In the decades since Friedan's book became a best seller, women have won the right to do as much as men do. They just haven't won the right to do as little as men do. Hence, effortless perfection.

While young women are given the impression that all doors are open, all boundaries down, empirical evidence is to the contrary. A study from Princeton issued at the same time as the Duke study showed that faculty women in the sciences reported less satisfaction in their jobs and less of a sense of belonging than their male counterparts. Maybe that's because they made up only 14 percent of the faculty in those disciplines or because one out of four reported their male colleagues occasionally or frequently engaged in unprofessional conduct focusing on gender issues.

Californians were willing to ignore Arnold Schwarzenegger's alleged career as a serial sexual bigot,[1] despite a total of 16 women coming forward to say he thought nothing of reaching up your skirt or into your blouse. (Sure, they're only allegations. But it was Arnold himself who said that where there's smoke, there's fire. In this case, there was a conflagration.) The fact that one of the actor's defenses was that he didn't realize this was objectionable—and that voters were OK with that—speaks volumes about enduring assumptions about women. What if he'd habitually publicly humiliated black men, or Latinos, or Jews? Yet the revelation that the guy often demeaned women with his hands was written off as partisan politics and even personal behavior. Personal behavior is when you have a girlfriend. When you touch someone intimately without her consent, it's sexual battery.

The point is not that the world has not changed for women since Friedan's book lobbed a hand grenade into the homes of pseudohappy housewives who couldn't understand the malaise that accompanied sparkling Formica and good-looking kids. Hundreds of arenas, from government office to the construction trades, have opened to working women. Of course, when it leaks out that the Vatican is proposing to scale back on the use of altar girls, it shows that the forces of reaction are always waiting, whether beneath hard hats or miters.

But the world hasn't changed as much as we like to tell ourselves. Otherwise *The Feminine Mystique* wouldn't feel so contemporary. Otherwise Duke University wouldn't find itself concentrating on eating disorders and the recruitment of female faculty. Otherwise the governor-elect of California wouldn't be a guy who thinks it's "playful" to grab and grope, and the voters wouldn't ratify that attitude. Part fair game, part perfection: that's a tough standard for 51 percent of

10

---

[1]The allegations surfaced during the 2003 election for governor.

174

everyone. The first women's rights activists a century ago set out to prove, in Friedan's words, "that woman was not a passive empty mirror." How dispiriting it would be to those long-ago heroines to read of the women at Duke focused on their "cute" reflections in the eyes of others. The F word is not an expletive but an ideal—one that still has a way to go.

STUDY QUESTIONS

1. What, according to Quindlen, does "feminism" mean? What does she say is the state of feminism today?

2. What EVIDENCE does Quindlen use to support her ARGUMENT about the need for feminism? How effective is it? Explain.

3. *For Writing.* In an essay, REFLECT on how and why feminism might carry negative cultural perceptions, and explain why you agree or disagree with these perceptions. Be sure to draw on your own experiences as well as to RESEARCH current feminist thinkers. You might begin at feministing.com or feminist.com.

GUY TREBAY ⎰ *The Vanishing Point*

GUY TREBAY (b. 1952), fashion columnist at the *New York Times,* writes about not only fashion trends but also the glitterati, designers, and models who make up the world of fashion. Whether his subject is fashion shows in Milan, London, Paris, or New York; Michelle Obama's style; or celebrity fundraisers for Madonna's African charity, he writes descriptively and, when need be, critically of the trends and people he observes. The *Guy Trebay Collection of Fashion Ephemera, 2000–2005* can be found in the library at the University of California, Los Angeles, in eleven boxes.

In this 2008 article from the *New York Times*, Trebay describes a recent trend in men's fashion that has been controversial in women's fashion for years: the incredible shrinking model. Trebay contrasts the chiseled, muscular look of male models that was long the standard with the gaunt, androgynous look of today. But with men's fashions as with women's, the designers say that they are simply meeting public demand. "In terms of image," Trebay writes, "the current preference is for beauty that is not fully evolved."

CREDIT HEDI SLIMANE OR BLAME him. The type of men Mr. Slimane promoted when he first came aboard at Dior Homme[1] some years back (he has since left) were thin to the point of resembling stick figures; the clothes he designed were correspondingly lean. The effects of his designs on the men's wear industry were radical and surprisingly persuasive. Within a couple of seasons, the sleekness of Dior Homme suits

[1]The menswear division of the Christian Dior fashion company (*homme* is French for "man").

made everyone else's designs look boxy and passé, and so designers everywhere started reducing their silhouettes.

Then a funny thing happened. The models were also downsized. Where the masculine ideal of as recently as 2000 was a buff 6-footer with six-pack abs, the man of the moment is an urchin, a wraith or an underfed runt.

Nowhere was this more clear than at the recent men's wear shows in Milan and Paris, where even those inured to the new look were flabbergasted at the sheer quantity of guys who looked chicken-chested, hollow-cheeked and undernourished. Not altogether surprisingly, the trend has followed the fashion pack back to New York.

Wasn't it just a short time ago that the industry was up in arms about skinny models? Little over a year ago, in Spain, designers were commanded to choose models based on a healthy body mass index; physicians were installed at Italian casting calls; Diane von Furstenberg, the president of the Council of Fashion Designers of America, and Anna Wintour, the editor of *Vogue,* called a conference to ventilate the issue of unhealthy body imagery and eating disorders among models.

The models in question were women, and it's safe to say that they 5 remain as waiflike as ever. But something occurred while no one was looking. Somebody shrunk the men.

"Skinny, skinny, skinny," said Dave Fothergill, a director of the agency of the moment, Red Model Management. "Everybody's shrinking themselves."

This was abundantly clear in the castings of models for New York shows by Duckie Brown, Thom Browne, Patrik Ervell, Robert Geller and Marc by Marc Jacobs, where models like Stas Svetlichnyy of Russia typified the new norm. Mr. Svetlichnyy's top weight, he said last week, is about 145 pounds. He is 6 feet tall with a 28-inch waist.

"Designers like the skinny guy," he said backstage last Friday at the Duckie Brown show. "It looks good in the clothes and that's the main thing. That's just the way it is now."

Even in Milan last month at shows like Dolce & Gabbana and Dsquared, where the castings traditionally ran to beefcake types, the models were leaner and less muscled, more light-bodied. Just as tellingly, Dolce & Gabbana's look-book for spring 2008 (a catalog of

the complete collection) featured not the male models the label has traditionally favored—industry stars like Chad White and Tyson Ballou,
who have movie-star looks and porn-star physiques—but men who
look as if they have never seen the inside of a gym.

"The look is different from when I started in the business eight   10
years ago," Mr. Ballou said last week during a photo shoot at the Milk
Studios in lower Manhattan. In many of the model castings, which
tend to be dominated by a handful of people, the body style that now
dominates is the one Charles Atlas[2] made a career out of trying to
improve.

"The first thing I did when I moved to New York was immediately
start going to the gym," the designer John Bartlett said. That was in the
long-ago 1980s. But the idea of bulking up now seems retro when
musicians and taste arbiters like Devendra Banhart boast of having
starved themselves in order to look good in clothes.

"The eye has changed," Mr. Bartlett said. "Clothes now are tighter
and tighter. Guys are younger and younger. Everyone is influenced by
what Europe shows."

What Europe (which is to say influential designers like Miuccia
Prada and Raf Simons at Jil Sander) shows are men as tall as Tom
Brady[3] but who wear a size 38 suit.

"There are designers that lead the way," said James Scully, a seasoned
casting agent best known for the numerous modeling discoveries he
made when he worked at Gucci under Tom Ford. "Everyone looks to
Miuccia Prada for the standard the way they used to look at Hedi
Slimane. Once the Hedi Slimanization got started, all anyone wanted to
cast was the scrawny kid who looked like he got sand kicked in his face.
The big, great-looking models just stopped going to Europe. They
knew they'd never get cast."

For starters, they knew that they would never fit into designers' sam-   15
ples. "When I started out in the magazine business in 1994, the sam-

---

[2]Italian-born American body-builder and businessman, born Angelo Siciliano
(1892–1972), who successfully marketed a fitness program "for the 97-pound weakling."
[3]American football player (b. 1977), quarterback of the New England Patriots. He is 6'4".

ple size was an Italian 50," said Long Nguyen of *Flaunt* magazine, referring to a size equivalent to a snug 40-regular.

"That was an appropriate size for a normal 6-foot male," Mr. Nguyen said. Yet just six years later—coincidentally at about the time Mr. Slimane left his job as the men's wear designer at YSL for Dior Homme—the typical sample size had dwindled to 48. Now it is 46.

"At that point you might as well save money and just go over to the boy's department," Mr. Nguyen said from his seat in the front row of the Benjamin Cho show, which was jammed as usual with a selection of reedy boys in Buffalo plaid jackets and stovepipe jeans, the same types that fill Brooklyn clubs like Sugarland. "I'm not really sure if designers are making clothes smaller or if people are smaller now," Mr. Nguyen said.

According to a study by the Centers for Disease Control and Prevention, Americans are taller and much heavier today than 40 years ago. The report, released in 2002, showed that the average height of adult American men has increased to 5–9 1/2 in 2002 from just over 5-8 in 1960. The average weight of the same adult man had risen dramatically, to 191 pounds from 166.3.

Nowadays a model that weighed in at 191 pounds, no matter how handsome, would be turned away from most agencies or else sent to a fat farm.

Far from inspiring a spate of industry breast-beating, as occurred 20 after the international news media got hold of the deaths of two young female models who died from eating disorders, the trend favoring very skinny male models has been accepted as a matter of course.

"I personally think that it's the consumer that's doing this, and fashion is just responding," said Kelly Cutrone, the founder of People's Revolution, a fashion branding and production company. "No one wants a beautiful woman or a beautiful man anymore."

In terms of image, the current preference is for beauty that is not fully evolved. "People are afraid to look over 21 or make any statement of what it means to be adult," Ms. Cutrone said.

George Brown, a booking agent at Red Model Management, said: "When I get that random phone call from a boy who says, 'I'm 6-foot-1 and I'm calling from Kansas,' I immediately ask, 'What do you weigh?'"

If they say 188 or 190, I know we can't use him. Our guys are 155 pounds at that height."

Their waists, like that of Mr. Svetlichnyy, measure 28 or 30 inches. They have, ideally, long necks, pencil thighs, narrow shoulders and chests no more than 35.5 inches in circumference, Mr. Brown said. "It's client driven," he added. "That's just the size that blue-chip designers and high-end editorials want."

For Patrik Ervell's show on Saturday, the casting brief called for new   25
faces and men whose bodies were suited to a scarecrow silhouette. "We had to measure their thighs," Mr. Brown said.

For models like Demián Tkach, a 26-year-old Argentine who was recently discovered by the photographer Bruce Weber, the tightening tape measure may cut off a career.

Mr. Tkach said that when he came here from Mexico, where he had been working, "My agency asked me to lose some muscle. I lost a little bit to help them, because I understand the designers are not looking for a male image anymore. They're looking for some kind of androgyne."

STUDY QUESTIONS

1. To what does Trebay attribute the current trend for skinny male models?

2. In a typical newspaper article, a journalist adopts a neutral, objective TONE that allows the AUDIENCE to make its own subjective judgments. Is Trebay's tone in this article objective or subjective? In other words, does he indicate whether he approves or disapproves of the fashion trend he describes? Give several examples from the article to support your RESPONSE.

3. How and how effectively does Trebay establish his CREDIBILITY with his readers? Refer to specific passages from the article in your response.

4. *For Writing.* Think about a SUBJECT with which you are familiar, such as music, cooking, fashion, sports, movies, or literature, and write an essay in which you ANALYZE a particular aspect of this subject. Determine who your audience will be, whether those who know a great deal about the topic, those who know very little about it, or a mixed general readership, and make sure your language and tone are appropriate for that audience. Remember to establish your credibility as an expert on your topic. Try to use appropriate language free from jargon, but if you have to use specialized terms be sure to DEFINE terms that will be unfamiliar to your audience.

KATHA POLLITT ⎰ *Why Boys Don't Play*
with Dolls

KATHA POLLITT (b. 1949), poet and essayist, was born in New York City
and educated at Harvard University, where she earned a BA in philosophy
in 1972, and at the Columbia School of the Arts, where she received an
MFA in writing in 1975. Pollitt writes the award-winning column "Subject
to Debate" for the *Nation*, in which she engages with cultural issues ranging
from identity politics to U.S. foreign policy. Her work is collected in a number of volumes, including *Reasonable Creatures: Essays on Women and
Feminism* (1994) and *Virginity or Death! And Other Social and Political
Issues of Our Time* (2006). Her book of poetry, *Antarctic Traveller*, won a
National Book Critics Circle Award in 1983.

In "Why Boys Don't Play with Dolls," Pollitt examines how parents raise
their children to adhere to "sex role conventions." She challenges adults to
be mindful of the roles they reinforce or subvert, because children will emu-
late and internalize them, and she argues that overblown reports of biological differences between boys and girls should not lessen our efforts to
consider what messages are going out to children. As you read, consider
your own upbringing: Were you encouraged to work in the kitchen? Mow
the lawn? Play with dolls? Trucks? If gender roles were not emphasized in
your home, what sorts of behaviors *were* encouraged—and discouraged—as
you were growing up?

IT'S 28 YEARS SINCE THE founding of NOW,[1] and boys still like trucks
and girls still like dolls. Increasingly, we are told that the source of these

[1] The National Organization for Women, the largest feminist group in the U.S., founded in
1966.

"Why Boys Don't Play with Dolls" by Katha Pollitt. Originally published in the *New York
Times Magazine*, October 8, 1995. Used by permission of the New York Times
Syndication.

robust preferences must lie outside society—in prenatal hormonal influences, brain chemistry, genes—and that feminism has reached its natural limits. What else could possibly explain the love of preschool girls for party dresses or the desire of toddler boys to own more guns than Mark from Michigan?[2]

True, recent studies claim to show small cognitive differences between the sexes: he gets around by orienting himself in space, she does it by remembering landmarks. Time will tell if any deserve the hoopla with which each is invariably greeted, over the protests of the researchers themselves. But even if the results hold up (and the history of such research is not encouraging), we don't need studies of sex-differentiated brain activity in reading, say, to understand why boys and girls still seem so unalike.

The feminist movement has done much for some women, and something for every woman, but it has hardly turned America into a playground free of sex roles. It hasn't even got women to stop dieting or men to stop interrupting them.

Instead of looking at kids to "prove" that differences in behavior by sex are innate, we can look at the ways we raise kids as an index to how unfinished the feminist revolution really is, and how tentatively it is embraced even by adults who fully expect their daughters to enter previously male-dominated professions and their sons to change diapers.

I'm at a children's birthday party. "I'm sorry," one mom silently   5
mouths to the mother of the birthday girl, who has just torn open her present—Tropical Splash Barbie. Now, you can love Barbie or you can hate Barbie, and there are feminists in both camps. But *apologize* for Barbie? Inflict Barbie, against your own convictions, on the child of a friend you know will be none too pleased?

Every mother in that room had spent years becoming a person who had to be taken seriously, not least by herself. Even the most attractive, I'm willing to bet, had suffered over her body's failure to fit the impossible American ideal. Given all that, it seems crazy to transmit Barbie to the next generation. Yet to reject her is to say that what Barbie rep-

[2]Hypothetical caller to a radio talk show.

resents—being sexy, thin, stylish—is unimportant, which is obviously not true, and children know it's not true.

Women's looks matter terribly in this society, and so Barbie, however ambivalently, must be passed along. After all, there are worse toys. The Cut and Style Barbie styling head, for example, a grotesque object intended to encourage "hair play." The grown-ups who give that probably apologize, too.

How happy would most parents be to have a child who flouted sex conventions? I know a lot of women, feminists, who complain in a comical, eyeball-rolling way about their sons' passion for sports: the ruined weekends, obnoxious coaches, macho values. But they would not think of discouraging their sons from participating in this activity they find so foolish. Or do they? Their husbands are sports fans, too, and they like their husbands a lot.

Could it be that even sports-resistant moms see athletics as part of manliness? That if their sons wanted to spend the weekend writing up their diaries, or reading, or baking, they'd find it disturbing? Too antisocial? Too lonely? Too gay?

Theories of innate differences in behavior are appealing. They let 10 parents off the hook—no small recommendation in a culture that holds moms, and sometimes even dads, responsible for their children's every misstep on the road to bliss and success.

They allow grown-ups to take the path of least resistance to the dominant culture, which always requires less psychic effort, even if it means more actual work: just ask the working mother who comes home exhausted and nonetheless finds it easier to pick up her son's socks than make him do it himself. They let families buy for their children, without *too* much guilt, the unbelievably sexist junk that the kids, who have been watching commercials since birth, understandably crave.

But the thing the theories do most of all is tell adults that the *adult* world—in which moms and dads still play by many of the old rules even as they question and fidget and chafe against them—is the way it's supposed to be. A girl with a doll and a boy with a truck "explain" why men are from Mars and women are from Venus, why wives do housework and husbands just don't understand.

The paradox is that the world of rigid and hierarchal sex roles evoked by determinist theories is already passing away. Three-year-olds may indeed insist that doctors are male and nurses female, even if their own mother is a physician. Six-year-olds know better. These days, something like half of all medical students are female, and male applications to nursing school are inching upward. When tomorrow's 3-year-olds play doctor, who's to say how they'll assign the roles?

With sex roles, as in every area of life, people aspire to what is possible, and conform to what is necessary. But these are not fixed, especially today. Biological determinism may reassure some adults about their present, but it is feminism, the ideology of flexible and converging sex roles, that fits our children's future. And the kids, somehow, know this.

That's why, if you look carefully, you'll find that for every kid who fits 15
a stereotype, there's another who's breaking one down. Sometimes it's the same kid—the boy who skateboards *and* takes cooking in his after-school program; the girl who collects stuffed animals *and* A-pluses in science.

Feminists are often accused of imposing their "agenda" on children. Isn't that what adults always do, consciously and unconsciously? Kids aren't born religious, or polite, or kind, or able to remember where they put their sneakers. Inculcating these behaviors, and the values behind them, is a tremendous amount of work, involving many adults. We don't have a choice, really, about *whether* we should give our children messages about what it means to be male and female—they're bombarded with them from morning till night.

The question, as always, is what do we want those messages to be?

STUDY QUESTIONS

1. According to Pollitt, how and why does society reinforce "sex role conventions"?

2. Pollitt notes that one mother, when giving a Barbie doll to a child as a birthday gift, apologizes to that child's mother. Reread Pollitt's penultimate paragraph, in which she discusses how adults "impose" their "agendas" on children. How does the Barbie doll incident fit into this discussion? What might the mother giving the gift have done instead? What seems to be Pollitt's ideal for raising children of either sex?

3. What is Pollitt's THESIS? What REASONS and EVIDENCE does she provide to support that thesis?

4. *For Writing.* Consider what messages about sex role conventions you have received from adults in your life—families, teachers, employers—and write an essay in which you ANALYZE how closely you adhere to or distance yourself from them.

CECILIA BALLÍ { *Ciudad de la Muerte*

CECILIA BALLÍ (b. 1976), an anthropology professor at the University of Texas at Austin, has written articles for *Harper's Monthly*, the *San Antonio Express-News*, and the *Los Angeles Times*, serving as the Washington, DC, correspondent for the *Times*. In addition to publishing scholarly articles, she serves as a senior editor at *Texas Monthly* magazine, contributing investigative stories about gender and violence, immigration, crime, and music in the U.S.–Mexico borderlands.

"Ciudad de la Muerte" ("City of Death") explores the numerous brutal murders of young Mexican women that have continued unabated since the early 1990s in Ciudad Juárez, Mexico, a city of 1.5 million across the Rio Grande from El Paso, Texas. In 2009 the city witnessed more than two thousand murders, most of which were unsolved, leading one of Juárez's newspapers to declare, "This is the most violent zone in the world outside of declared war zones." Ballí's article puts readers in this "zone," narrating her own visits to Juárez and offering insights about the mysterious killings and the dangers of a city she so clearly associates with death. As you read, note how Ballí uses techniques borrowed from fiction to create vivid scenes and moments of suspense.

DO YOU KNOW WHAT HAPPENS to a human body in the desert? If it's fresh, the intestines eat themselves out. The body swells, the lungs ooze fluids through the nostrils and mouth, and the decaying organs let out a cocktail of nauseating gases. Sometimes, scavengers leave their mark: a gnawed leg, a missing shoulder. Eventually, all that is left is a pile of white bones. But there is a cruel trick the dry weather will sometimes play on a corpse. It will dehydrate the skin before the bacteria can get to it, producing a mummy—a blackened girl with skin dry as cardboard, baring her teeth like a frightened animal.

• ○ •

In February 1996 a seventeen-year-old girl named María Guadalupe del Rio Vázquez went shopping in downtown Ciudad Juárez and vanished into thin air. Days later, her body was found in the desolate mountains of the Chihuahuan Desert—raped, strangled, her left breast mutilated. As girls continued to disappear, residents of the city formed bands and scoured the mountains for more bodies. The state police picked up the corpses—seventeen in all, an epidemic of murder—and quickly scurried away, leaving behind clothing, locks of hair, shoes curled like orange peels. The girls' hands were bound with their own shoelaces. All of the victims resembled each other: pretty, slim, medium to dark skin, long, straight dark hair. In a country that privileges men, whiteness, and wealth, these victims were female, brown, and poor. In a city that resents immigration and anything else from central and southern Mexico, these young women who had come to the northern border hoping to find work were social outcasts, strangers without names—especially now that they lay in silence in the sand, looking just like the ones before and the ones who would follow.

The deaths in the mountainous desert region known as Lomas de Poleo confirmed the worst fears of the women of Juárez: that something sinister had overcome their city. Beginning in 1993, there had been an unusual number of news reports in Juárez about the abduction and murder of women, an anomaly in Mexico. The grisly discoveries in the desert signaled that the worst crime wave in modern Mexican history had entered a new and more intense phase. Today, the toll of women who have been murdered in the past ten years is more than three hundred, staining the reputation of the country's fourth-largest city worldwide. Some of the women were murdered by their husbands and boyfriends. Other killings seemed to be random acts of violence. Around a third of the victims, however, were teenage girls whose deaths appear to be connected to a cryptic and chilling kind of serial killing. This crime is indisputably solvable: Evidence has been scattered like bread crumbs all over the crime scenes, but the state authorities have jailed no one who truly seems responsible. Be it incompetence or a cover-up, the lack of credible prosecution in these cases is perhaps the most blatant—and certainly the most baffling—illustration of the nearly flawless record of impunity that characterizes the Mexican justice system.

Who would commit such crimes? Juárez brims with rumor and suspicion. A serial killer with government protection is an obvious possibility. The indifference of the authorities charged with investigating the murders has focused suspicion on themselves. Maybe it's the Juárez police, some people say. They drive those white pickups with the campers, where they could easily hide a rotting body or a pile of bones, and they're always prowling around the shantytown of Anapra, on the edge of the desert, peering out their windows. The Chihuahua state police zoom about in sleek, unmarked SUVs capable of navigating the rugged desert terrain. Recently, federal investigators speculated that fourteen of the killings might be linked to an organ-smuggling ring.

Or maybe it's the drug dealers. The desert is, after all, their country, a frontier on the fringe of globalization. Between dips in the mountains, you glimpse El Paso to the north, its downtown towers gleaming like teeth. The Rio Grande cut through the mountains and created a valley that would in time birth the most densely populated border region in the world. But in Lomas de Poleo, there is only the sand and the desert scrub and a sea of trash—empty jugs, shabby toys, broken toilets, an unwound cassette of English lessons, plastic bags clinging to the brush like confetti. A frail man picks his way through a dumpster. An occasional small truck rattles off into the distance. They say that at night, this becomes the realm of gang members and drug runners, an army of men hauling their illicit goods into the United States. Rumor has it that if you wander far enough into the disorienting maze of primitive roads that have been scratched out of the sand, you will come upon a crude runway and a marvelous ranch with a swimming pool. If anybody sees you there, you should say you got lost and quickly turn around.

The obvious questions—who, why, how—remain unanswered. The abductions occur in mysterious moments, in quick, ghastly twists of fate that nobody seems—or at least wants to admit—to have witnessed. Most recently, they have transpired in the heart of the city in broad daylight. Some people believe the girls are taken by force, while others think it is more likely that the victims are lured by a seemingly innocent offer. A few mothers have said that their daughters disappeared a day or two after being approached about a job. Only one thing can be said with certainty, and it's that in Juárez, Mexico, the most barbarous things are possible.

• o •

The sun shimmers over downtown Juárez like white linen, but I have learned to march down its streets staring at the ground or ahead with icy, distant eyes. To do anything else is to acknowledge the lusty stares from men of all ages who stand at the corners of the city's busy thoroughfares waiting for nothing to happen. So begins the taunting. A skinny man with red eyes lets out a slow whistle through clenched teeth. Two young boys look at me, look at each other, and nod with a dirty grin. From among a group of men huddled on the steps of a shop, one calls out, "*¡Una como esa!*"—One like her!—and the rest burst out laughing, their mustaches spreading gleefully across their faces as they watch me walk by. This is everywhere in urban Mexico, I remind myself, but knowing what I do about the fate of women in Juárez, their glares begin to feel more predatory. I watch my feet skitter on the pavement and, with every step, wish I could shed these hips, this chest, this hair. To walk through downtown Juárez is to know and deeply regret that you are a young woman.

Juárez, though, is a city of young women. They run its shops; they keep its hundreds of factories humming. In 1964 the United States terminated the Bracero guest-worker program[1] with Mexico and deported many of its laborers, dumping thousands of men along the Mexican side of the border. In an effort to reemploy them, the Mexican government launched the Border Industrialization Program, which

---

[1] Diplomatic agreement starting in 1942 that allowed temporary contract laborers from Mexico to work in the U.S. in order to meet labor shortages caused by World War II. After the war, workers in the program primarily filled low-wage positions in the agriculture industry.

prodded American manufacturers to assemble their products in northern Mexico using cheap labor. The plan succeeded, but its main beneficiaries turned out to be women, who, it was determined, would make better workers for the new factories, or *maquiladoras*, because of their presumed superior manual dexterity. Word spread throughout Mexico that thousands of assembly-line jobs were cropping up in Juárez, and the nation's north quickly became the emblem of modernity and economic opportunity. In the seventies, factory-sponsored buses rumbled into the heartland and along the coasts and returned with thousands of hungry laborers. Among them were many single women with children in tow, who, aside from landing their own jobs in the *maquilas*,[2] began to staff the throngs of stores and restaurants that proliferated to satisfy the new consumerism of Juárez's formerly cash-strapped population.

And so, if the working women of this border city had once earned reputations as prostitutes or bartenders, they now earned paychecks as factory workers, saleswomen, police officers, teachers—a few even as managers and engineers in the concrete tilt-ups[3] that were constructed all around town to house around four hundred maquiladoras. For anywhere from $4 to $7 a day, they assembled automotive parts and electronic components and made clothing. Of the girls who couldn't afford to go to college—which is to say, the vast majority—some took computer classes, where they learned to use Microsoft Word and Excel so that they might become secretaries and administrative assistants. Juárez, after all, is a city that places a high premium on skills such as knowing how to use computers and speak English. Even in its most impoverished desert neighborhood, a dazed collection of impromptu homes stitched together from wood pallets, mattresses, cardboard boxes, and baling wire, I saw a tiny brick shack with a dozen mismatched chairs planted outside and a hand-painted sign that promised "*Clases de inglés*."[4]

But the migration was too fast, too disorganized. The population 10 shot up to an estimated 1.5 million. Gone was the charm Juárez had

[2] Factories (Spanish).

[3] That is, factories built cheaply and quickly with prefabricated concrete walls.

[4] English classes (Spanish).

possessed in the thirties, when its valley bore succulent grapes, or in the forties, when the music of Glenn Miller and Agustín Lara never stopped playing on Juárez Avenue, even as its neighboring country went to war. It was one of Mexico's biggest blunders to have planted its largest industrial experiment in the desert, in a city separated from the rest of the country not only symbolically, by its distinctly North American feel, but also physically, by the stunning but unforgiving Juárez Mountains. Cardboard shanties began to dot the landscape. Sewage spilled onto the streets. Power lines reproduced like parasites. Today, radio talk-show hosts ramble on about the ways in which immigrants ruined their beautiful community. I asked a well-bred young man what he felt were the virtues of his hometown, and despite a genuine effort, all he could name were the swank, cavernous clubs where the rich kids spend their weekends consuming alcohol by the bottle.

Even as the maquiladoras have begun relocating to China in the past two years, the reputation of Juárez as a city of opportunity lingers in impoverished rural Mexico. Inside the city, however, Mexico's economic vulnerability is exposed like raw flesh. The city is filled with broken people who crack open with the most innocent of questions. I met a woman from Zacatecas who lives in Anapra with her husband and three daughters in a minuscule house that they built out of wood pallets and thatched with black roofing material. They possess one bed, no refrigerator, and a tin washtub for bathing. State officials offered them this sliver of land, but the sliver is in the desert mountains, where life is not "beautiful," as the woman's brother had sent word home; it's shivery cold and always covered in a thin film of orange dirt. When I asked her how she liked living in this *colonia*[5] along the city's northwestern frontier, the woman's smile quivered and a puddle of tears instantly dribbled to her chin.

Still, the worst part about Juárez, she told me, is the threat of violence that hangs over the sprawling city like a veil of terror. For just a short distance from her home, the bodies of girls who resemble her

---

[5] Literally, colony (Spanish), colonias are low-income rural settlements along the U.S.-Mexico border, characterized by makeshift housing and lack of social, political, and physical infrastructures.

own sixteen-year-old Ana have appeared in the desert. Lured to their deaths—perhaps by promises of a job?—they lie abandoned like the heaps of trash that fleck this interminable sea of sand.

• o •

"Disculpe, señorita . . . "[6]

I turned toward the male voice that came from behind me and saw a dark-skinned, round-faced man in his thirties striding in my direction with a large basket of candies wedged between his neck and shoulder. He was heavyset, clad in light-brown slacks, a white, long-sleeved shirt with blue pinstripes, and a green windbreaker.

It was lunchtime, and I had walked out of a restaurant to return a call   15
to a source on my cell phone, leaving behind three journalists with whom I'd been roaming the city. Diana Washington Valdez, an *El Paso Times* reporter who has been chronicling the Juárez women's deaths, had thought I should meet an attorney who is defending one of the government's scapegoats for the murders. But when we had rattled the wrought-iron gates of his office, there had been no reply. We had decided to wait at a small restaurant next door, and since a peal of music was issuing from a nearby television, I had gone outside to return the call. After I'd finished, I'd dialed my sister's number.

He looked rather humble, and this, I thought, was confirmed by the apologetic smile he wore, as if he were sorry to be intruding for something as mundane as the time or how to find a street. I half-smiled at him. "Hold on," I told my sister. I was about to save him the trouble of asking by telling him that I was not from around here when he spoke once more.

"Are you looking for work?"

• o •

Journalists and activists and sociologists trying to explain the loss of hundreds of women in such violent ways have constructed a common narrative. The story tells that when the immigrants came to Juárez from the countryside, they brought with them traditional

---

[6] "Excuse me, Miss" (Spanish).

Mexican ideas about gender. Women were to stay home, obey their husbands, and raise their children. But when wives and girlfriends and daughters began earning their own paychecks, they tasted a new independence and savored it. They bought nice things for themselves. They went dancing. They decided when bad relationships needed ending. In many cases, because unemployment rates for men were higher, women even took on the role of breadwinner in their families. The men saw their masculinity challenged and lashed out. Their resentment, uncontained by weakened religious and community bonds, turned violent, into a rage that manifested itself in the ruthless killing of women. This story has become so popular that when I interviewed the director of the Juárez Association of Maquiladoras, he recited it for me almost as though he were delivering a pitch at a business convention.

Yet the violence in Juárez—against men as well as women—is at its barest a criminal act and the direct by-product of the lack of rule of law in the Mexican justice system. Killers know that the odds are overwhelming that they can get away with murder. Nationally, only two in every one hundred crimes are ever solved, including cases that are closed by throwing a scapegoat in jail. There are no jury trials, and it is easy to influence a judge with money. If not one of the Juárez girls' cases has been properly resolved in ten years, only two explanations are possible: Law enforcement is either inept or corrupt. Most people believe both are true.

"I got to witness the inefficiency," says Oscar Maynez, the chief of forensics in Juárez from 1999 to 2002. Maynez has been involved in the cases of the murdered women of Juárez from the beginning. In 1993, as an instructor at the state police academy, he was skimming criminal files to use in his class when something disturbing grabbed his attention: In three separate cases, it appeared that three young women had been raped and strangled. Fearing that a serial killer might be on the loose, he created a psychological profile of the killer. When he approached his superiors with the report, however, every one of them, including the Juárez police chief and the deputy attorney general in the state capital of Chihuahua, dismissed its importance.

Maynez left his job a year later to pursue a master's degree in Washington, D.C. When he returned to reorganize the state crime lab, in

New graves fill cemeteries on the edge of a stark and empty land.

1999, he was greeted by a growing pile of women's remains, along with case records and forensic evidence, all of it hopelessly confused. Though some of the bodies still had vital clues embedded, the lab had never done any follow-up on those that had appeared between 1993 and 1999, including DNA analyses of the rapists' semen. Maynez was certain now—and the thought enraged him—that either a serial killer or a well-funded criminal ring was systematically target-ing Juárez's youngest and poorest women. And yet, six years after his initial findings, neither the local nor the state authorities had made an effort to pursue an investigation according to Maynez's profile.

In early November 2001 eight female bodies were found in a cotton field across a busy street from the maquiladora association's air-conditioned offices. Five of them had been dumped in an old sewage canal, the other three in an irrigation ditch. Most followed a similar modus operandi: hands bound, apparently raped and strangled. Two days after the first corpses were found, Maynez and his crew began their work, dusting for evidence with tiny paintbrushes. As they did so, a man drove up in a bulldozer, saying that he'd been ordered by the attorney general's office to dig up the area to search for more bodies. Maynez sent him off to work elsewhere, preserving the crime scene.

Just a few days later, the police presented an edited videotape con-fession of two bus drivers who said they had killed the women, naming each of the eight. It seemed odd that the murderers would know the complete names of their victims—middle names, maternal and pater-nal names. When the accused were admitted to the city jail, it became obvious that they were scapegoats and had been forced to confess, for they showed multiple signs of torture, including electrical burns on their genitals. The cost of defending them turned out to be quite high. In February 2002 one of the two lawyers who was representing the drivers was shot and killed by state police officers as he drove his car; they say they mistook him for a fugitive. (An investigation was con-ducted, but the officers were never charged.) And a few days after the national human rights commission agreed to hear the drivers' cases, one of them mysteriously died in custody while undergoing an unau-thorized surgery based on forged documents for a hernia that he had developed from the torture.

To date, eighteen people have been arrested in connection with the murders, including an Egyptian chemist named Abdel Latif Sharif Sharif, who arrived in Juárez by way of the United States, where he had lived for 25 years. He had accumulated two convictions for sexual battery in Florida. Sharif, who has been jailed in Mexico since October 1995, was accused by Chihuahua state prosecutors of several of the

Juárez murders but convicted of only one. Though the conviction was overturned in 2000, a state judge ruled in favor of the prosecution's appeal, and Sharif remains imprisoned in Chihuahua City.

Judging from the lack of evidence, none of those eighteen individuals has been justly charged or convicted. The biggest testament to this is the fact that the murders continue unabated. At a press conference in jail in 1998, Sharif divulged information he had received from a police officer who claimed that the person behind the killings was Armando Martínez, the adopted son of a prominent Juárez bar owner. Sharif's source, Victor Valenzuela Rivera, said that he had overheard Martínez bragging about the murders at the Safari Club, one of his father's bars and a place frequented by police officers and *narcotraficantes*.[7] Valenzuela insisted that Martínez, who also goes by Alejandro Maynez, had said he was being protected by government officials and the police and that he had bragged about his involvement in the trafficking of drugs and jewelry. The following year, Valenzuela repeated this account before several federal legislators and reporters; again, there were bloody repercussions. After Irene Blanco, the woman who had defended Sharif in court, demanded that the press investigate the allegations against Martínez, her son was shot and nearly killed by unknown assailants. The police say the shooting was drug-related; others blame police officers themselves. Martínez's whereabouts are unknown.

Valenzuela's testimony was not the only suggestion that the murders might be linked to the drug world. In 1996 a group of civilians searching for women's remains in Lomas de Poleo came upon a wooden shack and inside it an eerie sight: red and white votive candles, female garments, traces of fresh blood, and a wooden panel with detailed sketches on it. On one side of the panel was a drawing of a scorpion—a symbol of the Juárez cartel—as well as depictions of three unclothed women with long hair and a fourth lying on the floor, eyes closed, looking sad. A handful of soldiers peered out from behind what looked like marijuana plants, and at the top there was an ace of spades. The other side showed similar sketches: two unclothed women with their legs spread, an ace of clubs, and a male figure that looked

---

[7] Drug traffickers (Spanish).

like a gang member in a trench coat and hat. The panel was handed over to Victoria Caraveo, a women's activist, who turned it in to state authorities. Though the incident was reported by the Mexican papers, today government officials refuse to acknowledge that the panel ever existed.

As Oscar Maynez sees it, the problem with the Mexican justice system begins with "a complete absence of scruples among the people at the top." The criminologist says that the state crime lab has become merely an office that signs death certificates. In the case of the eight girls' bodies discovered in 2001, Maynez told the *El Paso Times,* "We were asked to plant evidence against two bus drivers who were charged with the murders." Though the drivers were prosecuted, their evidence file, Maynez says, remained empty. Frustrated, he resigned in January 2002. Because it has become his life's mission to save Juárez—or at least reduce its death toll—he is still intent upon getting his job back some day. The only chance of this happening is if the National Action Party (PAN) retakes control of the state.

But the PAN-controlled federal government isn't doing much to solve the Juárez murders either. Some of Chihuahua's top leaders a decade ago now sit in the highest ranks of President Vicente Fox's administration. In December 2001 federal legislators formed a committee to investigate the issue; it has yet to release a report. The bad blood between political parties and the long history of turf wars between state and federal law enforcement groups have prevented any sort of interagency cooperation, a key to solving difficult crimes in the United States. (On one of my trips to Juárez, I watched news footage of a mob of men pummeling each other—it was the state and federal police, fighting over who was supposed to protect the governor of Chihuahua when he flew into the city.) Early this March, the federal attorney general finally sent his investigators to the border, and in May they announced their intention to reopen fourteen of the murder cases as part of an investigation into organ smuggling.

Activists in Juárez and El Paso believe that the only way the murders can ever be solved is for Mexican federal officials to invite the American FBI to investigate, but historically, neither side has seemed eager for this to occur. Nationalism runs high in Mexico, and the country's leaders do not want Americans meddling in their affairs. In El Paso, officials like outgoing mayor Ray Caballero hesitate to offend their peers in Chihuahua. Caballero, who has had little to say publicly about the murdered women, told me. "For me to come out and make one pronouncement does not solve the problem." Perhaps circumstances are changing. This spring his office announced the creation of a hotline that will allow people in Juárez to report information to the El Paso police, who will then turn it over to investigators in Chihuahua. In late April, two deputies of the Mexican federal attorney general asked the FBI to collaborate with them on their investigations of the Juárez murder cases and the Juárez drug cartel. FBI agents have also been training Mexican prosecutors and detectives in Juárez and El Paso.

• ○ •

"Are you looking for work?"   30

My heart stopped. I knew that line, knew it immediately. My eyes, frozen, terrified, locked onto his. "N-n-n-o," I believe I stuttered, but the man spoke again: "Where are you from?" His eyes crawled down my body and back up to my face. I was wearing leather boots, a black turtleneck, and fitted jeans—the last pair of clean pants I had managed to dig out of my suitcase that morning. And I regretted it immediately, because they might have been appropriate for trekking in mountains but not, I realized now, for walking around downtown. My heart was back, pounding furiously. Only then did I notice that as I had talked on the phone, I had absentmindedly paced half a block away from the restaurant's door. At that moment, there was nobody within sight, not even a single officer from the police station next door. I tried to envision the scenarios, tried to imagine some chance of safety. Would he ask me to follow him somewhere? Would someone drive up out of nowhere and force me into a vehicle? Did I have control of the situation or did he? If I darted toward the restaurant door, would I startle him, causing him to reach over and grab me? If I screamed, would my sister, who was now dangling by my thigh on the other end of a cell phone—listening, I hoped desperately, to this conversation—be able to help? Would Diana and the others inside the restaurant hear me over the music? If I was not able to escape, how much would I have to suffer before being killed? Was this it? Had I really—and the brief thought of this made me sad—gambled it all for a story?

For a few infinite seconds, nothing, and everything, was possible. But as my heart began to slow down and my mind sped up, I thought of another possibility. "I'm from El Paso," I said.

• ○ •

Irma Monrreal lives in a dust-tinged neighborhood known as Los Aztecas. The streets are unpaved, lined with tiny cement homes that peek out from behind clumsy cinder-block walls. Her home on Calle Grulla, which she bought on credit for $1,000, originally consisted of one room, in which she slept with seven children, but her eldest sons constructed another two rooms. Like so many immigrants in Juárez, Irma had hopped on a train and headed to the border with visions of prosperity flitting about in her head. In the fields of her state of Zacatecas, she had earned $3 a day hoeing beans and chiles. The big talk those days was of the factories in Juárez, where one could make nearly three times as much money. Since she and her husband had separated and her two eldest boys, who were thirteen and fourteen years old, would soon be needing jobs, she moved to Juárez and altered her sons' birth certificates so that they could immediately begin work in the maquiladoras.

Though Irma had a bundle of children to care for, she was closest to her third-youngest, Esmeralda, a blithe girl with a broad, round face and an unflinchingly optimistic attitude. At fifteen, she had completed middle school and was determined to keep studying so that someday she might work in a big place—like the airport, she told her mother— and earn lots of money. She was an excellent typist. She didn't date or spend much time with friends, but she was extremely close to her little sister Zulema, who was four years younger. The two pretended that they were television stars or models, and on special occasions they attended mass and treated themselves to lunch. When nighttime set in, they dreamed in bunk beds.

The only thing Esmeralda desired even more than an education was to have a *quinceañera*[8] and to wear, like every other girl in Juárez

[8] Celebration of a girl's fifteenth birthday (Spanish).

who turns fifteen, a white gown to her rite-of-passage celebration. Her mother, who earns about $30 a week at a plastics factory, was saving up what she could to pay for the party, but Esmeralda felt the urge to pitch in. When an acquaintance asked Irma if she could borrow her teenage daughter to help around the house, Esmeralda pleaded with her hesitant mother to say yes, promising that she would work only up until the December 15 ceremony.

A week went by, and Esmeralda was excited, chatty. One evening she confided to her mom that a young man who was a few years older than she and who worked at the printshop where she had ordered her invitations had asked her out to lunch. She seemed deeply flattered that someone would notice her, but Irma admonished her not to take any offers from strangers. Her daughter promised that she wouldn't. A second week passed. Esmeralda would finish working at about four o'clock and head straight home, arriving well before Irma departed for her overnight shift at the maquiladora.

But a few days later, something went terribly wrong. At four-thirty, there was no sign of Esmeralda. Then it was five o'clock. Then six. At ten minutes to seven, Irma was forced to leave for work, but she asked her other children to watch for their sister. In the factory, she punched her time card and began talking to God silently.

The night dragged. When her shift was finally over, at seven in the morning, Irma rushed home to see her daughter's face, but her world imploded when her children opened the door: *Esmeralda no llegó.*[9] The girl had vanished.

During the following ten days, Irma sometimes wondered whether her mind hadn't just taken a crazy turn. *Her* Esmeralda. How could this be happening? At night, she was overwhelmed with terror as she speculated where the girl might be, what she might be going through at that very moment. To lose a family member and not know what has happened to her is to live an existential anguish of believing fiercely and at the same time losing all notion of truth. I spoke with a psychologist at a Juárez women's crisis center who said that she finds it almost impossible to help the relatives of disappeared people heal

[9] Esmeralda didn't come (Spanish).

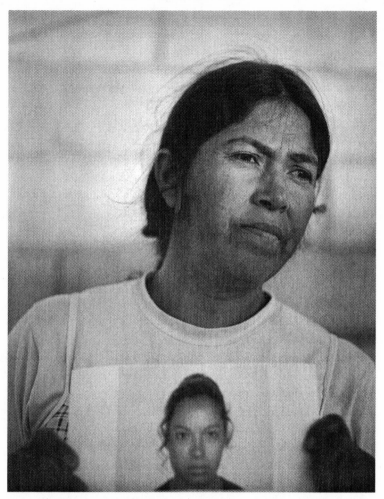

© Dan Winters

Elegy for Esmerelda: Irma Monrreal mourns her daughter.

because they are unable to discount that their abducted family member is either dead or alive. In El Paso I met Jaime Hervella, a Juárez native who runs a small accounting and consulting business as well as an organization for relatives of the disappeared on both sides of the border. "It's the worst of tragedies," he said, motioning with his wax-like hands over a cluttered desk. Then his bifocals fogged up, and he wept suddenly. "I just can't handle talking to the little old women, the mothers. Morning comes and they implore God, the Virgin, the man who drives the dump truck. Nighttime falls and they are still asking themselves. 'Where could my child be?' And the hours pass in this way, and the sun begins to disappear."

As she scavenged her memory for clues, Irma recalled the young 40 man who had invited her daughter to lunch and immediately sent her son to look for him. But the owner of the printshop said he'd left his job. He refused to give any more information. After several visits herself, Irma finally persuaded the shop owner's son to tell her where their former employee lived. She found the little house, but it was locked; she banged on the door, the windows, screaming loudly in case her daughter was inside, listening. Esmeralda had told her mother that the young man had asked her for her schedule and that he had wanted to know whether her mom always walked her home from work. As Irma circled the house, the man arrived. She explained who she was and asked if he knew anything about her daughter, but he brushed her away, saying that he was married.

A few days later, a co-worker at the maquiladora asked Irma if she'd heard the news: Eight bodies had been found in a couple of ditches at the intersection of Ejército Nacional and Paseo de la Victoria. Could one of them be Esmeralda? Next came the phone call from the state prosecutor's office, asking her to identify the body. At the morgue, however, Irma was told it was too gruesome to view. She would have to obtain signed permission from the prosecutor's office. They offered to bring out the blouse that was on the corpse when it was found; Irma's heart collapsed when she glimpsed the speckled yellow, pink, orange, and white. It was the blouse that Esmeralda's older sister Cecilia had sent from Colorado, where she had moved to with her husband.

Yet there was still that lingering doubt, so Irma requested the permit to see the body. Fearing the shock would be too great for their mother to bear, her two eldest sons insisted on identifying it themselves. When they arrived home from the morgue, they were silent, their heads hung low.

"So?" Irma asked anxiously. "Was it your sister?"

But the response was hesitant, brittle: "We don't know."

"What do you mean, you don't know?!" Irma sputtered.   45

"It's just that . . . she doesn't have a face."

The words shattered on the floor like a Christmas ornament. She burst: "But what about her hair—was it her hair?!"

"It's just that she doesn't have any hair," came the grief-stricken reply. "She doesn't have any ears. She doesn't have anything."

The corpse presumed to be Esmeralda's was one of the three found on November 6, a day before the other five were discovered a short distance away. All of the bodies were partially or wholly unclothed, some with their hands tied. But unlike the other girls, most of whom had been reduced to mere skeletal remains, Esmeralda's state of decomposition was particularly grisly and perplexing. She was missing most of the flesh from her collarbone up to her face. The authorities suggested that the rats in the fields had had their share, but Irma noted—and Oscar Maynez, the chief of forensics, concurred—that it would have made more sense for them to feast on the meatier parts of her body. The mystery deepened when the forensic workers took hair and blood from Esmeralda's mother and father and sent them to a laboratory in Mexico City. Even when DNA samples from the parents who had identified clothing were compared with those from the girls wearing the clothing, the results came back without a match. This opened up two possibilities: Either the samples had been grossly contaminated or, even more eerily, the murderers were switching clothes with other, as yet unfound, victims.

"Why?" Irma cried out as I sat with her one wintry afternoon in her   50 tidy home, which is crammed with curly-haired dolls and deflated balloons and stuffed animals her daughter had collected—the last traces of happiness left in her little house. "Do they want to drive me crazy or something? Is it her or isn't it?" In a silver frame on top of a brown armoire, Esmeralda sat squeezed into a strapless red top, her shoulder-length hair dyed a blondish brown. She was laughing irresistibly—cracking up—but across from the photo, Irma slumped in her chair in blue sweats and a denim shirt, her body heaving uncontrollably as I listened, speechless. "Why does God let the evil ones take the good ones away? Why the poor, if we don't bring any harm on anybody? Nobody can imagine what this trauma is like. I go to work and I don't know if my children are going to be safe when I return. It's a terror that's lived day by day, hour by hour."

Like numerous stories I had heard from other victims' families, Irma's included the lament that her family has fallen apart as her children struggle to confront the tragedy of losing their sister and try to assign blame. Unable to channel their newfound hate, they have begun hating each other. Her eldest sons have stopped talking to her. Zulema, who refuses to sleep in her bunk bed now, attempted to kill herself and her eight-year-old brother with tranquilizers a doctor had prescribed for Irma. Defeated, the woman spoke with the shame of a child who has discovered that she has made an irrevocably wrong choice. She wished, with all her might, that she had never made that fateful decision to come to Juárez. "They've destroyed my life," she said with vacant eyes and a flat voice, once she had regained her composure. "I don't believe in anything anymore. There is a saying that one comes here in search of a better life, but those are nothing but illusions."

Irma eventually claimed the body, she says, so that she would "have somewhere to cry." Instead of determining whether more lab work needed to be done, the authorities instantly handed it over. They never interrogated the suspicious young man Irma had reported, and in a tasteless act of disregard for her daughter, they ruled that the cause of the young woman's death was "undetermined," even though it seemed apparent that she had been strangled. On November 16 Irma buried the corpse, using the quinceañera savings to pay for the $600 coffin.

• o •

"Soy de El Paso,"[1] I said to the man outside the restaurant. I held my breath. I remembered what Diana had told me when we first met to talk about the story: "They know who to leave alone. They leave the Americans alone. They leave the rich girls alone, because there might be trouble. The other girls? A dime a dozen." And yes, his interest

---

[1] I'm from El Paso (Spanish).

faded instantly. "I'm sorry," he said, still bearing his apologetic smile, though somewhat more sheepishly. "I—I just saw you holding that piece of paper so I thought maybe you were looking for a job. Sorry." He turned around and began to walk away.

I was still frightened, but now that I felt a little safer, the journalist in me began to return. "Why?" I called out nervously. "Do you know of a job?" He turned around and stared at me. "I hire girls to work at a grocery store," he said. His eyebrows crinkled. "Where are you from?" Shaking my head, I stammered. "Oh, no—I'm from El Paso. My friends are waiting for me inside this restaurant." I brushed past him in a hurry, skipping up the restaurant's steps and to the table where the rest of the group was finishing their meal. Diana was gone. I took my seat. My legs, my hands, trembled violently.

"You'll never guess what happened to me," I said in a shaky voice. The others fell silent and looked at me with interest. "I just got offered a job." As the words spilled, one of the group nodded slowly. "You fit the profile," she said. When I described the man to her, she said that he had walked into the restaurant earlier, while I was on the phone. He had chatted with the woman who was cooking, taken some food, and left.

I jumped from my chair and stepped over to the counter. "Excuse me, *señora*," I said to the woman at the grill. "Do you know the man who just came in a few minutes ago?" "Not very well," she replied. "At night he guards the lawyer's office next door and by day he sells candies on the street."

At that moment, something blocked the light from the doorway. I turned around and found myself face to face with the same man from outside, this time without his basket. He looked nervous. "Let me buy you a Coke," he offered. "No, thanks," I replied firmly. Then I asked him, "Do you really have a store?"

"You're a journalist," he said, "aren't you?" His question caught me by surprise. I turned toward my table, then back to his intense gaze. "I—I'm here with some journalist friends," I stuttered. "No." he said forcefully, "but *you're* a journalist, aren't you?" It was obvious that he knew. "Well, yes, but I'm just here accompanying my friends, who are working on a story." His tone softened. "Come on, let's sit down. Let

55

me buy you a drink. *En confianza.*[2] *You can trust me.* "No," I repeated, "I'm with my friends and we're leaving." I walked back to the table. Diana had returned, unaware of what had transpired. Later I would learn that she had gone to the lawyer's office, encountered the candy man, and told him she was with a group of journalists who wanted to see his boss. But with the man standing there, all I wanted to do was get away. We all gathered our belongings and hurried toward the door. "The lawyer says he'll be here tomorrow, if you want to see him," we heard the man call out to us. I never turned back.

That night, safe in El Paso, I stared at the ceiling in the darkness of my hotel room and replayed the afternoon's events over and over. My family had worried when I told them that I was going to write about the women of Juárez, even after I assured them that plenty of other journalists had done so safely. But *you*, they shot back, as if I'd missed the most obvious point, *you* look just like those girls. I thought of how much care I had taken not to go to Juárez alone, even if it had meant sacrificing my journalistic independence. And yet, in that one brief instant I had let my guard down, and I had been approached by someone mysterious. I will never know for sure if that was it—if, as I have told colleagues I felt at that moment, I really touched the story, my own life colliding with those of the girls whose lives I had been hoping to preserve. What I do know is this: that I had felt my heart beat, the way they must have felt it beat too.

As I thought this, warm tears spilled down the sides of my face and trickled into my ears. And I realized that I was crying not for myself, but for the women of Juárez—for the girls who had died and for the mothers who survived them. They say that whenever a new body is found, every grieving mother relives her pain. I was crying for the girls who had stayed on the other side of the border. For the ones who couldn't leave their reflections on paper and run far, far away, as I was going to do. I cried because I realized how easy it would have been to believe the man who approached me; because I understood that the girls were not naive, or careless, or as a former attorney general of Chihuahua once said, asking for it. They were simply women—poor

2. In private (Spanish).

women, brown women. Fighters, dreamers. And they weren't even dreaming of all that much, by our standards: a secretarial job, a bedroom set, a fifteenth-birthday party. A little chance to live.

I cried because of the absurdity of it all, because it was possible for a life to be worth less than a brief taste of power. I cried thinking of how we had failed them.

STUDY QUESTIONS

1. The title of Ballí's article implies that Juárez is an extremely violent city, but none of the people she interviews there are the actual perpetrators of this violence. How would you characterize the various individuals that Ballí speaks to in Juárez—their different situations and social positions, as well as the emotional effects they create in you as a reader? Explain by referring to specific passages from the text.

2. "Ciudad de la Muerte" mixes different RHETORICAL STRATEGIES, or modes, including DESCRIPTION of places, NARRATION of Ballí's own experiences, ETHNOGRAPHIC observations of people, and historical background. How does each of these modes contribute to the sense of place, and how effective is this multimodal approach overall?

3. Ballí recounts several moments of discomfort and fear during her visit to Juárez. How do her own gender, age, and skin color influence her experiences in Juárez, her conversations with residents there, and her thoughts and feelings about the murders? In what ways might this article be different if researched and written by a man?

4. *For Writing.* Ballí concludes that, after returning to the safety of El Paso, "I cried because of the absurdity of it all, because it was possible for a life to be worth less than a brief taste of power. I cried thinking of how we had failed them." Whom exactly does Ballí implicate here as "we"—Ballí and her fellow journalists? Her American AUDIENCE? Write an essay that explores Ballí's sense of who might be responsible for the failure to protect the young women of Juárez. What are some ARGUMENTS for and against her implication that Americans bear part of this responsibility?

FAREED ZAKARIA { *The Islamic Threat*

FAREED ZAKARIA (b. 1964) grew up in Mumbai, India, in an intellectual family—his father was a politician and Islamic scholar; his mother was the editor of the Sunday *Times of India*. He journeyed west for his education, earning a BA from Yale University and a PhD from Harvard University. His doctoral research into American foreign policy led to his position as editor of *Foreign Affairs* magazine. In 2000 he joined *Newsweek International* as both editor and weekly columnist on international relations. His books include *From Wealth to Power: The Unusual Origins of America's World Role* (1998) and *The Post-American World* (2008). He has been a news analyst for ABC's *This Week with George Stephanopoulos* and has also hosted his own weekly shows on foreign affairs.

"The Islamic Threat," a selection from *The Post-American World*, addresses misperceptions in the United States about threats of Islamic terrorism. Using statistics and historical examples, Zakaria puts Al Qaeda and other jihadist groups in context to argue that, although Islamic terrorism is real, it is not as great a threat as is commonly perceived. As you read, consider whether or not you agree that the threat of terrorism in America has been overblown. Notice the possible objections that Zakaria anticipates and how he acknowledges and refutes them.

ISLAMIC TERROR, WHICH MAKES THE headlines daily, is a large and persistent problem, but one involving small numbers of fanatics. It feeds on the dysfunctions of the Muslim world, the sense (real and imagined) of humiliation at the hands of the West, and easy access to technologies of violence. And yet, does it rank as a threat on the order of Germany's drive for world domination in the first half of the twentieth century? Or Soviet expansionism in the second half? Or Mao's efforts to foment war and revolution across the Third World in the 1950s and 1960s? These were all challenges backed by the power and purpose of major countries, often with serious allies, and by an ideology that was seen as a plausible alternative to liberal democracy. By comparison, consider the jihadist[1] threat. Before 9/11, when groups like Al Qaeda operated under the radar, governments treated them as minor annoyances, and they roamed freely, built some strength, and hit symbolic, often military targets, killing Americans and other foreigners. Even so, the damage was fairly limited. Since 2001, governments everywhere have been aggressive in busting terrorists' networks, following their money, and tracking their recruits—with almost immediate results. In Indonesia, the largest Muslim nation in the world, the government captured both the chief and the military leader of Jemaah Islamiah, the country's deadliest jihadist group and the one that carried out the Bali bombings in 2002. With American help, the Filipino army battered the Qaeda-style terrorist outfit Abu Sayyaf. The group's leader was killed by Filipino troops in January 2007, and its membership has declined from as many as two thousand guerrillas six years ago to a few hundred today. In Egypt and Saudi Arabia—Al Qaeda's original bases and targets of attack—terrorist cells have been rounded up, and those still at large have been unable to launch any new attacks in three years. Finance ministries—especially the U.S. Department of the Treasury—have made life far more difficult for terrorists. Global organizations cannot thrive without being able to move money around, and so the more terrorists' funds are tracked and targeted, the more they have to resort to small-scale and hastily improvised operations. This struggle, between governments and terrorists, will persist, but it is the former who have the upper hand.

In Iraq, where terrorist attacks have declined, a complication that is revealing has weakened Al Qaeda. In its original fatwas and other state-

---

[1] To most Muslims, the word *jihad* (Arabic for "struggle") denotes the inner struggle to live a moral life, not the "holy war" against nonbelievers espoused by extremists.

ments, Al Qaeda made no mention of Shiites,[2] condemning only the
"Crusaders" and "Jews." But Iraq changed things. Searching for ways
to attract Sunni support, Al Qaeda morphed into an anti-Shiite group,
espousing a purist Sunni worldview. The late Abu Mussab al-Zarqawi,
the head of Al Qaeda in Mesopotamia, bore a fierce hatred for Shiites
derived from his Wahhabi-style[3] puritanism. In a February 2004 letter
to Osama bin Laden,[4] he claimed, "The danger from the Shia . . . is
greater . . . than the Americans. . . . [T]he only solution is for us to
strike the religious, military, and other cadres among the Shia with
blow after blow until they bend to the Sunnis." If there ever was a
debate between him and bin Laden, Zarqawi won. As a result, a movement that had hoped to rally the entire Muslim world to jihad against
the West was dragged into a dirty internal war within Islam.

The split between Sunnis and Shiites is only one of the divisions
within the Islamic world. Within that universe are Shiites and Sunnis,
Persians and Arabs, Southeast Asians and Middle Easterners, and,
importantly, moderates and radicals. Just as the diversity within the
communist world ultimately made it less threatening, so do the many
varieties of Islam undermine its ability to coalesce into a single, mono-
lithic foe. Some Western leaders speak of a single worldwide Islamist
movement—absurdly lumping together Chechen separatists in Russia,
Pakistani-backed militants in India, Shiite warlords in Lebanon, and
Sunni jihadists in Egypt. In fact, a shrewd strategist would emphasize
that all these groups are distinct, with differing agendas, enemies, and
friends. That would rob them of their claim to represent Islam. It
would also describe them as they often really are: small local gangs of
misfits hoping to attract attention through nihilism and barbarism.

[2]Islam split into two principal denominations almost immediately after the death of its
founder, the prophet Muhammad. Those who believed that political and spiritual leadership should go only to direct descendants of Muhammad and his family became known as
Shiites; those who believed that leaders should be those most qualified to lead, such as
Muhammad's friend and advisor Abu Bakr, became known as Sunnis. Today Sunni Islam
is by far the largest denomination, Shia Islam the second largest. *Fatwas*: decrees or legal
opinions pronounced by Islamic clerics (Arabic).
[3]The Wahhabis are a particularly strict sect of Sunni Islam, founded in what is now Saudi
Arabia in the eighteenth century.
[4]The Saudi-born founder of Al Qaeda (b. 1957), the terror organization responsible for the
September 11, 2001, attacks on the United States.

Conflicts involving radical Islamic groups persist, but these typically have more to do with specific local conditions than with global aspirations. Although North Africa has seen continued terror, particularly in Algeria, the main group there, the Salafist[5] Group for Call and Combat (known by its French abbreviation, GSPC), is part of a long war between the Algerian government and Islamic opposition forces and cannot be seen solely through the prism of Al Qaeda or anti-American jihad. The same is true of the main area where there has been a large and extremely dangerous increase in the strength of Al Qaeda, the Afghanistan-Pakistan borderlands. It is here that Al Qaeda Central, if there is such an entity, is housed. But the group has been able to sustain itself despite the best efforts of NATO troops because it had dug deep roots in the area during the years of the anti-Soviet campaign. Its allies, the Taliban,[6] are a local movement that has long been supported by a section of the Pashtuns, an influential ethnic group in Afghanistan and Pakistan.

Here is the bottom line. In the six years since 9/11, Al Qaeda   5 Central—the group led by Osama bin Laden and Ayman Zawahiri—has been unable to launch a major attack anywhere. It was a terrorist organization; it has become a communications company, producing the occasional videotape rather than actual terrorism.[7] Jihad continues, but the jihadists have had to scatter, make do with smaller targets, and operate on a local level—usually through groups with almost no connection to Al Qaeda Central. And this improvised strategy has a crippling weakness: it kills locals, thus alienating ordinary Muslims—a process that is well underway in countries as diverse as Indonesia, Iraq, and Saudi Arabia. Over the last six years, support for bin Laden and his goals has fallen steadily throughout the Muslim world. Between 2002 and 2007, approval of suicide bombing as a tactic—a

---

[5]Zakaria refers to a Sunni Islam fundamentalist movement; the term is sometimes used interchangeably with "Wahhabist."

[6]Literally, "Students" (Pashto), a Sunni Islamist group that held power in Afghanistan from 1996 until they were ousted in 2001 by Afghan and NATO forces led by the United States.

[7]Even if an attack were to take place tomorrow, the fact that, for six years, Al Qaeda Central has been unable to organize one explosion anywhere is surely worth noting. [Author's note.]

figure that was always low—has dropped by over 50 percent in most Muslim countries that have been tracked. There have been more denunciations of violence and fatwas against bin Laden than ever before, including from prominent clerics in Saudi Arabia. Much more must happen to modernize the Muslim world, but the modernizers are no longer so scared. They have finally realized that, for all the rhetoric of the madrassas[8] and mosques, few people want to live under the writ of Al Qaeda. Those who have, whether in Afghanistan or Iraq, have become its most dedicated opponents. In contrast to Soviet socialism or even fascism in the 1930s, no society looks with admiration and envy on the fundamentalist Islamic model. On an ideological level, it presents no competition to the Western-originated model of modernity that countries across the world are embracing.

A cottage industry of scaremongering has flourished in the West—especially in the United States—since 9/11. Experts extrapolate every trend they don't like, forgoing any serious study of the data. Many conservative commentators have written about the impending Islamization of Europe (Eurabia, they call it, to make you even more uncomfortable). Except that the best estimates, from U.S. intelligence agencies, indicate that Muslims constitute around 3 percent of Europe's population now and will rise to between 5 and 8 percent by 2025, after which they will probably plateau. The watchdogs note the musings of every crackpot Imam,[9] search the archives for each reference to the end of days, and record and distribute the late-night TV musings of every nutcase who glorifies martyrdom. They erupt in fury when a Somali taxi driver somewhere refuses to load a case of liquor into his car, seeing it as the beginning of sharia[1] in the West. But these episodes do not reflect the basic direction of the Muslim world. That world is also modernizing, though more slowly than the rest, and there are those who try to become leaders in rebellion against it. The reactionaries in the world of Islam are more numerous and extreme than those in other cultures—that world does have its dysfunctions. But they remain a tiny minority

---

[8]Religious schools (Arabic).
[9]Islamic cleric or prayer leader (Arabic).
[1]An Islamic legal system based on the Koran.

of the world's billion-plus Muslims. And neglecting the complicated context in which some of these pseudoreligious statements are made—such as an internal Iranian power struggle among clerics and non-clerics—leads to hair-raising but absurd predictions, like Bernard Lewis's[2] confident claim that Iran's President Mahmoud Ahmadinejad planned to mark an auspicious date on the Islamic calendar (August 22, 2006) *by ending the world.* (Yes, he actually wrote that.)

The ideological watchdogs have spent so much time with the documents of jihad that they have lost sight of actual Muslim societies. Were they to step back, they would see a frustration with the fundamentalists, a desire for modernity (with some dignity and cultural pride for sure), and a search for practical solutions—not a mass quest for immortality through death. When Muslims travel, they flock by the millions to see the razzle-dazzle of Dubai, not the seminaries of Iran. The minority that wants jihad is real, but it operates within societies where such activities are increasingly unpopular and irrelevant.

In the West, the effects of terrorism have diminished with each additional attack. After September 11, global financial markets collapsed and did not return to September 10 levels for two months. After the Madrid bombings in 2004, the Spanish market took a month to recover. After the London bombings in July 2005, British stocks were back to prebombing levels in twenty-four hours. The broader economic picture is similar. After 9/11, the United States lost hundreds of billions of dollars in economic activity. The next large attack, the Bali nightclub bombing in 2002, had a similarly dramatic effect on the Indonesian economy, with tourism vanishing and trade and investment drying up for months. A year later, after another Indonesian bombing, this time at the Marriott hotel in Jakarta, the market dropped only briefly, and the Indonesian economy suffered little damage. Bombings in Morocco and Turkey in 2003 had similarly small effects. The 2004 bombings in Spain and 2005 bombings in Britain did nothing to undermine growth.

Of course, things would be different if a major terrorist organization were to acquire significant weapons of mass destruction. A nuclear

---

[2]British American commentator, scholar, and historian of Islam (b. 1916).

attack could result in mass panic and a broader breakdown. But such weapons are harder to get than many think, and a more sustained effort from Washington could make it nearly impossible to acquire them in any quantity. Biological terror may seem most worrying because of the ease of acquiring biological agents, but dispersing them effectively is difficult and may lack the dramatic results terrorists crave. And none of this is to suggest that anti-terror activities are unnecessary, but rather that careful, calibrated, intelligent policies are likely to be quite successful.

In some unspoken way, people have recognized that the best coun-　10 terterrorism policy is resilience. Terrorism is unusual in that it is a military tactic defined by the response of the onlooker. If we are not terrorized, then it doesn't work. And, from New York and London to Mumbai and Jakarta, people are learning this fact through experience and getting on with life even amid the uncertainty. The most likely scenario—a series of backpack or truck bombings in the United States—would be a shock, but in a couple of weeks its effects would fade and the long-term consequences would likely be minimal. In vast, vigorous, and complex societies—the American economy is now $13 trillion—problems in a few places do not easily spill over. Modern civilization may be stronger than we suspect.

The challenges from rogue states are also real, but we should consider them in context. The GDP of Iran is 1/68 that of the United States, its military spending 1/110 that of the Pentagon.[3] If this is 1938,[4] as many conservatives argue, then Iran is Romania, not

[3]A note on terminology: For such a straightforward idea, gross domestic product (GDP) is a surprisingly complicated measurement. Although tradable items like iPods or Nikes cost roughly the same from one country to the next, goods that can't flow across borders—such as haircuts in Beijing—cost less in developing economies. So the same income goes much further in India than in Britain. To account for this, many economists use a measure of GDP called purchasing power parity (PPP), which substantially inflates the incomes of developing countries. Proponents say this better reflects quality of life. Still, when it comes to the stuff of raw national power, measuring GDP at market exchange rates makes more sense. You can't buy an aircraft carrier, fund a UN peacekeeping mission, announce corporate earnings, or give foreign aid with dollars measured in PPP. This is why, in general, throughout this book I will calculate GDP using market exchange rates. Where PPP is more appropriate, or when the only numbers one can find are in that form, I will make a note of it. [Author's note.]
[4]That is, the eve of World War II (1939–45).

Germany. North Korea is even more bankrupt and dysfunctional. Its chief threat—the one that keeps the Chinese government awake at night—is that it will implode, flooding the region with refugees. That's power? These countries can cause trouble in their neighborhood and must be checked and contained, but we need to keep in mind the larger world of which they are a relatively small part. Look at Latin America. Venezuela is a troublemaker, but what has that meant on the ground? The broad trend in the region—exemplified by the policies of the major countries like Brazil, Mexico, and Chile—has been toward open markets, trade, democratic governance, and an outward orientation. And that trend, not Hugo Chávez's[5] insane rants, represents the direction of history.

• • •

[5]The president of Venezuela (b. 1954), famed for his fiery denunciations of the United States.

STUDY QUESTIONS

1. According to Zakaria, why do people in the United States think that Islamic terrorism is a greater threat than it really is? How does the author CHARACTERIZE Al Qaeda? What does he say are Al Qaeda's most pressing concerns?

2. What is Zakaria's CLAIM? What REASONS does he supply to prove that claim? What kinds of EVIDENCE does he supply? Are these effective? Why or why not?

3. *For Writing.* RESEARCH how, in the years since September 11, 2001, the threat of terrorism has been presented and discussed in the media, from newspaper articles to color-coded "threat advisory levels" (high, medium, low) reported on television news. In an essay, ANALYZE how the media has characterized the threat of terrorism and what the EFFECT of this coverage has been.

THOMAS L. FRIEDMAN ⎰ *Globalization: The Super-Story*

THOMAS L. FRIEDMAN (b. 1953), a columnist for the *New York Times*, was
born in St. Louis Park, Minnesota. He earned his BA at Brandeis University
and an MA in modern Middle Eastern studies at Oxford University. In 1981
Friedman joined the *New York Times* as a financial reporter covering the oil
industry; he went on to serve that paper as chief correspondent for the
Middle East, for the White House, and for international economics. He
currently writes a nationally syndicated, twice-weekly column for the *Times*.
Friedman has won three Pulitzer Prizes, two for international reporting
and one for commentary.His best-selling books *The Lexus and the Olive
Tree* (1999) and *The World Is Flat* (2005) both explore the process of
globalization, a concept that Friedman advocates, though with the caveat
that a country must preserve its sense of self. His other books include *From
Beirut to Jerusalem* (1989) and *Hot, Flat, and Crowded: Why We Need a
Green Revolution—And How It Can Renew America* (2008).

Friedman has also published a collection of his columns about his
international post-9/11 travels, *Longitudes and Attitudes: Exploring the
World after September 11* (2002). In this selection, the prologue to that
book, Friedman sets out to define globalization, as part of his claim that it
is the "super-story" of our age—the lens through which we view the
world. Friedman compares globalization to what he calls the "cold war
system," defining the new system in part by contrasting it with what it
replaces. Take note of the transitions Friedman uses to structure his essay.
How does he connect each of his points, and how do they lead to his larger
conclusion?

I AM A BIG BELIEVER in the idea of the super-story, the notion that we all carry around with us a big lens, a big framework, through which we look at the world, order events, and decide what is important and what is not. The events of 9/11 did not happen in a vacuum. They happened in the context of a new international system—a system that cannot explain everything but *can* explain and connect more things in more places on more days than anything else. That new international system is called globalization. It came together in the late 1980s and replaced the previous international system, the cold war system, which had reigned since the end of World War II. This new system is the lens, the super-story, through which I viewed the events of 9/11.

I define globalization as the inexorable integration of markets, transportation systems, and communication systems to a degree never witnessed before—in a way that is enabling corporations, countries, and individuals to reach around the world farther, faster, deeper, and cheaper than ever before, and in a way that is enabling the world to reach into corporations, countries, and individuals farther, faster, deeper, and cheaper than ever before.

Several important features of this globalization system differ from those of the cold war system in ways that are quite relevant for understanding the events of 9/11. I examined them in detail in my previous book, *The Lexus and the Olive Tree,* and want to simply highlight them here.

The cold war system was characterized by one overarching feature—and that was *division.* That world was a divided-up, chopped-up place, and whether you were a country or a company, your threats and opportunities in the cold war system tended to grow out of who you were divided from. Appropriately, this cold war system was symbolized by a single word—*wall,* the Berlin Wall.

The globalization system is different. It also has one overarching feature—and that is *integration.* The world has become an increasingly interwoven place, and today, whether you are a company or a country, your threats and opportunities increasingly derive from who you are connected to. This globalization system is also characterized by a single word—*web,* the World Wide Web. So in the broadest sense we have gone from an international system built around division and

5

walls to a system increasingly built around integration and webs. In the cold war we reached for the hotline, which was a symbol that we were all divided but at least two people were in charge—the leaders of the United States and the Soviet Union. In the globalization system we reach for the Internet, which is a symbol that we are all connected and nobody is quite in charge.

Everyone in the world is directly or indirectly affected by this new system, but not everyone benefits from it, not by a long shot, which is why the more it becomes diffused, the more it also produces a backlash by people who feel overwhelmed by it, homogenized by it, or unable to keep pace with its demands.

The other key difference between the cold war system and the globalization system is how power is structured within them. The cold war system was built primarily around nation-states. You acted on the world in that system through your state. The cold war was a drama of states confronting states, balancing states, and aligning with states. And, as a system, the cold war was balanced at the center by two super-states, two superpowers: the United States and the Soviet Union.

The globalization system, by contrast, is built around three balances, which overlap and affect one another. The first is the traditional balance of power between nation-states. In the globalization system, the United States is now the sole and dominant superpower and all other nations are subordinate to it to one degree or another. The shifting balance of power between the United States and other states, or simply between other states, still very much matters for the stability of this system. And it can still explain a lot of the news you read on the front page of the paper, whether it is the news of China balancing Russia, Iran balancing Iraq, or India confronting Pakistan.

The second important power balance in the globalization system is between nation-states and global markets. These global markets are made up of millions of investors moving money around the world with the click of a mouse. I call them the Electronic Herd, and this herd gathers in key global financial centers—such as Wall Street, Hong Kong, London, and Frankfurt—which I call the Supermarkets. The attitudes and actions of the Electronic Herd and the Supermarkets can have a huge impact on nation-states today, even to the point of triggering the downfall of governments. Who ousted Suharto in Indonesia in 1998? It wasn't another state, it was the Supermarkets, by withdrawing their support for, and confidence in, the Indonesian economy. You also will not understand the front page of the newspaper today unless you bring the Supermarkets into your analysis. Because the United States can destroy you by dropping bombs, but the Supermarkets can destroy you by downgrading your bonds. In other words, the United States is the dominant player in maintaining the globalization game board, but it is hardly alone in influencing the moves on that game board.

The third balance that you have to pay attention to—the one that is   10
really the newest of all and the most relevant to the events of 9/11—is the balance between individuals and nation-states. Because globalization has brought down many of the walls that limited the movement and reach of people, and because it has simultaneously wired the world into networks, it gives more power to *individuals* to influence both markets and nation-states than at any other time in history. Whether by enabling people to use the Internet to communicate instantly at almost no cost over vast distances, or by enabling them to use the Web to transfer money or obtain weapons designs that normally would have been controlled by states, or by enabling them to go into a hardware store now and buy a five-hundred-dollar global positioning device, connected to a satellite, that can direct a hijacked airplane—globalization can be an incredible force-multiplier for individuals. Individuals can increasingly act on the world stage directly, unmediated by a state.

So you have today not only a superpower, not only Supermarkets, but also what I call "super-empowered individuals." Some of these super-empowered individuals are quite angry, some of them quite wonderful—but all of them are now able to act much more directly and much more powerfully on the world stage.

Osama bin Laden declared war on the United States in the late 1990s. After he organized the bombing of two American embassies in Africa, the U.S. Air Force retaliated with a cruise missile attack on his bases in Afghanistan as though he were another nation-state. Think about that: on one day in 1998, the United States fired 75 cruise missiles at bin Laden. The United States fired 75 cruise missiles, at $1 million apiece, at a person! That was the first battle in history between a superpower and a super-empowered angry man. September 11 was just the second such battle.

Jody Williams won the Nobel Peace Prize in 1997 for helping to build an international coalition to bring about a treaty outlawing land mines. Although nearly 120 governments endorsed the treaty, it was opposed by Russia, China, and the United States. When Jody Williams was asked, "How did you do that? How did you organize one thousand different citizens' groups and nongovernmental organizations on five continents to forge a treaty that was opposed by the major powers?" she had a very brief answer: "E-mail." Jody Williams used e-mail and the networked world to super-empower herself.

Nation-states, and the American superpower in particular, are still hugely important today, but so too now are Supermarkets and super-empowered individuals. You will never understand the globalization system, or the front page of the morning paper—or 9/11—unless you see each as a complex interaction between all three of these actors: states bumping up against states, states bumping up against Supermarkets, and Supermarkets and states bumping up against super-empowered individuals—many of whom, unfortunately, are super-empowered angry men.

STUDY QUESTIONS

1. SUMMARIZE Friedman's DEFINITION of globalization in your own words.

2. Friedman CONTRASTS globalization to the "cold war system." What are some of the differences between the two? Is the COMPARISON an effective way of defining globalization? Explain.

3. How would you DESCRIBE Friedman's TONE? Is it effective and appropriate for his RHETORICAL SITUATION? Explain.

4. *For Writing.* This selection was published in 2002. In the years since then, has globalization taken on new meanings? Write an essay in which you update Friedman's definition of globalization, using examples from recent history and your own life to give it as current a definition as possible.

PICO IYER   { *The Burning House*

PICO IYER (b. 1957) writes books and articles about travel, cultural mixing, and globalization, publishing in magazines such as *Time, Harper's*, and the *New York Review of Books*. Born to Indian parents in Oxford, England, Iyer and his family moved to California when he was seven, though the family traveled back and forth between the two places (and others) frequently during his childhood. These global travels prompted Iyer to question notions of stability, home, displacement, and disorientation in the world, topics central to much of his subsequent writing. Once referring to himself as a "global village on two legs," Iyer seeks not just to capture the realities of different places around the globe, but also to show them from an outsider's perspective.

This selection, excerpted from Iyer's *The Global Soul: Jet Lag, Shopping Malls, and the Search for Home* (2000), combines personal experiences and perspectives as a means of exploring the consequences of what is variously known as "our shrinking world" or "globalism" in the twenty-first century. As a world traveler who says that "taking planes is as natural for me as picking up the phone or going to school," Iyer criticizes many of the outcomes of globalism, particularly as it contributes to disparities in wealth and misunderstandings among cultures.

THE CENTURY JUST ENDED, MOST of us agree, was the century of movement, with planes and phones and even newer toys precipitating what the secretary-general of the UN's Habitat II conference in 1996 called the "largest migration in history"; suddenly, among individuals and among groups, more bodies were being thrown more widely across the planet than ever before. Therein lay many of the new excitements of our time, and therein lay the pathos: in Cambodia recently, I heard that the second city of the Khmer people had been a refugee camp; even in relatively settled Central Europe, the number of refugees is greater than the populations of Vienna and Berlin combined.

For more and more people, then, the world is coming to resemble a diaspora, filled with new kinds of beings—Gastarbeiters and boat people and *marielitos*[1]—as well as new kinds of realities: Rwandans in Auckland and Moroccans in Iceland. One reason why Melbourne looks ever more like Houston is that both of them are filling up with Vietnamese *pho* cafés;[2] and computer technology further encourages us to believe that the remotest point is just a click away. Everywhere is so made up of everywhere else—a polycentric anagram—that I hardly notice I'm sitting in a Parisian café just outside Chinatown (in San Francisco), talking to a Mexican-American friend about biculturalism while a Haitian woman stops off to congratulate him on a piece he's just delivered on TV on St. Patrick's Day. "I know all about those Irish nuns," she says, in a thick patois, as we sip our Earl Grey tea near signs that say CITY OF HONG KONG, EMPRESS OF CHINA.

Up the hill, in my hotel, a woman named Madame Nhu is waiting in a corner of the lobby to talk to me.

"Are you from Vietnam?" I ask as we introduce ourselves, following the implication of her name.

"No. America."   5

"You never lived in Vietnam?" I press on, not very diplomatically (and mostly because I want to share with her my enthusiasm for her country).

"I'm from Hue."

"But"—I don't want to make it hard for her—"you left when you were young?"

"Yes. I never lived there; I am American."

[1] Members of a 1980 exodus of some 125,000 Cubans, most of them poor, who left Cuba's Mariel Harbor by boat and were admitted into the United States. *Gastarbeiters*: guest workers (German). *Boat people*: usually a reference to the many Vietnamese refugees who fled Vietnam by boat in the late 1970s and early 1980s.

[2] Restaurants featuring Vietnamese beef noodle soup.

I feel a little uneasy about this line of questioning, knowing that I   10
would squirm just as restlessly if someone asked the same of me: those
of us who live between categories just tend to pick the nearest (or handi-
est) answer so we can move the conversation along. In any case, "Where
do you come from?" is coming to seem as antiquated an inquiry as
"What regiment do you belong to?"

"I remember once, in Vietnam," this highly cultured woman goes
on, understanding, perhaps, that I'm only looking for a point of contact
and, in fact, that I probably have more in common with her than someone from Hue or from the Berkeley Hills might, "the chambermaid at
my hotel finally picked up the courage to ask, 'Are you one of us?'"

"In English?"

"No, in Vietnamese."

"And you must have found it difficult to answer?"

"No. I said, 'Yes. Definitely. Yes, I *am* one of you!'"   15

"Even though, when I asked just now, you didn't sound so sure.
Maybe it depends on whom you're talking to?"

Unfair again, though doubtless true: after all, nearly all the cultures
of which she'd been a member had been at war with one another during her lifetime, and wherever she was, whether it was Paris or English
boarding school, New York or San Francisco, she must have felt that
many of her lives were far away. The previous night, I'd met a man at
dinner who'd told me that he dreamed in Swedish, English, and Italian (though only his Italian dreams were in black and white).

The surprising thing about such encounters, really, is that they
don't seem surprising anymore. Already we're taking yesterday's
astonishments for granted.

Though none of these mixtures are new, as I say—Homer and Dante[3]
tell us everything we need to know about exile and abandoned homes—
what is changing, surely, is the speed at which the world is turning, and
sometimes I feel as if I'm going through the existential equivalent of that
game I used to play as a child, in which I'd spin myself around and

[3] Homer, an ancient Greek poet, and Dante Alighieri (1265–1321), an Italian poet, both
wrote of characters who left home and went on epic journeys.

around where I stood, till I collapsed in a dizzy heap on the floor. The two great engines of our age—technology and travel (now the largest industry in the world)—give fuel to each other, our machines prompting us to prize speed as an end in itself, and the longing for speed quickening a hunger for new technologies.

The external effects of this are everywhere—1 million transactions every minute on the New York Stock Exchange, and the speed of silicon chips doubling (as their price diminishes) every eighteen months. Yet the internal effects may be even more disquieting, as memory itself seems accelerated, and yesterday's dramas become as remote as ancient history. At times, it can feel as if the whole planet is joyriding in somebody else's Porsche, at ninety miles per hour, around blind curves. As even Marshall McLuhan,[4] the hopeful (if somewhat absent-minded) godfather of the "electronic cottage," confessed, "You get going very quickly and you end up in the wrong place."

In the final winter of the old millennium, to see what the official caretakers of our global order make of all this, I accepted an invitation to go as a Fellow to the annual meeting of the World Economic Forum in Davos, Switzerland. The Forum gathers hundreds of "leaders of global security" in Davos each year—captains of industry, heads of state, computer billionaires, and a few token mortals such as me—to map out the future of the planet. For six days in the tightly sealed mountain village, surrounded by teams of armed Swiss guards (the same village, skeptics always note, where Thomas Mann[5] placed his sanatorium in *The Magic Mountain*), we walked through heavy snowfall, met for panels amidst the buzzing screens of the Congress Centre, gathered for lunch and dinner in elegant hotels.

If globalism has a formal, corporate face, it was surely here, amongst the pinstriped CEOs and faces familiar from our TV screens gathered to discuss the theme of "Responsible Globality." Fellows were given "global calendars" on which they could compute the time in

20

---

[4] Canadian scholar and critic (1911–80), whose writing focused on communications and media theory. McLuhan is best known for his catchphrases "the medium is the message" and the "global village."

[5] German novelist (1875–1955); author of the novels *The Magic Mountain* and *Death in Venice*; recipient of the 1929 Nobel Prize for literature.

Karachi, Rio, and Sydney, and a World Electronic Community was set up to allow us to network on-line as well as off. The first session on the opening day was devoted to the perils of jet lag, a scientist telling his groggy audience that attention skills fall 500 percent after a long-distance flight. Beside the narrow, slushy road, along which Bill Gates and Warren Beatty and Yasir Arafat[6] could be seen trudging, one Institutional Partner had erected an enormous snow sculpture in the shape of a Coca-Cola bottle cap.

Of all the bodies on the planet, multinationals have the greatest stake—quite literally an investment—in telling us that the world is one (and Everyman, therefore, a potential consumer). CNN, part of the new media conglomerate for which I work—the largest such in the world—forbids the use of the word *foreign* on its broadcasts, and IBM, aiming, like most large companies, to be local everywhere, tells us in reassuring tones, "Somehow the word *foreign* seems foreign these days." Globalism has become the convenient way of saying that all the world's a single market.

Yet what the members of the Forum were contemplating in 1999 was the fact that a small world is a precarious one; and in our closely linked planet, a fire in one place soon becomes a blaze in another. Day after day, flanked by large-screen images of themselves, leaders came out onto the main stage of the Congress Hall to assure us of what Al Gore[7] had called the "wisdom of connectedness," and to say that the conflagration was under control. We were all joined now, they said, for richer and for poorer, in sickness and in health; all we could do was make the most of it.

Yet as the days went on, another strain began to rise up from the corners of the gathering as spokesmen for the world's poorer nations began to address us, somewhat in the manner of children with their hands extended outside a private party in some Fashion Café. "Our   25

---

[6] Palestinian leader (1929–2004); chairman of the Palestine Liberation Organization (PLO) and recipient of the 1994 Nobel Peace Prize. *Bill Gates:* American entrepreneur (b. 1955), founder of Microsoft. *Warren Beatty:* American film actor and director (b. 1937).

[7] American politician (b. 1948); forty-fifth vice president of the United States and recipient of 2004 Nobel Peace Prize for his work to draw public attention to the dangers of global climate change.

global village has caught fire," Hosni Mubarak[8] said in the fluent English that almost everyone seemed to use, "from where we do not know. We have put out some of the flames . . . but we do not know where to begin rebuilding." Kofi Annan[9] told us that a quarter of the human race seemed condemned to starvation, and one of his colleagues reminded us that more than a quarter of the human race was actually poorer now than before the end of the Cold War.[1] "Is globalism only going to benefit the powerful?" asked Nelson Mandela,[2] in his farewell address to the gatekeepers of the new world order. "Does it offer nothing to men, women and children ravaged by the violence of poverty?"

The other sound I heard, unmistakably rising up in the shadows of the Congress Centre, under the collective breath almost, was an undercurrent of anxiety about what the global order was doing to those parts of us that do not show up on screens. Even Global Man cannot live on bread alone, the Ecumenical Patriarch of Constantinople[3] reminded us; values do not figure on the currency charts, and all the globalism in the world could not add up to universalism.

Such whispers, to my surprise, were coming even from those most in tune with the planet's synergies. A young scientist credited with the invention of massive parallel computers held a dinner at which he outlined his dream of creating a "Millennium Clock," an instrument that would toll every thousand years, to remind us, in our accelerating world, of the virtue of slowness, and of the need to think of generations we could not see. A futurist spoke of "High Touch" as the necessary complement to "High Tech": consumer technology was the largest industry in America, he said, but the flight from consumer technology

---

[8] Egyptian politician (b. 1928); president of the Arab Republic of Egypt from 1981–2011.

[9] Ghanaian-born diplomat (b. 1938); secretary-general of the United Nations from 1997 to 2006 and recipient of the 2001 Nobel Peace Prize.

[1] Period of diplomatic, economic, and military tension between, on the one hand, the Soviet Union and its satellites, and on the other, the United States and its Western European allies (1947–91).

[2] South African leader (b. 1918); elected president of South Africa in 1994 after serving 27 years in prison for opposing the former apartheid government; recipient of the 1993 Nobel Peace Prize.

[3] That is, Bartholomew I (b. 1940), the archbishop of Constantinople, head of the Eastern Orthodox Church.

was the second. A film producer led a dinner at which he asked, straight out, "What happened to home?" The only home he knew, he said, had come in two unexpected moments of stillness—spiritual epiphanies, really—while traveling through rural Ireland.

At least along its fringes, the unspoken message of the conference, for me, was that it was not just goods and data (or even "gypsy capital") that were being sent around the world in ever greater quantities, but souls, and souls not always used to living without a sense of orientation; and that the "global" we so readily attach to every product we wish to make seem desirable struck a less happy note when it came to "global hearts" or "global loyalties." All the new joint ventures we celebrated so happily in the public sphere had private correspondences, and sometimes, I suspected, they were the more significant precisely because they were the less considered. Borders, after all, were collapsing in lives as much as on the map (borders between now and then, or here and there; borders between public and private). The way in which nearly all the world's conflicts now were internal ones—twenty out of thirty in 1995, according to a Swedish agency—had a counterpart, surely, in the way in which more and more of us had to negotiate a peace within, in our own private Sarajevos or Cape Towns, made up in many cases (as in Madame Nhu's) of several clashing worlds. And the fact that the world was moving in two directions at once (countries breaking down into smaller units, while companies straddle more and more continents) had a parallel in our lives, where we may find that we have more and more "connections" in the telephone, or airplane, senses, and fewer and fewer in the classic human sense.

It made me wonder, not for the first time, whether humans were really meant to cross five continents in an afternoon, and what effect it must have on us to be (in Mr. Toad's[4] immortal phrase), "here today—in next week to-morrow!" And I couldn't help but notice that in the midst of all the talk of a world without borders, the most recent Nobel laureate in economics was detained for ninety minutes at Zurich's

---

[4] Character in the children's book *The Wind in the Willows*, by Scottish author Kenneth Grahame (1859–1932).

airport—prevented from joining the global discussion—because his (Indian) passport lacked a (Swiss) visa.

One day, as I was listening to all the talk of open markets and the Euro, a pioneer in artificial intelligence leaned over to me and said, quietly, that he'd never forgotten a trip he'd taken to a monastery. What had moved him most, he said, was just the way the stone on the monastery steps had been worn down, by centuries of monastic feet, all anonymous, but all walking on the same path to the chapel, to sing the same hymns every morning.

My own steadying point, ever since I could remember, had been the essays of Emerson,[5] with their translation of Asian and ancient Greek wisdom into a code of New World optimism that turned into a private declaration of independence. Experience, but also something deeper and more innate, led me to believe that there was a higher component to the collective unconscious—that we converge as we rise, as Teilhard[6] says—and that, in fact, almost everyone, in his better moments, longed to subscribe to the creed of universal loyalty voiced by Thomas Paine[7] ("My country is the world, and my religion is to do good"). There is a "universal soul" behind us, Emerson writes in *Nature*, and shining through us, that is "not mine, or thine, or his, but we are its; we are its property and men." We are "children of the fire, made of it," he declares in "The Poet," and "only the same divinity transmuted and at two or three removes, when we know least about it."

The key to this global soul, for Emerson, lay entirely in perception: it was not so much that man had been exiled from the Garden as that he had ceased to notice that it was all around him. In that sense, our shrinking world gave more and more of us a chance to see, in palpable, unanswerable ways, how much we had in common, and how much we could live, in the grand Emersonian way, beyond petty allegiances and labels, outside the reach of nation-states. When Edward

---

[5] Ralph Waldo Emerson (1803–82); American poet, essayist, and philosopher.

[6] Pierre Teilhard de Chardin (1881–1955); French philosopher, Jesuit priest, and paleontologist.

[7] English-born American writer and revolutionary (1737–1809); author of *Common Sense*, a series of influential pamphlets urging American independence from Great Britain.

Bellamy,[8] inspired by the same impulse, envisaged the year 2000 in his novel of 1888, *Looking Backward*, he saw us all united by a system he called "Nationalism" (in which, ironically, there was "neither selling nor buying," neither money nor trade).

Yet the chance to rise to this higher sense of kinship was shadowed by the fact that more and more of what we seemed to share was on the merest surface, and global unity was most often defined in terms of common markets and linked networks; sometimes it could seem that the main force carrying the "Novus Ordo Seclorum"[9] around the world—our new order of man—was the dollar bill (on which that noble motto is inscribed above the Masonic seal). And though the world was available to many of us in ways inconceivable to our grandparents, that also meant that all the age-old human problems played out now on a planetary stage, with "centers everywhere and margins nowhere" (in McLuhan's digital upgrade of Augustine's God).

When my parents were growing up, in the heart of an old-style empire (their hometown of Bombay the largest "British" city outside London), they were part, willy-nilly, of a worldwide web of such schoolchildren, learning the same poems and reciting the same catechisms, thousands of miles away from London; the British Empire exported Shakespeare and the hymns of Wesley[1] around the globe just as determinedly as the Disney Company distributes *Aladdin* or *Mulan*. By the nineteenth century, in fact (not least because its origins lay in the commercial undertakings of the East India Company), the Raj[2] had set up a global transportation and staffing system—linking Wellington to the Falkland Islands, and Kingston to Nairobi—that was not so different from a multinational's today.

---

[8] American author and socialist (1850–98).

[9] A New Cycle of the Ages (Latin), motto on the reverse of the Great Seal of the United States.

[1] Charles Wesley (1707–88), Methodist clergyman who published more than 6,000 hymns.

[2] The British Raj was that period of direct British colonial dominion over modern-day Pakistan, India, Bangladesh, and Burma, lasting from 1857 until these nations became fully independent in the 1940s.

What was different, though, was that in the British Empire every
child was born to the immigrant's bifurcation—torn between the
home he carried in his blood and the one he had on paper; colonials
were all condemned to living with two faces. Yet in the modern world,
which I take to be an International Empire, the sense of home is not
just divided, but scattered across the planet, and in the absence of any
center at all, people find themselves at sea. Our ads sing of Planet
Reebok and Planet Hollywood—even my monthly telephone bill in
Japan speaks of "One World One Company"—yet none of us necessarily feels united on a deeper level.

Reflecting on all this, I began to wonder whether a new kind of being
might not be coming to light—a citizen of this International Empire—
made up of fusions (and confusions) we had not seen before: a "Global
Soul" in a less exalted (and more intimate, more vexed) sense than
the Emersonian one. This creature could be a person who had grown
up in many cultures all at once—and so lived in the cracks between
them—or might be one who, though rooted in background, lived and
worked on a globe that propelled him from tropic to snowstorm in three
hours. She might have a name that gave away nothing about her nation-
ality (a name like Kim, say, or Maya, or Tara), and she might have a
porous sense of self that changed with her location. Even the most age-
less human rites—scattering his father's ashes, or meeting the woman
who might be his wife—he might find himself performing six thousand
miles from the place he now called home.

This Global Soul, to use the convenient tag, lived in the metaphorical
equivalent of international airspace (the human version of cyberspace,
in a sense): his currency might be "air miles" (40 percent of which are
now earned on the ground), and the main catechism he knew by heart
might involve "fastening your seat-belt low and tight across your lap."
His memories might be set in airports that looked more and more like
transnational cities, in cities that looked like transnational airports.
Lacking a binding sense of "we," he might nonetheless remain fiercely
loyal to a single airline.

High above the clouds, in an alternative plane of existence—a duty-
free zone, in a way, in which everyone around him was a stranger—
the Global Soul would be facing not just new answers to the old

questions but a whole new set of questions, as he lived through shifts that the traditional passenger on ocean liner or long-distance train could never have imagined. His sense of obligation would be different, if he felt himself part of no fixed community, and his sense of home, if it existed at all, would lie in the ties and talismans he carried round with him. Insofar as he felt a kinship with anyone, it would, most likely, be with other members of the Deracination-state.

"One country's not enough," said a sweet, unplaceable soul who approached me one night at a gathering in rural Japan, introducing himself as half-English and half-Japanese, though he thought of himself as Malaysian (he'd spotted me, clearly, as a fellow in-betweener). "When I'm in England, there's a part of me that's not fulfilled; that's why I come here—to find the other part."

One spring day in London, I went to see Kazuo Ishiguro[3] in his home along the Northern line, near "J.J. Town," as he wryly calls it (for its large population of Jewish and Japanese émigrés), a house he shares with the Glaswegian wife he met while both of them were working with the homeless, and a young daughter. "Ish," as he is generally known (like many a Graham Greene character, he goes usually by his last name), seems in many ways a quintessential Global Soul, not quite a part of the Japan he left when he was five and not really a part of an England where his name and face (though not his manner) brand him instantly as a "foreigner." One reason his fiction speaks to readers across the world is that Ish is a seasoned translator of sorts, used to converting the values of Japan into terms the West can understand, while bringing to both his not-quite homes a nostalgia and an amused detachment that few natives could quite muster.

Ish in conversation, I soon notice, uses "they" for both his apparent homelands, calling the English the "natives" even as he pronounces Nagasaki with the short *a*'s no Japanese would ever use; he speaks only a child's Japanese, he keeps assuring me, yet in English he uses the word *aeroplane* with the careful articulation of one who's learned it as a

40

---

[3] Japanese British author (b. 1954); best known for his 1989 novel *The Remains of the Day*.

foreign term, while a boy (and at a time when the things themselves were not so common). In recent months, he says, he's been spending much of his time trying to find the perfect name for a half-Japanese, half-Scottish daughter who will be growing up in an England very likely full of Muslim fundamentalists (and their enemies). His prose, of course, is of the classic, antique sort you seldom find in England anymore, and bespeaks the keen attentiveness of a lifelong mimic.

"I can actually remember this process," he says, "of listening to words I didn't know the meaning of and literally copying the sounds." The only "un-English" boy at all the schools where he found himself, he realized that his survival depended on impersonating an English boy, while also putting his exoticism to occasional good use. "Whenever it was convenient for me to become very Japanese, I could become very Japanese," he says disarmingly. "And then, when I wanted to drop it, I would just become this ordinary Englishman."

And suddenly, in a flash, I am taken back to myself at the age of nine, going back and forth (three times a year) between my parents' home in California and my boarding school in England and realizing that, as a member of neither culture, I could choose between selves at will, wowing my Californian friends with the passages of Greek and Latin I'd already learned in England, and telling my breathless housemates in Oxford how close I lived to the Grateful Dead.[4] The tradition denoted by my face was something I could erase (mostly) with my voice, or pick up whenever the conversation turned to the Maharishi[5] or patchouli oil. With any of my potential homes, in fact, I could claim or deny attachment when I chose; and where the traditional being knew that his home, his past, and his community were all givens, often to an oppressive degree, someone like me—or Ish, or Madame Nhu—could select even the most fundamental details of our lives.

The other striking thing about Ish, I'd already seen, was that I'd closed both his last two novels without knowing the protagonist's first name; in his most recent one, *The Unconsoled*, five hundred pages of

---

[4] California-based American rock & roll band popular from the 1960s through the 1990s.

[5] Maharishi Mahesh Yogi (1914–2008); Indian yoga teacher and developer of Transcendental Meditation technique.

action, or its absence, had taken place more or less in a hotel, in some unnamed foreign town through which a touring artist walks as through a labyrinth in a dream, surrounded by people and passions he can't begin to fathom. The book is a novel about a state akin to jet lag, a nightmare of disorientation and disconnection, and its main character, at some level, doesn't know where he is, whom he's among, or who he is taken to be. Ish deliberately keeps all colloquialisms and local references out of his books, he tells me in his surprisingly open, precisely affable way, because he knows, from eighteen-month promotional tours around his global markets, that most of his readers will greet him in Norwegian, or Mandarin, or Portuguese.

As I listen to him, I think that with this new kind of lifestyle is coming to light a whole new way of writing (and dressing and eating), as Global Souls face their equivalent of the same issue that confronts nations at the end of the old world order. The heroes of many contemporary novels are multicultural foundlings—one typical one, in Bharati Mukherjee's[6] *Leave It to Me,* is called "Devi" now (she was once "Debby" and once "Faustine") and, in search of her mother, finds that her forebear carried six different passports at least; this child of Eurasian parents learns about the mysterious East from a Chinese lover in San Francisco. The person reading such a book, I suspect, will be equally mixed up often (in terms of national name tags) as she listens to "Norwegian Wood"[7] sung in Punjabi (and wreathed in sitars), and dines on French-Korean food from down the street. All that her parents could take for granted, she has to create from scratch.

In a way, it seemed, the central issue before us offshore beings (as before the floating world around us) was how to keep the soul intact in the face of pell-mell globalism; and how to preserve a sense of universality in a world that was apt to define unity in more divisive ways. I think, for example, of the man from the Punjab who picked me up recently at Lester B. Pearson Airport in Toronto, and for whom all the traditional immigrant questions were complicated many times over as members of his family, his community, set up on different continents.

[6] Indian-born American writer (b. 1940); best known for the novel *Jasmine* (1989).
[7] Song (1966) written and performed by the Beatles.

"Here not like home, sir," he assured me, as almost every Indian cabdriver in Toronto did. "Here is no corruption. Indian picture we have here, sir; Indian market. Even Indian street name, sir." (I think he meant Albion and Dundas.) But when I asked him if he felt at home in the adopted city whose praises he was singing, his voice turned soft, and gathered feeling.

"Where you spent your childhood, sir, you can never forget that place. I am here, sir, and I like it here. But"—and I could hear the ache—"I love my India."

I know a little about the Global Soul in part because, having grown up simultaneously in three cultures, none of them fully my own, I acquired very early the sense of being loosed from time as much as from space—I had no history, I could feel, and lived under the burden of no home; and when I look at many of the most basic details of my life, I realize that even though they look hardly strange to me, they would have seemed surreal to every one of my grandparents. Growing up, I had no relatives on the same continent as myself, and I never learned a word of my mother's tongue or my father's (because, coming from different parts of India, they had no common language save that of British India). To this day, I can't pronounce what is technically my first name, and the name by which I go is an Italian one (though often mistaken for Spanish, Portuguese, female), mostly because my parents, realizing I'd be living among people foreign to Indian polysyllables, named me after a fifteenth-century Italian neo-Platonist whose name was easy to spell and to pronounce.[8]

As a permanent alien, I've never been in a position to vote, and, in fact, I've never held a job in the country where I more or less live; I thought relatively little (though my parents were middle-class academics, far from rich) of going to school over the North Pole, and have never had a partner who belongs to the same race. ("Miscegenation is the great hope and future of mankind," an optimistic soul in San Francisco

50

[8] Reference to Italian Renaissance philosopher Giovanni Pico della Mirandola (1463–94), here associated with neo-Platonism, a body of religious and mystical thought developed by the Greek philosopher Plotinus in the third century CE, attempting to reconcile Christian doctrine with the philosophy of Plato.

tells me. "It's not possible to hate your grandson.") The son of Hindu-born Theosophists, I was educated entirely in Christian schools and spend most of my time now in Buddhist lands (the Caribbean islanders would call me a "Nowherian"), and, though I spend most of my year in rural Japan or in a Catholic monastery, I've nonetheless accumulated 1.5 million miles on one American airline alone.

A person like me can't really call himself an exile (who traditionally looked back to a home now lost), or an expatriate (who's generally posted abroad for a living); I'm not really a nomad (whose patterns are guided by the seasons and tradition); and I've never been subject to the refugee's violent disruptions: the Global Soul is best characterized by the fact of falling between all categories (and at college, for example, I counted neither as a local, who could receive a government grant, nor as a foreigner, who was subject to a specially inflated fee). The country where people look like me is the one where I can't speak the language, the country where people sound like me is a place where I look highly alien, and the country where people live like me is the most foreign space of all. And though, when I was growing up, I was nearly always the only mongrel in my classroom or neighborhood, now, when I look around, there are more and more people in a similar state, the children of blurred boundaries and global mobility.

I've grown up, too, with a keen sense of the blessings of being unaffiliated; it has meant that almost everywhere is new and strange to me (as I am new and strange to it), and nearly everywhere allows me to keep alive a sense of wonder and detachment. Besides, the foreigner is in the rare position of being able to enjoy the facilities of a place without paying the taxes, and can appreciate the virtues of anywhere without being wholly subject to its laws. My complexion (like my name) allows me to pass as a native in Cuba, or Peru, or Indonesia, and none of them, in any case, is more foreign to me than the England where I don't look like a native, the America where I'm classified as an alien, and the India where I can't speak a word of any of the almost two hundred languages. Enabled, I hope, to live a little bit above parochialisms, I exult in the fact that I can see everywhere with a flexible eye; the very notion of home is foreign to me, as the state of foreignness is the closest thing I know to home.

Yet deeper than such tidy formulations, any number of questions begin to gather, and the fact remains that humans have never lived with quite this kind of mobility and uprootedness before (indeed, the questions themselves may be the closest thing we have to home: we live in the uncertainties we carry round with us). A lack of affiliation may mean a lack of accountability, and forming a sense of commitment can be hard without a sense of community. Displacement can encourage the wrong kinds of distance, and if the nationalism we see sparking up around the globe arises from too narrow and fixed a sense of loyalty, the internationalism that's coming to birth may reflect too roaming and undefined a sense of belonging. The Global Soul may see so many sides of every question that he never settles on a firm conviction; he may grow so used to giving back a different self according to his environment that he loses sight of who he is when nobody's around. Even the most basic questions have to be answered by him alone, and when, on the planes where he may make his home the cabin attendant passes down the aisle with disembarkation forms, it may be difficult for him to fill in any of the boxes: "Home Address," "Citizenship," "Purpose of Visit," even "Marital Status."

I can answer almost any of these questions from a variety of perspectives, I often feel (depending on whether I'm calling myself Indian in Cuba, or English-born in Burma, or affiliated with California in the Philippines). But though this can be a natural- and useful-enough impulse in response to the question, "Where do you come from?" it becomes more treacherous in answer to the question "Where do you stand?"

Every one of these concerns is, of course, still the province of a tiny minority (and a relatively comfortable minority at that); the most urgent issues in the world today, as the plaintive voices of Davos remind us, are still the same ones they've always been: how to get food on the table, and find shelter for your children; how to live beyond tomorrow. Indeed, one of the most troubling features of the globalism we celebrate is that the so-called linking of the planet has, in fact, intensified the distance between people: the richest 358 people in the world, by UN calculations, have a financial worth as great as that of 2.3 billion others, and even in the United States, the prosperous home of egalitarianism, the most wired man in the land (Bill Gates) has a net worth larger than that of 40 percent of the country's households, or perhaps 100 million of his compatriots combined (according to Robert Reich). The rich have the sense that they can go anywhere tomorrow, while 95 percent of the new beings on the planet are among the poor; I worry about the effects of E-mail and transprovincialism, while two-thirds of the people in the world have never used a telephone.

Not long ago, I flew to Haiti, just two hours from New York City, and, stepping off the plane, I walked into the pages of the Bible. Women were relieving themselves along the main streets and the principal sights on view along National Highway One were tombstones. The sidewalks were crowded with people around the Centre de Formation Intellectuelle, but that was mostly because unemployment was running at 70 percent; the sign that said Tomorrow Belongs to Haiti was all but obscured by mountains of trash. Most of the adults I saw around me, I learned, had never had a day of formal schooling, and the average man would be dead by the age of forty-four. Though only 5 percent of the people I saw would vote in the coming elections, it was unsafe for anyone to go out at night, people said, "because of democracy."

Haiti still remains the globe's rule more than its exception—more and more of the countries I visit are descending into anarchy—and it makes a mockery of the concerns of the Global Soul, as of the airline's happy talk of "15,000 travellers transcending borders every minute." There are more telephones in Tokyo, it's often said, than on the entire continent of Africa. But these very discrepancies are one of the by-products of the age, and more and more of us, moving between countries as easily as between channels on our screens, are tempted to underestimate the distances between them. My parents, when they traveled to the England that seemed the end point of an educated Indian's destiny, had to travel by boat, through the Suez Canal, or around the Cape of Good Hope, and the two weeks at sea, on the Peninsular and Oriental lines, gave them time to measure the distance between the two countries; now, such shifts are instantaneous, and it's not always easy to differentiate between traveling from Seventh

Avenue to Eighth Avenue and traveling to a place that has no tradition or values in common with our own.

I woke up one morning last month in sleepy, never-never Laos (where the center of the capital is unpaved red dirt and a fountain without water), and went to a movie that same evening in the Westside Pavilion in Los Angeles, where a Korean at a croissanterie made an iced cappuccino for a young Japanese boy surrounded by the East Wind snack bar and Panda Express, Fajita Flats and the Hana Grill; two weeks later, I woke up in placid, acupuncture-loving Santa Barbara, and went to sleep that night in the broken heart of Manila, where children were piled up like rags on the pedestrian overpasses and girls scarcely in their teens combed, combed their long hair before lying down to sleep under sheets of cellophane on the central dividers of city streets. It is hard not to think that such quick transitions bring conflicts, and sometimes illusions that we haven't confronted before, and though I, as a sometime journalist, travel more than many people I know the planes on which I travel are full of management consultants and computer executives and international aid workers and tribal backpackers who fly much more than I do.

And what complicates the confusions of the Global Soul is that, as fast as we are moving around the world, the world is moving around us; it is not just the individual but the globe with which we're interacting that seems to be in constant flux. So even the man who never leaves home may feel that home is leaving him, as parents, children, lovers scatter around the map, taking pieces of him wherever they go. More and more of us may find ourselves in the emotional or metaphysical equivalent of that state we know from railway stations, when we're sitting in a carriage waiting to pull out and can't tell, often, whether we're moving forwards, or the train next to ours is pulling back.

Thus even those people whose lives haven't changed are subject, at times, to a universe increasingly shaped and colored by the Global Soul, and the Bangladeshi who's never moved from his village finds himself visited by images of Hong Kong (on-screen), and videos from Bombay, and phone calls from Toronto, perhaps, while the Torontonian who's never left the city walks out of his grandmother's house, only to see signs he can't read and hear words he can't understand, 60 among people whose customs are strange to him. Never before in human history, I suspect, have so many been surrounded by so much that they can't follow.

The temptation in the face of all this can be (as the great analyst of the modern condition, Graham Greene,[9] saw) to try to lay anchor anywhere, even in a faith one doesn't entirely believe, just so one will have a home and solid ground under one's feet. To lack a center, after all, may be to lack something essential to the state of being human; "to be rooted," as Greene's fellow admirer of Catholicism, Simone Weil[1] said, "is perhaps the most important and least recognized need of the human soul."

* * *

[9] English novelist, playwright, and critic (1904–91); best known for his novels set in "trouble spots" around the world.

[1] French author, critic, and activist (1909–43) whose work often dealt with the plight of the working class.

STUDY QUESTIONS

1. Iyer acknowledges that globalism is nothing new. In what ways does Iyer suggest, however, that today's globalism is different from what it was in the past? What specific examples does he use in order to help support his ARGUMENT about contemporary forms of globalism?

2. Iyer writes in paragraph 53 that "A lack of affiliation may mean a lack of accountability, and forming a sense of commitment can be hard without a sense of community." He argues throughout that unaffiliated people like himself have difficulties because traditional connections between people (culture, ethnicity, and community, for example) become scattered and disoriented. Although Iyer never explicitly DEFINES the words "culture" and "community" in the essay, what can you infer about them and what about them does he appear to deem important in our contemporary era?

3. In this selection, drawn from his book *The Global Soul*, Iyer frequently refers to people like himself as "Global Souls." What does he mean by this phrase? And do you think it an effective phrase to describe the condition of people like Iyer? What else might be meant by the phrase "Global Soul"?

4. *For Writing.* Much has changed in the world since *The Global Soul* was published in 2000. Write an essay that explains what you believe is still relevant about Iyer's notion of globalism and what is no longer relevant in the post-9/11 world. You may RESEARCH and refer to specific global issues since 2000 that will help you evaluate Iyer's arguments and assert your own CLAIMS.

BRENT STAPLES

$\left\{\begin{array}{l}\end{array}\right.$ *What Adolescents Miss*
When We Let Them
Grow Up in Cyberspace

BRENT STAPLES (b. 1951) grew up in Chester, Pennsylvania, the eldest in a family of nine children. He did not expect to go to college but ultimately earned a PhD in psychology from the University of Chicago. After teaching briefly at Widener University, where he did his undergraduate studies, he worked as a reporter for the *Chicago Sun-Times* and then joined the *New York Times* as a reporter in 1985. Five years later, he was appointed to the *Times* editorial board, and he continues to write for that paper and for other publications, frequently focusing on politics and race in American culture. His memoir, *Parallel Time: Growing Up in Black and White* (1994), details his childhood in Chester and the death of his younger brother.

In this *Times* editorial, Staples writes about how very different socializing was when he was growing up compared to what it has become for today's adolescents, who cultivate relationships in cyberspace. As he explores why young people are drawn to the Internet and what might be the benefits and consequences of that behavior, notice the evidence Staples presents to support his thesis.

MY TENTH-GRADE HEARTTHROB WAS the daughter of a fearsome steel-worker who struck terror into the hearts of fifteen-year-old boys. He made it his business to answer the telephone—and so always knew who was calling—and grumbled in the background when the conversation went on too long. Unable to make time by phone, the boy either gave up or appeared at the front door. This meant submitting to the intense scrutiny that the girl's father soon became known for.

He greeted me with a crushing handshake, then leaned in close in a transparent attempt to find out whether I was one of those bad boys who smoked. He retired to the den during the visit, but cruised by the living room now and then to let me know he was watching. He let up after some weeks, but only after getting across what he expected of a boy who spent time with his daughter and how upset he'd be if I disappointed him.

This was my first sustained encounter with an adult outside my family who needed to be convinced of my worth as a person. This, of course, is a crucial part of growing up. Faced with same challenge today, however, I would probably pass on meeting the girl's father—and outflank him on the Internet.

Thanks to e-mail, online chat rooms and instant messages—which permit private, real-time conversations—adolescents have at last succeeded in shielding their social lives from adult scrutiny. But this comes at a cost: teenagers nowadays are both more connected to the world at large than ever, and more cut off from the social encounters that have historically prepared young people for the move into adulthood.

The Internet was billed as a revolutionary way to enrich our social 5 lives and expand our civic connections. This seems to have worked well for elderly people and others who were isolated before they got access to the World Wide Web. But a growing body of research is showing that heavy use of the Net can actually isolate younger socially connected people who unwittingly allow time online to replace face-to-face interactions with their families and friends.

Online shopping, checking e-mail and Web surfing—mainly solitary activities—have turned out to be more isolating than watching television, which friends and family often do in groups. Researchers have found that the time spent in direct contact with family members drops by as much as half for every hour we use the Net at home.

This should come as no surprise to the two-career couples who have seen their domestic lives taken over by e-mail and wireless tethers that keep people working around the clock. But a startling body of research from the Human-Computer Interaction Institute at Carnegie Mellon has shown that heavy Internet use can have a stunting effect outside the home as well.

Studies show that gregarious, well-connected people actually lost friends, and experienced symptoms of loneliness and depression, after joining discussion groups and other activities. People who communicated with disembodied strangers online found the experience empty and emotionally frustrating but were nonetheless seduced by the novelty of the new medium. As Professor Robert Kraut, a Carnegie Mellon researcher, told me recently, such people allowed low-quality relationships developed in virtual reality to replace higher-quality relationships in the real world.

No group has embraced this socially impoverishing trade-off more enthusiastically than adolescents, many of whom spend most of their free hours cruising the Net in sunless rooms. This hermetic existence has left many of these teenagers with nonexistent social skills—a point widely noted in stories about the computer geeks who rose to prominence in the early days of Silicon Valley.

Adolescents are drawn to cyberspace for different reasons than adults. As the writer Michael Lewis observed in his book *Next: The Future Just Happened,* children see the Net as a transformational device that lets them discard quotidian identities for more glamorous ones. Mr. Lewis illustrated the point with Marcus Arnold, who, as a 15-year-old, adopted a pseudonym a few years ago and posed as a 25-year-old legal expert for an Internet information service. Marcus did not feel the least bit guilty, and wasn't deterred, when real-world lawyers discovered his secret and accused him of being a fraud. When asked whether he had actually read the law, Marcus responded that he found books "boring," leaving us to conclude that he had learned all he needed to know from his family's big-screen TV.

Marcus is a child of the Net, where everyone has a pseudonym, telling a story makes it true, and adolescents create older, cooler, more socially powerful selves any time they wish. The ability to slip easily into a new, false self is tailor-made for emotionally fragile adolescents, who can consider a bout of acne or a few excess pounds an unbearable tragedy.

But teenagers who spend much of their lives hunched over computer screens miss the socializing, the real-world experience that would allow them to leave adolescence behind and grow into adulthood. These vital experiences, like much else, are simply not available in a virtual form.

STUDY QUESTIONS

1. What appeals to adolescents about online communication—chat rooms, social networks, text messaging? What does Staples CLAIM that people, especially adolescents, miss when they communicate online?

2. Why does Staples begin his ARGUMENT with a DESCRIPTION of a man he knew from his past? How effective is it? How does Staples's encounter with the man and his daughter CONTRAST with the kinds of relationships that are cultivated online?

3. *For Writing.* Consider the amount of time you spend online (surfing the Internet, sending emails, text messaging) compared to how much time you spend socializing in person. Drawing on your own experience, write an essay in which you RESPOND to Staples's argument that adolescents' socialization is hampered when it becomes predominantly virtual.

THOMAS L. FRIEDMAN { *Generation Q*

THOMAS FRIEDMAN (b. 1953), journalist and author, was born in St.
Louis Park, Minnesota. He holds degrees from Brandeis and Oxford.
Since he began writing for the *New York Times* in 1981 he has won three
Pulitzer Prizes, for international reporting and for commentary. Friedman,
who has served as the *Times* chief correspondent for the Middle East, for
the White House, and for international economics, currently writes a
nationally syndicated, twice-weekly column mainly addressing foreign
affairs. His best-selling books include *From Beirut to Jerusalem* (1989),
The Lexus and the Olive Tree (1999), *The World Is Flat* (2005), and *Hot,
Flat, and Crowded: Why We Need a Green Revolution—And How It Can
Renew America* (2008).

In "Generation Q," which appeared in the *New York Times* in 2007,
when U.S. presidential candidates were campaigning for the 2008 election,
Friedman continues the tradition of giving distinctive names to
generations (such as Baby Boomers or Gen Xers) by suggesting a name
for young Americans currently in college: the Quiet Americans. According
to Friedman, today's twenty-somethings will inherit unprecedented
challenges—potentially devastating climate change, a bankrupt Social
Security system, and an immense national budget deficit—and he worries
that they're not as outraged as they should be, or as they need to be.
As you read, consider whether or not you agree with Friedman's
assessment of "Generation Q" and how you might respond to the
author.

"Generation Q" by Thomas Friedman from *The New York Times*, October 10, 2007. Used
by permission of The New York Times.

I JUST SPENT THE PAST week visiting several colleges—Auburn, the University of Mississippi, Lake Forest and Williams—and I can report that the more I am around this generation of college students, the more I am both baffled and impressed.

I am impressed because they are so much more optimistic and idealistic than they should be. I am baffled because they are so much less radical and politically engaged than they need to be.

One of the things I feared most after 9/11—that my daughters would not be able to travel the world with the same carefree attitude my wife and I did at their age—has not come to pass.

Whether it was at Ole Miss or Williams or my alma mater, Brandeis, college students today are not only going abroad to study in record numbers, but they are also going abroad to build homes for the poor in El Salvador in record numbers or volunteering at AIDS clinics in record numbers. Not only has terrorism not deterred them from traveling, they are rolling up their sleeves and diving in deeper than ever.

The Iraq war may be a mess, but I noticed at Auburn and Ole Miss 5 more than a few young men and women proudly wearing their R.O.T.C. uniforms. Many of those not going abroad have channeled their national service impulses into increasingly popular programs at home like "Teach for America," which has become to this generation what the Peace Corps was to mine.

It's for all these reasons that I've been calling them "Generation Q"—the Quiet Americans, in the best sense of that term, quietly pursuing their idealism, at home and abroad.

But Generation Q may be too quiet, too online, for its own good, and for the country's own good. When I think of the huge budget deficit, Social Security deficit and ecological deficit that our generation is leaving this generation, if they are not spitting mad, well, then they're just not paying attention. And we'll just keep piling it on them.

There is a good chance that members of Generation Q will spend their entire adult lives digging out from the deficits that we—the "Greediest Generation," epitomized by George W. Bush—are leaving them.

When I was visiting my daughter at her college, she asked me about a terrifying story that ran in this newspaper on October 2, reporting that the Arctic ice cap was melting "to an extent unparalleled in a century or more"—and that the entire Arctic system appears to be "heading toward a new, more watery state" likely triggered by "human-caused global warming."

"What happened to that Arctic story, Dad?" my daughter asked me.   10
How could the news media just report one day that the Arctic ice was melting far faster than any models predicted "and then the story just disappeared?" Why weren't any of the candidates talking about it? Didn't they understand: this has become the big issue on campuses?

No, they don't seem to understand. They seem to be too busy raising money or buying votes with subsidies for ethanol farmers in Iowa. The candidates could actually use a good kick in the pants on this point. But where is it going to come from?

Generation Q would be doing itself a favor, and America a favor, if it demanded from every candidate who comes on campus answers to three questions: What is your plan for mitigating climate change? What is your plan for reforming Social Security? What is your plan for dealing with the deficit—so we all won't be working for China in twenty years?

America needs a jolt of the idealism, activism and outrage (it must be in there) of Generation Q. That's what twentysomethings are for—to light a fire under the country. But they can't e-mail it in, and an online petition or a mouse click for carbon neutrality won't cut it. They have to get organized in a way that will force politicians to pay attention rather than just patronize them.

Martin Luther King and Bobby Kennedy didn't change the world by asking people to join their Facebook crusades or to download their platforms. Activism can only be uploaded, the old-fashioned way—by young voters speaking truth to power, face to face, in big numbers, on campuses or the Washington Mall. Virtual politics is just that—virtual.

Maybe that's why what impressed me most on my brief college   15
swing was actually a statue—the life-size statue of James Meredith at the University of Mississippi. Meredith was the first African-American to be admitted to Ole Miss in 1962. The Meredith bronze is posed as

if he is striding toward a tall limestone archway, re-enacting his fateful step onto the then-segregated campus—defying a violent, angry mob and protected by the National Guard.

Above the archway, carved into the stone, is the word "Courage." That is what real activism looks like. There is no substitute.

STUDY QUESTIONS

1. What attributes does Friedman ascribe to "Generation Q"? Do you agree with his CHARACTERIZATION? If not, explain why not. If so, offer two or three examples of how you or people you know fit his characterization.

2. Publicly characterizing and naming a generation is a bold act. Is Friedman qualified to make such an assessment? How does he seek to establish his ETHOS—that is, his credibility with his readers? Is he successful?

3. *For Writing.* Write an opinion piece that responds to Friedman. Be sure to establish your credibility with your readers. Consider the following questions to help you get started: With what parts of Friedman's assessment do you agree or disagree? What, if anything, do you believe he leaves out or doesn't fully address?

ROB FISHMAN { *The Generation*
of Generation Q

ROB FISHMAN (b. 1986) graduated from Cornell University in 2007.
While a student there he joined the *Cornell Daily Sun*, the university's
independent newspaper, as a staff writer and weekly columnist. Upon
graduating, he entered the Journalism School at Columbia University in
New York City, and he is a research assistant at the Peter G. Peterson
Foundation, an organization dedicated to increasing political and
personal fiscal responsibility.

In this *Daily Sun* editorial from 2007, Fishman argues that if his
generation of college-age Americans is indeed "quiet," as *New York
Times* columnist Thomas Friedman argued when he dubbed them
"Generation Q," it's because technology has made them complacent:
instant replay resolves a dispute during a sporting event; Google
instantly provides the forgotten lyrics to a song. Using examples ranging
from commonplaces like these to significant moments in recent history,
Fishman redefines "Generation Q" by showing how they are all too
ready to defer to technology. Do you recognize your own behavior in his
examples?

LAST WEEK, THOMAS FRIEDMAN[1] DUBBED us "Generation Q"—the
Quiet Americans, so plugged in (and tuned out) that our idealism stops
at the computer monitor. With so much interconnectedness among the
Facebook-YouTube-MySpace cohort, and so much wrong in the world,
Friedman wonders why our generation looks so complacent.

[1]*New York Times* columnist and author (b. 1953).

"The Generation of Generation Q" by Rob Fishman from *The Cornell Daily Sun*, October 15, 2007. Used by permission of *The Cornell Daily Sun*.

255

The twentysomethings fire back that their technological moving and shaking is being mistaken for indolence; as a recent *Sun* editorial argued, activism has "transformed from sensationalized 1960s tear-gas rallies to online petitions and Internet discussion boards."

Yet for Friedman—and, I suspect, many among the Baby Boomers and the "Greatest Generation"—we come off as apologists, hiding our apathy behind a high tech façade: "Martin Luther King and Bobby Kennedy didn't change the world by asking people to join their Facebook crusades or to download their platforms," Friedman chides us nostalgically.

In truth, we are complacent—and if you look around, for good reason.

For my generation, technology *has* had a distinctively quieting 5 effect. In nearly every walk of life, technological advancements have instilled this generation with a deep sense of inevitability that encourages us to look inward. In a sense, Friedman has it backwards: we don't lazily hide behind technology, so much as technology inspires us to stay quiet.

Take sports. In an edge-of-your-seat final quarter between the Dallas Cowboys and the Buffalo Bills last week, a few of the thrills came from great catches and kicks, to be sure, but the real drama resulted from technicalities—from an instant replay review of a twenty-yard pass and from a split-second time out that voided a field goal kick that made the victory "one of the most implausible in the Cowboys' illustrious history," according to an ESPN recap of the game.

It's strange, watching these hippo-sized linemen beating the hell out of each other . . . all until a flag drops, at which point they respectfully defer to a high-definition replay.

Much the same in other sports: as the *Daily Scotsman* noted when FIFA[2] sanctioned a trial run for a soccer ball that "beeps" when it crosses the goal line, football fans can't quibble with technology that "ensure[s] justice and eradicate[s] controversy."

---

[2]The Fédération Internationale de Football Association, the international governing body for association football (professional soccer).

For sports fans and players alike, technology has obviated the important human element of competition. The exciting disputes are no longer about "bad" or "close" calls, but about close-up high-definition simulacra of the plays in question; as controversy is eradicated, sports fans are, for lack of a better option, quiet.

Consider a seminal American experience for my generation: the O. J. Simpson trial. In an adversarial procedure that (we now know) failed to capture the truth (if he did it, of course), the determining factor was DNA evidence, which, according to a *New York Times* article at that time, was not challenged by the defense at all on the basis of its "validity as a science."

Though the DNA evidence may not have been "clear or convincing to a jury of non-scientists," according to the *Times* article, it was ultimately presented as indisputable fact. Where Clarence Darrow drew on philosophy, religion and, yes, science to defend Leopold and Loeb in the "Trial of the Century," Johnnie Cochran's famous catchphrase was "if it doesn't fit, you must acquit."[3] Like the instant replay, DNA evidence isn't up for debate, it's a foregone conclusion.

Perhaps the most glaring example was the 2000 presidential election, when the Supreme Court upheld the voting tabulations accrued by the disputed ballots in Florida to hand the election to George W. Bush. The Court, while lamenting the "unfortunate number of ballots which [were] not punched in a clean, complete way" in *Bush v. Gore* (2000), ruled that the technology of the day would have to suffice, and that it could not read into the intent of voters—even if half a chad was clearly punched.[4]

---

[3]The courtroom words of defense attorney Johnnie Cochran (1937-2005), addressing the jury in the 1995 murder trial of O. J. Simpson after Simpson was unable to squeeze his hand into a glove found at the crime scene. *Clarence Darrow*: American lawyer (1857-1938) famed for representing thrill killers Nathan Freudenthal Leopold Jr. and Richard A. Loeb in criminal proceedings dubbed the "Trial of the Century" in 1924.

[4]In a ruling that determined the outcome of the 2000 presidential election, the U.S. Supreme Court declined to overrule Florida election officials and the Florida Supreme Court after supporters of Democratic Party candidate Al Gore argued that faulty vote-tabulating machinery had tainted the Florida vote count. (A "chad" is the tiny piece of paper displaced when a hole is punched in a computer card; such cards were used as ballots in Florida in the 2000 election.)

What's dangerous in these cases is not the technology itself—for surely, we applaud fairness in sports, exonerations based on DNA evidence, and new digital voting platforms—but the excesses and unintended consequences of these innovations.

Thus, dinner-table disputes end as quickly as one can BlackBerry the answer; road-side directions are relics of history thanks to GPS technology; and those impossible-to-understand song lyrics no longer require funny substitutions because you can Google them straightaway. Because information is so readily accessible, technology has made us close-minded, more attuned to what's for lunch than what's on the news (though, like CNN.com, menupages.com is a mere click away).

The direst consequences of a technocracy are the stuff of entertainment: the Orwellian[5] justice system in the blockbuster hit *Minority Report* and the simulated boxing match which precedes the actual fight in *Rocky Balboa* being two prominent examples of technology meting out results before the parties have spoken. When Tom Cruise or ESPN can anticipate outcomes before events, deliberation loses meaning. 15

Is it any wonder that Generation Q, which saw the guilty O. J. vindicated by DNA evidence and the calamitous Bush crowned by faulty ballots, appears so apathetic?

Faced with the most bitter and divisive of conflicts, our societal "referees" regularly defer to technological precepts of justice over human concepts of fairness. With the world on fire, Generation Q isn't questioning the lies of WMDs in Iraq[6] or global climate change—no, we're keeping our mouths shut and burying ourselves further in our computers.

---

[5]An allusion to George Orwell's 1949 novel *Nineteen Eighty-Four,* depicting life under an oppressive totalitarian government.

[6]U.S. President George W. Bush famously cited the presence in Iraq of forbidden WMDs—weapons of mass destruction—as justification for the American invasion of 2003. Such weapons were never found.

STUDY QUESTIONS

1. Why did columnist Thomas Friedman call today's college-age Americans "Generation Q?" How does technology have what Fishman calls "unintended consequences?"

2. How does Fishman DEFINE Generation Q through its behavior? Consider the examples that Fishman uses to support his ARGUMENT. How effective are they? How might they appeal to a college AUDIENCE?

3. *For Writing.* Drawing on your own experience, write an essay in which you either defend or critique—or both defend *and* critique—Fishman's argument about how Generation Q relies on technology.

{ *Literacy Debate: Online,*
R U Really Reading? }

MOTOKO RICH (b. 1970) was born in Los Angeles, California, but grew up primarily in Petaluma. She graduated from Yale University in 1991 and received an MA in English from Cambridge University. Rich was a reporter at the *Wall Street Journal* for six years before moving in 2003 to the *New York Times,* where she reviews books and writes about culture and the arts.

In "Literacy Debate: Online, R U Really Reading?" Rich presents proponents' and opponents' views about children and teenagers reading online. Education scholars and researchers correlate falling standardized test scores among children and teens and a drop in the percentage of teens who say they read for fun with the amount of time children and teens spend on computers. On the other hand, Web enthusiasts argue that the reading strategies gained through online reading prepare students for work in today's digital society, and that Internet proficiency should be tested in the same way students are tested in print material for reading comprehension. As you read, determine whether Rich draws any conclusions.

BOOKS ARE NOT NADIA KONYK'S thing. Her mother, hoping to entice her, brings them home from the library, but Nadia rarely shows an interest.

Instead, like so many other teenagers, Nadia, 15, is addicted to the Internet. She regularly spends at least six hours a day in front of the computer here in this suburb southwest of Cleveland.

A slender, chatty blonde who wears black-framed plastic glasses, Nadia checks her e-mail and peruses myyearbook.com, a social networking site, reading messages or posting updates on her mood. She searches for music videos on YouTube and logs onto Gaia Online, a role-playing site where members fashion alternate identities as cutesy cartoon characters. But she spends most of her time on quizilla.com or fanfiction.net, reading and commenting on stories written by other users and based on books, television shows or movies.

Her mother, Deborah Konyk, would prefer that Nadia, who gets A's and B's at school, read books for a change. But at this point, Ms. Konyk said, "I'm just pleased that she reads something anymore."

Children like Nadia lie at the heart of a passionate debate about just what it means to read in the digital age. The discussion is playing out among educational policy makers and reading experts around the world, and within groups like the National Council of Teachers of English and the International Reading Association. 5

As teenagers' scores on standardized reading tests have declined or stagnated, some argue that the hours spent prowling the Internet are the enemy of reading—diminishing literacy, wrecking attention spans and destroying a precious common culture that exists only through the reading of books.

But others say the Internet has created a new kind of reading, one that schools and society should not discount. The Web inspires a teenager like Nadia, who might otherwise spend most of her leisure time watching television, to read and write.

Even accomplished book readers like Zachary Sims, 18, of Old Greenwich, Connecticut, crave the ability to quickly find different points of view on a subject and converse with others online. Some children with dyslexia or other learning difficulties, like Hunter Gaudet, 16, of Somers, Connecticut, have found it far more comfortable to search and read online.

At least since the invention of television, critics have warned that electronic media would destroy reading. What is different now, some literacy experts say, is that spending time on the Web, whether it is looking up something on Google or even britneyspears.org, entails some engagement with text.

SETTING EXPECTATIONS

Few who believe in the potential of the Web deny the value of books.   10
But they argue that it is unrealistic to expect all children to read *To Kill
a Mockingbird* or *Pride and Prejudice* for fun. And those who prefer
staring at a television or mashing buttons on a game console, they say,
can still benefit from reading on the Internet. In fact, some literacy experts say that online reading skills will help children fare better when
they begin looking for digital-age jobs.

Some Web evangelists say children should be evaluated for their
proficiency on the Internet just as they are tested on their print reading comprehension. Starting next year, some countries will participate
in new international assessments of digital literacy, but the United
States, for now, will not.

Clearly, reading in print and on the Internet are different. On paper,
text has a predetermined beginning, middle and end, where readers
focus for a sustained period on one author's vision. On the Internet,
readers skate through cyberspace at will and, in effect, compose their
own beginnings, middles and ends.

Young people "aren't as troubled as some of us older folks are by
reading that doesn't go in a line," said Rand J. Spiro, a professor of educational psychology at Michigan State University who is studying
reading practices on the Internet. "That's a good thing because the
world doesn't go in a line, and the world isn't organized into separate
compartments or chapters."

Some traditionalists warn that digital reading is the intellectual
equivalent of empty calories. Often, they argue, writers on the Internet
employ a cryptic argot that vexes teachers and parents. Zigzagging
through a cornucopia of words, pictures, video and sounds, they say,
distracts more than strengthens readers. And many youths spend most
of their time on the Internet playing games or sending instant messages, activities that involve minimal reading at best.

Last fall the National Endowment for the Arts issued a sobering report   15
linking flat or declining national reading test scores among teenagers with
the slump in the proportion of adolescents who said they read for fun.

According to Department of Education data cited in the report, just over a fifth of 17-year-olds said they read almost every day for fun in 2004, down from nearly a third in 1984. Nineteen percent of 17-year-olds said they never or hardly ever read for fun in 2004, up from 9 percent in 1984. (It was unclear whether they thought of what they did on the Internet as "reading.")

"Whatever the benefits of newer electronic media," Dana Gioia, the chairman of the N.E.A., wrote in the report's introduction, "they provide no measurable substitute for the intellectual and personal development initiated and sustained by frequent reading."

Children are clearly spending more time on the Internet. In a study of 2,032 representative 8- to 18-year-olds, the Kaiser Family Foundation found that nearly half used the Internet on a typical day in 2004, up from just under a quarter in 1999. The average time these children spent online on a typical day rose to one hour and 41 minutes in 2004, from 46 minutes in 1999.

The question of how to value different kinds of reading is complicated because people read for many reasons. There is the level required of daily life—to follow the instructions in a manual or to analyze a mortgage contract. Then there is a more sophisticated level that opens the doors to elite education and professions. And, of course, people read for entertainment, as well as for intellectual or emotional rewards.

It is perhaps that final purpose that book champions emphasize 20 the most.

"Learning is not to be found on a printout," David McCullough, the Pulitzer Prize–winning biographer, said in a commencement address at Boston College in May. "It's not on call at the touch of the finger. Learning is acquired mainly from books, and most readily from great books."

WHAT'S BEST FOR NADIA?

Deborah Konyk always believed it was essential for Nadia and her 8-year-old sister, Yashca, to read books. She regularly read aloud to the girls and took them to library story hours.

"Reading opens up doors to places that you probably will never get to visit in your lifetime, to cultures, to worlds, to people," Ms. Konyk said.

Ms. Konyk, who took a part-time job at a dollar store chain a year and a half ago, said she did not have much time to read books herself. There are few books in the house. But after Yashca was born, Ms. Konyk spent the baby's nap time reading the Harry Potter novels to Nadia, and she regularly brought home new titles from the library.

Despite these efforts, Nadia never became a big reader. Instead, she 25 became obsessed with Japanese anime cartoons on television and comics like "Sailor Moon." Then, when she was in the sixth grade, the family bought its first computer. When a friend introduced Nadia to fanfiction.net, she turned off the television and started reading online.

Now she regularly reads stories that run as long as 45 Web pages. Many of them have elliptical plots and are sprinkled with spelling and grammatical errors. One of her recent favorites was "My absolutely, perfect normal life . . . ARE YOU CRAZY? NOT!," a story based on the anime series "Beyblade."

In one scene the narrator, Aries, hitches a ride with some masked men and one of them pulls a knife on her. "Just then I notice (Like finally) something sharp right in front of me," Aries writes. "I gladly took it just like that until something terrible happen. . . ."

Nadia said she preferred reading stories online because "you could add your own character and twist it the way you want it to be."

"So like in the book somebody could die," she continued, "but you could make it so that person doesn't die or make it so like somebody else dies who you don't like."

Nadia also writes her own stories. She posted "Dieing Isn't Always 30 Bad," about a girl who comes back to life as half cat, half human, on both fanfiction.net and quizilla.com.

Nadia said she wanted to major in English at college and someday hopes to be published. She does not see a problem with reading few books. "No one's ever said you should read more books to get into college," she said.

The simplest argument for why children should read in their leisure time is that it makes them better readers. According to federal statistics, students who say they read for fun once a day score significantly higher on reading tests than those who say they never do.

Reading skills are also valued by employers. A 2006 survey by the Conference Board, which conducts research for business leaders, found that nearly 90 percent of employers rated "reading comprehension" as "very important" for workers with bachelor's degrees. Department of Education statistics also show that those who score higher on reading tests tend to earn higher incomes.

Critics of reading on the Internet say they see no evidence that increased Web activity improves reading achievement. "What we are losing in this country and presumably around the world is the sustained, focused, linear attention developed by reading," said Mr. Gioia of the N.E.A. "I would believe people who tell me that the Internet develops reading if I did not see such a universal decline in reading ability and reading comprehension on virtually all tests."

Nicholas Carr sounded a similar note in "Is Google Making Us 35 Stupid?" in the current issue of the *Atlantic* magazine. Warning that the Web was changing the way he—and others—think, he suggested that the effects of Internet reading extended beyond the falling test scores of adolescence. "What the Net seems to be doing is chipping away my capacity for concentration and contemplation," he wrote, confessing that he now found it difficult to read long books.

Literacy specialists are just beginning to investigate how reading on the Internet affects reading skills. A recent study of more than 700 low-income, mostly Hispanic and black sixth through 10th graders in Detroit found that those students read more on the Web than in any other medium, though they also read books. The only kind of reading that related to higher academic performance was frequent novel reading, which predicted better grades in English class and higher overall grade point averages.

Elizabeth Birr Moje, a professor at the University of Michigan who led the study, said novel reading was similar to what schools demand already. But on the Internet, she said, students are developing new reading skills that are neither taught nor evaluated in school.

One early study showed that giving home Internet access to low-income students appeared to improve standardized reading test scores and school grades. "These were kids who would typically not be reading in their free time," said Linda A. Jackson, a psychology professor at Michigan State who led the research. "Once they're on the Internet, they're reading."

Neurological studies show that learning to read changes the brain's circuitry. Scientists speculate that reading on the Internet may also affect the brain's hard wiring in a way that is different from book reading.

"The question is, does it change your brain in some beneficial   40
way?" said Guinevere F. Eden, director of the Center for the Study of Learning at Georgetown University. "The brain is malleable and adapts to its environment. Whatever the pressures are on us to succeed, our brain will try and deal with it."

Some scientists worry that the fractured experience typical of the Internet could rob developing readers of crucial skills. "Reading a book, and taking the time to ruminate and make inferences and engage the imaginational processing, is more cognitively enriching, without doubt, than the short little bits that you might get if you're into the 30-second digital mode," said Ken Pugh, a cognitive neuroscientist at Yale who has studied brain scans of children reading.

BUT THIS IS READING TOO

Web proponents believe that strong readers on the Web may eventually surpass those who rely on books. Reading five Web sites, an op-ed article and a blog post or two, experts say, can be more enriching than reading one book.

"It takes a long time to read a 400-page book," said Mr. Spiro of Michigan State. "In a 10th of the time," he said, the Internet allows a reader to "cover a lot more of the topic from different points of view."

Zachary Sims, the Old Greenwich, Connecticut, teenager, often stays awake until 2 or 3 in the morning reading articles about technology or politics—his current passions—on up to 100 Web sites.

"On the Internet, you can hear from a bunch of people," said   45
Zachary, who will attend Columbia University this fall. "They may not be pedigreed academics. They may be someone in their shed with a conspiracy theory. But you would weigh that."

Though he also likes to read books (earlier this year he finished, and loved, *The Fountainhead* by Ayn Rand), Zachary craves interaction with fellow readers on the Internet. "The Web is more about a conversation," he said. "Books are more one-way."

The kinds of skills Zachary has developed—locating information quickly and accurately, corroborating findings on multiple sites—may seem obvious to heavy Web users. But the skills can be cognitively demanding.

Web readers are persistently weak at judging whether information is trustworthy. In one study, Donald J. Leu, who researches literacy and technology at the University of Connecticut asked 48 students to look at a spoof Web site (http://zapatopi.net/treeoctopus/) about a mythical species known as the "Pacific Northwest tree octopus." Nearly 90 percent of them missed the joke and deemed the site a reliable source.

Some literacy experts say that reading itself should be redefined. Interpreting videos or pictures, they say, may be as important a skill as analyzing a novel or a poem.

"Kids are using sound and images so they have a world of ideas to 50 put together that aren't necessarily language oriented," said Donna E. Alvermann, a professor of language and literacy education at the University of Georgia. "Books aren't out of the picture, but they're only one way of experiencing information in the world today."

A LIFELONG STRUGGLE

In the case of Hunter Gaudet, the Internet has helped him feel more comfortable with a new kind of reading. A varsity lacrosse player in Somers, Connecticut, Hunter has struggled most of his life to read. After learning he was dyslexic in the second grade, he was placed in special education classes and a tutor came to his home three hours a week. When he entered high school, he dropped the special education classes, but he still reads books only when forced, he said.

In a book, "they go through a lot of details that aren't really needed," Hunter said. "Online just gives you what you need, nothing more or less."

When researching the 19th-century Chief Justice Roger B. Taney for one class, he typed Taney's name into Google and scanned the Wikipedia entry and other biographical sites. Instead of reading an entire page, he would type in a search word like "college" to find Taney's alma mater, assembling his information nugget by nugget.

Experts on reading difficulties suggest that for struggling readers, the Web may be a better way to glean information. "When you read online there are always graphics," said Sally Shaywitz, the author of *Overcoming Dyslexia* and a Yale professor. "I think it's just more comfortable and—I hate to say easier—but it more meets the needs of somebody who might not be a fluent reader."

Karen Gaudet, Hunter's mother, a regional manager for a retail $_{55}$ chain who said she read two or three business books a week, hopes Hunter will eventually discover a love for books. But she is confident that he has the reading skills he needs to succeed.

"Based on where technology is going and the world is going," she said, "he's going to be able to leverage it."

When he was in seventh grade, Hunter was one of 89 students who participated in a study comparing performance on traditional state reading tests with a specially designed Internet reading test. Hunter, who scored in the lowest 10 percent on the traditional test, spent weeks learning how to use the Web for a science class before taking the Internet test. It was composed of three sets of directions asking the students to search for information online, determine which sites were reliable and explain their reasoning.

Hunter scored in the top quartile. In fact, about a third of the students in the study, led by Professor Leu, scored below average on traditional reading tests but did well on the Internet assessment.

THE TESTING DEBATE

To date, there have been few large-scale appraisals of Web skills. The Educational Testing Service, which administers the SAT, has developed a digital literacy test known as iSkills that requires students to solve informational problems by searching for answers on the Web. About 80 colleges and a handful of high schools have administered the test so far.

But according to Stephen Denis, product manager at ETS, of the 60
more than 20,000 students who have taken the iSkills test since 2006,
only 39 percent of four-year-college freshmen achieved a score that
represented "core functional levels" in Internet literacy.

Now some literacy experts want the federal tests known as the
nation's report card to include a digital reading component. So far,
the traditionalists have held sway: The next round, to be administered to fourth and eighth graders in 2009, will test only print reading
comprehension.

Mary Crovo of the National Assessment Governing Board, which
creates policies for the national tests, said several members of a committee that sets guidelines for the reading tests believed large numbers
of low-income and rural students might not have regular Internet access, rendering measurements of their online skills unfair.

Some simply argue that reading on the Internet is not something
that needs to be tested—or taught.

"Nobody has taught a single kid to text message," said Carol Jago of
the National Council of Teachers of English and a member of the testing guidelines committee. "Kids are smart. When they want to do
something, schools don't have to get involved."

Michael L. Kamil, a professor of education at Stanford who lobbied 65
for an Internet component as chairman of the reading test guidelines
committee, disagreed. Students "are going to grow up having to be
highly competent on the Internet," he said. "There's no reason to make
them discover how to be highly competent if we can teach them."

The United States is diverging from the policies of some other
countries. Next year, for the first time, the Organization for Economic
Cooperation and Development, which administers reading, math and
science tests to a sample of 15-year-old students in more than 50 countries, will add an electronic reading component. The United States,
among other countries, will not participate. A spokeswoman for the
Institute of Education Sciences, the research arm of the Department of
Education, said an additional test would overburden schools.

Even those who are most concerned about the preservation of
books acknowledge that children need a range of reading experiences.
"Some of it is the informal reading they get in e-mails or on Web sites,"

said Gay Ivey, a professor at James Madison University who focuses on adolescent literacy. "I think they need it all."

Web junkies can occasionally be swept up in a book. After Nadia read Elie Wiesel's Holocaust memoir *Night* in her freshman English class, Ms. Konyk brought home another Holocaust memoir, *I Have Lived a Thousand Years*, by Livia Bitton-Jackson.

Nadia was riveted by heartbreaking details of life in the concentration camps. "I was trying to imagine this and I was like, I can't do this." she said. "It was just so—wow."

Hoping to keep up the momentum, Ms. Konyk brought home another book, *Silverboy*, a fantasy novel. Nadia made it through one chapter before she got engrossed in the Internet fan fiction again. 70

STUDY QUESTIONS

1. Rich begins and ends her article with PROFILES of particular teenagers; in between, she presents ARGUMENTS about the Internet's effect on reading. What is the relationship between the RESEARCH Rich cites and Nadia's and Zachary's reading experiences? How do the profiles of individuals contribute to the rest of the article?

2. What is the significance of the way the title is written? Does the title suggest the author's POSITION? Explain. Does the author provide a definitive answer to the question in the title? If so, what is it?

3. Rich sets up her essay as a Rogerian argument: one that presents multiple sides of an issue, from both proponents and opponents. Does she ever provide a CLAIM? Why or why not?

4. LIST the EVIDENCE that supports electronic media as a legitimate method of reading and the evidence that opposes it. Based on the evidence presented in the article, which side do you agree with—or do you find a middle ground? Write your own claim and be prepared to defend it in class.

5. *For Writing.* Write a LITERACY NARRATIVE about one or more early experiences you had reading in print and online. Include your attitude toward reading, your favorite reading material, and when and where you read. REFLECT on your enjoyment of reading or lack thereof—if you enjoyed reading, what did you enjoy about it? If you didn't, why didn't you?

JESSICA BENNETT { *The Flip Side of Internet Fame*

JESSICA BENNETT (b. 1981) earned a journalism degree from Boston
University and a certificate in cultural anthropology from the University of
Buenos Aires. She has been a reporter for the *Boston Globe,* an investigative
researcher for New York political reporter Wayne Barrett, and a junior
reporter for *Newsweek International.* She is currently an associate editor for
Newsweek magazine, where she writes about culture, technology, and health
for both the print edition and Newsweek.com.

   "The Flip Side to Internet Fame" first appeared in *Newsweek* in 2008. In
it, Bennett explores the ethical implications of posting personal information
on the Web—especially personal information about other people. As you
read, consider how posting such material can bring either celebrity or
shame—or both—to the subject of such postings, and whether or not this
is fair.

IN 2002, GHYSLAIN RAZA, A chubby Canadian teen, filmed himself
acting out a fight scene from *Star Wars* using a makeshift light saber.
His awkward performance was funny, in part because it wasn't meant
to be. And it certainly was never meant to be public: for nearly a year
the video remained on a shelf in Raza's school's TV studio, where he'd
filmed it. Sometime in 2003, though, another student discovered the
video, digitized it and posted it online—and Raza's nightmare began.
Within days, "Star Wars Kid" had become a viral frenzy. It was posted
on hundreds of blogs, enhanced by music and special effects, and
watched by millions. Entire Web sites were dedicated to the subject;

one, jedimaster.net, was even named one of *Time*'s 50 best sites of 2003. Had that teenager wanted to be famous, he couldn't have asked for anything better. But in Raza's case it became a source of public humiliation, precisely what every kid fears the most.

Razas of the world take note: among the generation that's been reared online, stories like this are becoming more and more common. They serve as important reminders of a dark side of instant Internet fame: humiliation. Already dozens of Web sites exist solely to help those who would shame others. There are sites for posting hateful rants about ex-lovers (DontDateHimGirl.com) and bad tippers (the S—ty Tipper Database), and for posting cell-phone images of public bad behavior (hollabackNYC.com) and lousy drivers. As a new book makes clear in powerful terms, such sites can make or break a person, in a matter of seconds.

"Anybody can become a celebrity or a worldwide villain in an instant," says Daniel Solove, a law professor at George Washington University and author of *The Future of Reputation: Gossip, Rumor and Privacy on the Internet* (Yale). "Some people may revel in that. But others might say that's not the role they wanted to play in life."

"Dog poop girl" wasn't the public role a South Korean student had in mind when, in 2005, she refused to clean up after her dog in the subway in Seoul. A minor infraction, perhaps, but another passenger captured the act on a cell-phone camera, posted it online and created a viral frenzy. The woman was harassed into dropping out of college. More recently a student at Lewis & Clark University in Portland, Oregon, was publicly accused—on Facebook, the social-networking site—of sexually assaulting another student. Normally, such allegations on campus are kept confidential. But in this case a Facebook group revealed his name, with the word "rapist" for the world to see, before the incident was ever even reported to the authorities. The accused teen was never arrested or charged, but he might as well have been: bloggers picked up the story, and a local alt-weekly put it on its cover, revealing graphic details of the encounter as described by the alleged victim, without including the supposed perpetrator's version of events.

Public shaming, of course, is nothing new. Ancient Romans punished wrongdoers by branding them on the forehead—slaves caught

5

stealing got *fur* (Latin for thief) and runaways got *fug* (fugitive). In Colonial America heretics were clamped into stocks in the public square, thieves had their hands or fingers cut off, and adulterers were forced to wear a scarlet A. More recently a U.S. judge forced a mail thief to wear a sign announcing his crime outside a San Francisco post office; in other places sex offenders have to post warning signs on their front lawns.

Although social stigma can be a useful deterrent, "the Internet is a loose cannon," says ethicist Jim Cohen of Fordham University School of Law in New York. Online there are few checks and balances and no due process—and validating the credibility of a claim is difficult, to say the least. Moreover, studies show that the anonymity of the Net encourages people to say things they normally wouldn't. JuicyCampus, a gossip Web site for U.S. college students, has made headlines by tapping into this urge. The site solicits juicy rumors under the protection of anonymity for sources. But what may have begun as fun and games has turned into a venue for bigoted rants and stories about drug use and sex that identify students by name. "Anyone with a grudge can maliciously and sometimes libelously attack defenseless students," Daniel Belzer, a Duke senior, told *Newsweek* in December.

Regulators find sites like JuicyCampus hard to control. Laws on free speech and defamation vary widely between countries. In the United States, proving libel requires the victim to show that his or her persecutor intended malice, while the British system puts the burden on the defense to show that a statement is not libelous (making it much easier to prosecute). A 1996 U.S. law—Section 230 of the Communications Decency Act—specifically protects the operators of Web sites from liability for the speech of their users. As long as the host of a site doesn't post or edit content, it has no liability. (If AOL,[1] say, were held responsible for every poster, it would quickly go out of business.)

So, then, what's to stop a person from posting whatever he wants about you, if he can do so anonymously and suffer no repercussions? For people who use blogs and social-networking sites like diaries, putting their personal information out there for the world to see, this pres-

[1]America Online, an Internet service provider.

ents a serious risk. "I think young people are seduced by the citizen-media notion of the Internet: that everyone can have their minutes of fame," says Barry Schuler, the former CEO of AOL who is now the coproducer of a new movie, *Look,* about public video surveillance. "But they're also putting themselves out there—forever."

Shaming victims, meanwhile, have little legal recourse. Identifying posters often means having to subpoena an anonymous IP address.[2] But that could lead nowhere. Many people share IP addresses on college networks or Wi-Fi hotspots, and many Web sites hide individual addresses. Even if a victim identifies the defamer, bloggers aren't usually rich enough to pay big damage awards. Legal action may only increase publicity—the last thing a shaming victim wants. "The law can only do so much," warns Solove.

Once unsavory information is posted, it's almost impossible to retrieve. The family of the "Star Wars Kid," who spent time in therapy as a result of his ordeal, filed suit against the students who uploaded his video, and settled out of court. But dozens of versions of his video are still widely available, all over the Net. One of the bad boyfriends featured on DontDateHimGirl.com also sued, but his case was dismissed due to lack of jurisdiction. The accused rapist at Lewis & Clark has also hired lawyers. But Google his name today, and the first entry has the word "rapist" in its title. If the "Star Wars Kid" has anything to teach us, it's that shame, like the force, will always be with you.

[2]That is, Internet Protocol address, a numerical identification assigned to each device on a computer network.

STUDY QUESTIONS

1. According to Bennett, what control does an individual have over what personal information is posted online? What are the limits of the law in preventing or punishing those who post information about someone else?

2. Bennett writes that the Internet is a modern tool for the longstanding practice of public shaming. What makes the Internet different from previous ways of public shaming? Does Bennett PERSUADE you that it is more dangerous? Why or why not?

3. *For Writing.* Colleges and universities often counsel students to be mindful of what they post on the Web because of the consequences to their personal or professional lives. Compose an essay in which you explore the ethics of posting information about yourself or someone else on the Web. What guidelines, if any, should be established? How might they be enforced? What should be the legal recourse for victims of online misconduct? Support your ARGUMENT about guidelines with EVIDENCE, either with ANECDOTES about yourself or others you know, or with RESEARCH.

MARK BITTMAN $\left\{\begin{array}{l}\textit{I Need a Virtual Break.} \\ \textit{No, Really.}\end{array}\right.$

MARK BITTMAN (b. 1950) is a food writer, cookbook author, and
television personality. He writes a weekly cooking column, "The
Minimalist," and a regular blog, "Bitten," for the *New York Times*; in
addition, he films himself preparing food for the online version of the
Times. Twice a month he appears on NBC's *Today* show, and he has his
own television series on PBS, the third season of which followed famed
chef Mario Batali and actress Gwyneth Paltrow on their eating adventures in Spain. Bittman's acclaimed cookbook *How to Cook Everything*
(1998) won the IACP/Julia Child Award, the James Beard Award, and
three international cookbook awards; its follow-up, *How to Cook
Everything Vegetarian,* was published in 2007. He has also published
Fish: The Complete Guide to Buying and Cooking (1980) and *The Best
Recipes in the World: More Than 1000 International Dishes to Cook at
Home* (2005).

   Imagine all the computers, cameras, telephones, and other electronic
devices that make such a publicly engaged life possible. In the following
essay, Bittman reveals his need for a break from technology. After he
finds himself "plugging in" even on an airplane, he sets new rules
regulating his use of technology—and then he adapts to these rules.
Watch for Bittman's use of religious terms and concepts in a thoroughly
secular context.

──────────────

I TOOK A REAL DAY off this weekend: computers shut down, cellphone left in my work bag, land-line ringer off. I was fully disconnected for 24 hours.

The reason for this change was a natural and predictable back-breaking straw. Flying home from Europe a few months ago, I swiped a credit card through the slot of the in-seat phone, checked my e-mail, and robbed myself of one of my two last sanctuaries.

At that point, the only other place I could escape was in my sleep. Yet I had developed the habit of leaving a laptop next to my bed so I could check my e-mail, last thing and first thing. I had learned how to turn my P.D.A. into a modem, the better to access the Web from my laptop when on a train. Of course I also used that P.D.A. in conventional ways, attending to it when it buzzed me.

In short, my name is Mark, and I'm a techno-addict.[1] But after my airplane experience, I decided to do something about it. Thus began my "secular Sabbath"—a term I found floating around on blogs—a day a week where I would be free of screens, bells and beeps. An old-fashioned day not only of rest but of relief.

Like many, though, I wondered whether breaking my habit would   5
be entirely beneficial. I worried about the colleagues, friends, daughters, parents and so on who relied on me, the people who knew that whether I was home or away I would get back to them, if not instantly then certainly before the end of the day. What if something important was happening, something that couldn't wait 24 hours?

Or was I just one of those Americans who've developed the latest in American problems, Internet addiction disorder?

As a baby boomer, I knew mine was no unique thought; we've always been part of some trend or other. And sure enough, as soon as I started looking I found others who felt the need to turn off, to take a stab at reconnecting to things real rather than virtual, a moderate but carefully observed vacation from ubiquitous marketing and the awesome burden of staying in touch.

---

[1] An allusion to the way members of Alcoholics Anonymous introduce themselves at their meetings.

Nor is this surprising, said David Levy, a professor in the information school at the University of Washington. "What's going on now is insane," he said, assuring me that he used the term intentionally. "Living a good life requires a kind of balance, a bit of quiet. There are questions about the limits of the brain and the body, and there are parallels here to the environmental movement." (Dr. Levy coined the term "information environmentalism.")

"Who," he then asked, "would say you don't need time to think, to reflect, to be successful and productive?"

This movement to unplug appears to be gaining traction everywhere, 10 from the blogosphere, where wired types like Ariel Meadow Stallings (http://electrolicious.com/unplugged) brag about turning off the screen one day a week (and how many books they've read so far this year), to the corporate world.

For example, Nathan Zeldes, a principal engineer at Intel (employees there read or send three million e-mail messages daily), is running a couple of experiments, one in which people spend a morning a week at work but offline, another in which people consciously reduce their e-mail output. Though he's not reporting results, he's encouraged and he says people are participating.

"Even many corporate leaders now believe you need time to hear the voice of the new inside," said Anne Dilenschneider, a spirituality consultant in Montara, Calif., a coastal town 17 miles south of San Francisco. "And this time need not be a day, or even a specific period, activity or lack of one. It doesn't necessarily mean a Zen sit, just some time of solitude."

Even without a Zen sit (enough to scare me away from anything) or a phrase like "the voice of the new," I found that the secular Sabbath was not all that easy to maintain. Something as simple as turning off the electronics is easy, but try to make a habit of it.

On my first weekend last fall, I eagerly shut it all down on Friday night, then went to bed to read. (I chose Saturday because my rules include no television, and I had to watch the Giants on Sunday.) I woke up nervous, eager for my laptop. That forbidden, I reached for the phone. No, not that either. Send a text message? No. I quickly realized that I was feeling the same way I do when the electricity goes out and, finding one appliance nonfunctional, I go immediately to the next. I was jumpy, twitchy, uneven.

I managed. I read the whole paper, without hyperlinks. I tried to let 15 myself do nothing, which led to a long, MP3-free walk, a nap and some more reading, an actual novel. I drank herb tea (caffeine was not helpful) and stared out the window. I tried to allow myself to be less purposeful, not to care what was piling up in my personal cyberspace, and not to think about how busy I was going to be the next morning. I cooked, then went to bed, and read some more.

Gradually, over this and the next couple of weekends—one of which stretched from Friday night until Monday morning, like the old days—I adapted.

But recidivism quickly followed; there were important things to do— deadlines, urgent communications. You know how it is. I called Andrea Bauer, an executive and career development coach in San Carlos, Calif. She assured me that, oddly enough, it takes work to stop working. "It takes different formats for different people, and you have to build up to it; you can't run five miles if you've never run at all." Increasingly, I realized that there is more to the secular Sabbath than an impulse, or even a day off from e-mail. And there are reasons that nonsecular Sabbaths— the holy days of Christians, Jews and Muslims—have rules that require discipline. Even for the nonreligious, those rules were once imposed: You need not be elderly to remember when we had no choice but to reduce activity on Sundays; stores and offices—even restaurants— were closed, there were certainly no electronics, and we were largely occupied by ourselves or our families.

Now it's up to us, and, as Dr. Levy says, there's little encouragement. "One of the problems with needing to slow down is that within the climate of our primary culture it sounds wishy-washy," he said.

But what's wishy-washy about taking time off? It didn't seem to me that I had to collect Social Security before I realized that a 70-hour week was nearly as productive as an 80-hour one, and if I couldn't get it all done in either, it certainly wasn't because I was taking too much time off.

I went back to nonwork, diligently following my rules to do less one 20 day a week. The walks, naps and reading became routine, and all as enjoyable as they were before I had to force myself into doing them. It's been more than six months, and while I'm hardly a new man—no one has yet called me mellow—this achievement is unlike any other in my life. And nothing bad has happened while I've been offline; the e-mail and phone messages, RSS feeds, are all there waiting for me when I return to them.

I would no more make a new-agey call to find inner peace than I would encourage a return to the mimeograph. But I do believe that there has to be a way to regularly impose some thoughtfulness, or at least calm, into modern life—or at least my version. Once I moved beyond the fear of being unavailable and what it might cost me, I experienced what, if I wasn't such a skeptic, I would call a lightness of being. I felt connected to myself rather than my computer. I had time to think, and distance from normal demands. I got to stop.

STUDY QUESTIONS

1. Why does Bittman say he needs to take a break from technology? Why is it difficult for him to turn off his gadgets? What does his "break" consist of—that is, what rules does he set for himself? How successful is he?

2. What are some of the REASONS that Bittman cites for reducing the amount of time he spends engaging with technology? What kinds of EVIDENCE does he supply to support those reasons? How effectively does he make his point?

3. *For Writing.* Drawing on your own experience, write a PERSONAL ESSAY in which you advocate for being plugged in, unplugged, or a particular combination of both. What are the benefits to your solution? What are the drawbacks?

APPENDIX

USING SOURCES IN YOUR WRITING

WHATEVER your purpose, academic research requires "poking and prying" into sources of information that go well beyond your own immediate knowledge of a subject. If you're examining the student loan controversy of 2007, for example, you'll consult news stories and blog commentary published at that time. Or if you're analyzing a poem by Rita Dove, you'll study Dove's other poetry and read critical interpretations of her work in literary journals. This appendix shows how to find reliable sources, use what you learn in your own writing, and document your sources accurately.

FINDING AND EVALUATING SOURCES

As you do your research, you will encounter a wide range of potential sources—print and online, general and specialized, published and firsthand. You'll need to evaluate these sources carefully, choose the ones that best support your thesis, and decide how to incorporate each source into your own paper.

Finding Appropriate Sources

The kinds of sources you turn to will depend on your topic. If you're doing research on a literary or historical topic, you might consult scholarly books and articles and standard reference works such as *The Dictionary of American Biography* or the *Literary History of the United States*. If your research is aimed at a current issue, you would likely consult newspapers and other periodicals, websites, and recent books.

Check your assignment to see if you are required to use primary or secondary sources—or both. PRIMARY SOURCES are original works, such as historical documents, literary works, eyewitness accounts, diaries, letters, and lab studies, as well as any original field research you do. SECONDARY SOURCES include books and articles, reviews, biographies, and other works that interpret or discuss primary sources. For example, novels and poems are primary sources; articles interpreting them are secondary sources.

Whether a work is considered primary or secondary often depends on your topic and purpose. If you're analyzing a poem, a critic's article analyzing the poem is a secondary source—but if you're investigating the critic's work, the article would be a primary source.

LIBRARY-BASED SOURCES

When you conduct academic research, it is often better to start with your library's website rather than with a commercial search engine such as *Google*. Library websites provide access to a range of well-organized resources, including scholarly databases through which you can access authoritative articles that have been screened by librarians or specialists in a particular field. In general, there are three kinds of sources you'll want to consult: reference works, books, and periodicals.

- *Reference works.* The reference section of your school's library is the place to find encyclopedias, dictionaries, atlases, almanacs, bibliographies, and other reference works. Remember, though, that reference works are only a starting point, a place where you can get an overview of your topic or basic facts about it. Some reference works are *general,* such as *The New Encyclopaedia Britannica* or the *Statistical Abstract of the United States.* Others are *specialized,* providing in-depth information on a single field or topic.

- *Books.* The library catalog is your main source for finding books. Most catalogs are computerized and can be accessed through the library's website. You can search by author, title, subject, or keyword. When you click on a specific source, you'll find more bibliographic data about author, title, and publication; the call number (which identifies the book's location on the library's shelves); related subject headings (which may lead to other useful materials in the library)—and more.

- *Periodicals.* To find journal and magazine articles, you will need to search periodical indexes and databases. Indexes (such as the *New York Times Index*) provide listings of articles organized by topics; databases (such as LexisNexis) provide the full texts. Although some databases are available for free, many can be accessed by subscription through your library.

WEB-BASED SOURCES

The Web offers countless sites sponsored by governments, educational institutions, organizations, businesses, and individuals. Because it is so vast and dynamic, however, finding useful information can be a challenge. There are several ways to search the Web:

- *Keyword searches. Google, Bing, Ask.com, Yahoo!, AltaVista,* and *Lycos* all scan the Web looking for the keywords you specify.
- *Metasearches. Copernic Agent, SurfWax,* and *Dogpile* let you use several search engines simultaneously.
- *Academic searches.* For peer-reviewed academic writing in many disciplines, try *Google Scholar;* or use *Scirus* for scientific, technical, and medical documents.

Although many websites provide authoritative information, keep in mind that Web content varies greatly in its stability and reliability: what you see on a site today may be different (or gone) tomorrow. So save or make copies of pages you plan to use, and carefully evaluate what you find. Here are just a few of the many resources available on the Web.

- *Indexes, databases, and directories.* Information put together by specialists and grouped by topics can be especially helpful. You may want to consult *Librarians' Internet Index* (an annotated subject directory of more than 20,000 websites selected by librarians); *Infomine* (a huge collection of databases, mailing lists, catalogs, articles, directories, and more); or *The World Wide Web Virtual Library* (a catalog of websites on numerous subjects, compiled by experts).
- *News sites.* Many newspapers, magazines, and radio and TV stations have websites that provide both up-to-the-minute information and also archives of older news articles. Through *Google News* and *NewsLink,* for example, you can access current news worldwide, whereas *Google News Archive Search* has files going back to the 1700s.
- *Government sites.* Many government agencies and departments maintain websites where you can find government reports, statistics, legislative

information, and other resources. *USA.gov* offers information, services, and other resources from the U.S. government.

- *Digital archives.* These sites collect and organize materials from the past—including drawings, maps, recordings, speeches, and historic documents—often focusing on a particular subject or country. For example, the National Archives and Records Administration and the Library of Congress both archive items relevant to the culture and history of the United States.

- *Discussion lists and forums.* Online mailing lists, newsgroups, discussion groups, and forums let members post and receive messages from other members. To join a discussion with people who are knowledgeable about your topic, try searching for your topic—for example, for "E. B. White discussion forum." Or consult a site such as *Google Groups.*

SEARCHING ELECTRONICALLY

When you search for subjects on the Web or in library catalogs, indexes, or databases, you'll want to come up with keywords that will lead to the information you need. Specific commands vary among search engines and databases, but most search engines now offer "Advanced Search" options that allow you to narrow your search by typing keywords into text boxes labeled as follows:

- All of these words
- The exact phrase
- Any of these words
- None of these words

In addition, you may filter the results to include only full-text articles (articles that are available in full online); only certain domains (such as *.edu*, for educational sites; *.gov*, for government sites; or *.org*, for nonprofit sites); and, in library databases, only scholarly, peer-reviewed sites. Type quotation marks around words to search for an exact phrase: "Twitter revolution" or "Neil Gaiman."

Some databases may require you to limit searches through the use of various symbols or Boolean operators (AND, OR, NOT). See the Advanced Search instructions for help with such symbols, which may be called *field tags.*

If a search turns up too many sources, be more specific (*homeopathy* instead of *medicine*). If your original keywords don't generate good results, try synonyms (*home remedy* instead of *folk medicine*). Keep in mind that searching requires flexibility, both in the words you use and the methods you try.

Evaluating Sources

Searching the *Health Source* database for information on the incidence of meningitis among college students, you find seventeen articles. An "exact words" *Google* search yields thirty-seven. How do you decide which sources to read? The following questions can help you select reliable and useful sources.

- *Is the source relevant?* Look at the title and at any introductory material to see what it covers. Does the source appear to relate directly to your purpose? What will it add to your work?

- *What are the author's credentials?* Has the author written other works on this subject? Is he or she known for taking a particular position on it? If the author's credentials are not stated, you might do a Web search to see what else you can learn about him or her.

- *What is the stance?* Does the source cover various points of view or advocate only one perspective? Does its title suggest a certain slant? If you're evaluating a website, check to see whether it includes links to sites expressing other perspectives.

- *Who is the publisher?* Books published by university presses and articles in scholarly journals are peer-reviewed by experts in the field before they are published. Those produced for a general audience do not always undergo such rigorous review and factchecking. At well-established publishing houses, however, submissions are usually vetted by experienced editors or even editorial boards.

- *If the source is a website, who is the sponsor?* Is the site maintained by an organization, interest group, government agency, or individual? If the site doesn't give this information on its homepage, look for clues in the URL domain: *.edu* is used mostly by colleges and universities, *.gov* by government agencies, *.org* by nonprofit organizations, *.mil* by the military, and *.com* by commercial organizations. Be aware that the sponsor may have an agenda—to argue a position, present biased information, or sell a product—and that text on the site does not necessarily undergo rigorous review or factchecking.

- *What is the level of the material?* Texts written for a general audience might be easier to understand but may not be authoritative enough for academic work. Scholarly texts will be more authoritative but may be harder to comprehend.

- *How current is the source?* Check to see when books and articles were published and when websites were last updated. (If a site lists no date, see if links to other sites still work; if not, the site is probably too dated to use.) A recent publication date or updating, however, does not necessarily mean the source is better—some topics require current information whereas others call for older sources.

- *Does the source include other useful information?* Is there a bibliography that might lead you to additional materials? How current or authoritative are the sources it cites?

Taking Notes

When you find material that will be useful to your argument, take careful notes.

- *Use index cards, a computer file, or a notebook,* labeling each entry with information that will allow you to keep track of where it comes from—author, title, the pages or the URL, and (for online sources) the date of access.

- *Take notes in your own words and use your own sentence patterns.* If you make a note that is a detailed paraphrase, label it as such so that you'll know to provide appropriate documentation if you use it.

- *If you find wording that you'd like to quote,* be sure to enclose the exact words in quotation marks to distinguish your source's words from your own words.

- *Label each note with a subject heading* so you can organize your notes easily when constructing an outline for your paper.

INCORPORATING SOURCE MATERIALS INTO YOUR TEXT

There are many ways to incorporate source materials into your own text. Three of the most common are quoting, paraphrasing, or summarizing. Let's look at the differences among these three forms of reference, and then consider when to use each one and how to work these references into your text.

Quoting

When you quote someone else's words, you reproduce his or her language exactly, in quotation marks—though you can add your own words in brackets or omit unnecessary words in the original by using ellipsis marks (. . .). This example from Mary Roach's "How to Know If You Are Dead" uses all of these conventions:

> In her analysis of the life-saving role of human cadavers, Mary Roach notes that "a gurney with a [newly deceased] cadaver commands no urgency. It is wheeled by a single person, . . . like a shopping cart" (167).

Paraphrasing

When you paraphrase, you restate information from a source in your own words, using your own sentence structures. Because a paraphrase includes all the main points of the source, it is usually about the same length as the original.

Here is a paragraph from Diane Ackerman's essay "Why Leaves Turn Color in the Fall," followed by two sample paraphrases. The first demonstrates some of the challenges of paraphrasing.

ORIGINAL SOURCE

Where do the colors come from? Sunlight rules most living things with its golden edicts. When the days begin to shorten, soon after the summer solstice on June 21, a tree reconsiders its leaves. All summer it feeds them so they can process sunlight, but in the dog days of summer the tree begins pulling nutrients back into its trunk and roots, pares down, and gradually chokes off its leaves. A corky layer of cells forms at the leaves' slender petioles, then scars over. Undernourished, the leaves stop producing the pigment chlorophyll, and photosynthesis ceases. Animals can migrate, hibernate, or store food to prepare for winter. But where can a tree go? It survives by dropping its leaves, and by the end of autumn only a few fragile threads of fluid-carrying xylem hold leaves to their stems.

UNACCEPTABLE PARAPHRASE

Ackerman tells us where the colors of leaves come from. The amount of sunlight is the trigger, as is true for most living things. At the end of June, as daylight lessens, a tree begins to treat its leaves differently. It feeds them all summer so they can turn sunlight into food, but in August a tree begins to redirect its food into its trunk and roots, gradually choking the leaves. A corky group of cells develops at the petioles, and a scar forms. By autumn, the leaves don't have enough food, so they stop producing chlorophyll, and photosynthesis also stops. Although animals are able to migrate, hibernate, or stow food for the winter, a tree cannot go anywhere. It survives only by dropping its leaves, and by the time winter comes only a few leaves remain on their stems (257).

This first paraphrase borrows too much of the language of the original or changes it only slightly. It also follows the original sentence structure too closely. The following paraphrase avoids both of these pitfalls.

ACCEPTABLE PARAPHRASE

Ackerman explains why leaves change color. Diminishing sunlight is the main instigator. A tree nourishes its leaves—and encourages photosynthesis—for most of the summer. By August, however, as daylight continues to lessen, a tree starts to reroute its food to the roots and trunk, a process that saves the tree but eventually kills the leaves. In autumn, because the leaves are almost starving, they can neither manufacture chlorophyll to stay green nor carry out photosynthesis. By this time, the base of the petiole, or leaf's stem, has hardened, in preparation for the final drop. Unlike animals, who have many ways to get ready for winter—hiding food ahead of time, moving to a warm climate, sleeping through winter—a tree is immobile. It can make it through the winter only by losing its leaves (257).

Summarizing

Unlike a paraphrase, a summary does not present all the details in the original source, so it is generally as brief as possible. Summaries may boil down an entire book or essay into a single sentence, or they may take a paragraph or more to present the main ideas. Here, for example, is a summary of the Ackerman paragraph:

> In late summer and fall, Ackerman explains, trees put most of their food into their roots and trunk, which causes leaves to change color and die but enables trees to live through the winter (257).

Deciding Whether to Quote, Paraphrase, or Summarize

Follow these rules of thumb to determine whether you should quote a source directly, paraphrase it in detail, or merely summarize the main points.

- *Quote* a text when the exact wording is critical to making your point (or that of an authority you wish to cite), or when the wording itself is part of what you're analyzing.

- *Paraphrase* when the meaning of a text is important to your argument but the original language is not essential, or when you're clarifying or interpreting the ideas (not the words) in the text.

- *Summarize* when the main points of the text are important to your argument but the details can be left out in the interest of conciseness.

Using Signal Phrases

When you quote, paraphrase, or summarize a source, identify your source clearly and use a signal phrase ("she says," "he thinks") to distinguish the words and ideas of your source from your own. Consider this example:

> Professor and textbook author Elaine Tyler May claims that many high-school history textbooks are too bland to interest young readers (531).

This sentence summarizes a general position about the effectiveness of certain textbooks ("too bland"), and it attributes that view to a particular authority (Elaine Tyler May), citing her credentials (professor, textbook author) for speaking as an authority on the subject. By using the signal phrase "claims that," the sentence also distinguishes the words and ideas of the source from those of the writers.

The verb you use in a signal phrase can be neutral (*says* or *thinks*), or it can indicate your (or your source's) stance toward the subject. In this case, the use of the verb *claims* suggests that what the source says is arguable (or that the writer of the sentence believes it is). The signal verb you choose can influence your reader's understanding of the sentence and of your attitude toward what it says.

ACKNOWLEDGING SOURCES AND AVOIDING PLAGIARISM

As a writer, you must acknowledge any words and ideas that come from others. There are numerous reasons for doing so: to give credit where credit is due, to recognize the various authorities and many perspectives you have considered, to show readers where they can find your sources, and to situate your own arguments in the ongoing academic conversation. Using other people's words and ideas without acknowledgment is plagiarism, a serious academic and ethical offense.

MATERIAL THAT DOESN'T HAVE TO BE ACKNOWLEDGED

- Facts that are common knowledge, such as the name of the current president of the United States
- Well-known statements accompanied by a signal phrase: "As John F. Kennedy said, 'Ask not what your country can do for you; ask what you can do for your country.'"

MATERIAL THAT REQUIRES ACKNOWLEDGMENT

- Direct quotations, paraphrases, and summaries
- Arguable statements and any information that is not commonly known (statistics and other data)
- Personal or professional opinions and assertions of others
- Visuals that you did not create yourself (charts, photographs, and so on)
- Collaborative help you received from others

Plagiarism is (1) using another writer's exact words without quotation marks, (2) using another writer's words or ideas without in-text citation or other documentation, (3) paraphrasing or summarizing someone else's ideas using language or sentence structure that is close to the original. The following practices will help you avoid plagiarizing:

- *Take careful notes,* clearly labeling quotations and using your own phrasing and sentence structure in paraphrases and summaries.

- *Check all paraphrases and summaries* to be sure they are stated in *your* words and sentence structures—and that you put quotation marks around any of the source's original phrasing.

- *Know what sources you must document,* and identify them both in the text and in a works-cited list.

- *Check to see that all quotations are documented;* it is not enough just to include quotation marks or indent a block quotation.

- *Be especially careful with online material*—copying source material directly into a document you are writing invites plagiarism. Like other sources, information from the Web must be acknowledged.

- *Recognize that plagiarism has consequences.* A scholar's work will be discredited if it too closely resembles the work of another scholar. Journalists who plagiarize lose their jobs, and students routinely fail courses or are dismissed from school when they are caught cheating—all too often by submitting essays that they have purchased from online "research" sites.

So, don't take the chance. If you're having trouble with an assignment, ask your instructor for assistance. Or visit your school's writing center. Writing centers can help with advice on all aspects of your writing, including acknowledging sources and avoiding plagiarism.

DOCUMENTATION

Taken collectively, all the information you provide about sources is your *documentation.* Many organizations and publishers—for example, the American Psychological Association (APA), the University of Chicago Press, and the Council of Science Editors (CSE)—have their own documentation styles. The focus here is on the documentation system of the Modern Language Association (MLA) because it is one of the most common systems used in college courses, especially in the liberal arts.

The MLA's documentation system has two basic parts (1) brief in-text references for quotations, paraphrases, or summaries and (2) more detailed information for each in-text reference in a list of works cited at the end of the text. MLA style requires that each item in your works-cited list include the following information: author, editor, or organization; title of work; place of publication; publisher; date of publication; medium of publication; and, for online sources, date when you accessed the source. Here is an example of how the two parts work together. Note that you can identify the author either in a signal phrase or in parentheses:

IN-TEXT CITATIONS (WITH AND WITHOUT SIGNAL PHRASE)

As Lester Faigley puts it, "The world has become a bazaar from which to shop for an individual 'lifestyle'" (12).

As one observer suggests, "The world has become a bazaar from which to shop for an individual 'lifestyle'" (Faigley 12).

CORRESPONDING WORKS-CITED REFERENCE

Faigley, Lester. *Fragments of Rationality: Postmodernity and the Subject of Composition*. Pittsburgh: U of Pittsburgh P, 1992. Print.

MLA IN-TEXT DOCUMENTATION

1. Author in signal phrase
2. Author in parentheses
3. After a block quotation
4. Two or more authors
5. Organization as author
6. Author unknown
7. Literary works
8. Works cited together
9. Source in another source
10. Work without page numbers
11. An entire work

Brief documentation in your text makes clear to your reader what you took from a source and where within the source you found the information. As you cite each source, you will need to decide whether or not to name the author in a signal phrase—"as Toni Morrison writes"—or in parentheses—"(Morrison 24)." For either style of reference, try to put the parenthetical citation at the end

of the sentence or as close as possible to the material you've cit
wardly interrupting the sentence. When citing a direct quotat
note that the parenthetical reference comes after the closing c
but before the period at the end of the sentence.

1. AUTHOR NAMED IN A SIGNAL PHRASE

If you mention the author in a signal phrase, put only the page number(s) in parentheses. Do not write *page* or *p.*

> McCullough describes John Adams as having "the hands of a man accustomed to pruning his own trees, cutting his own hay, and splitting his own firewood" (18).

2. AUTHOR NAMED IN PARENTHESES

If you do not mention the author in a signal phrase, put his or her last name in parentheses along with the page number(s). Do not use punctuation between the name and the page number(s).

> One biographer describes John Adams as someone who was not a stranger to manual labor (McCullough 18).

3. AFTER A BLOCK QUOTATION

When quoting more than three lines of poetry, more than four lines of prose, or dialogue between two or more characters from a drama, set off the quotation from the rest of your text, indenting it one inch (or ten spaces) from the left margin. Do not use quotation marks, and place any parenthetical documentation *after* the final punctuation.

> In *Eastward to Tartary*, Kaplan captures ancient and contemporary Antioch:
>
>> At the height of its glory in the Roman-Byzantine age, when it had an amphitheater, public baths, aqueducts, and sewage pipes, half a million people lived in Antioch. Today the population is only 125,000. With sour relations between Turkey and Syria, and unstable politics throughout the Middle East, Antioch is now a backwater—seedy and tumbledown, with relatively few tourists. I found it altogether charming. (123)

4. TWO OR MORE AUTHORS

For a work by two or three authors, name all the authors, either in a signal phrase or in parentheses.

> Carlson and Ventura's stated goal is to introduce Julio Cortázar, Marjorie Agosín, and other Latin American writers to an audience of English-speaking adolescents (5).

For a work with four or more authors, you can mention all their names *or* just the name of the first author followed by *et al.*, which means "and others."

> One popular survey of American literature breaks the contents into sixteen thematic groupings (Anderson, Brinnin, Leggett, Arpin, and Toth 19–24).

> One popular survey of American literature breaks the contents into sixteen thematic groupings (Anderson et al. 19–24).

5. ORGANIZATION OR GOVERNMENT AS AUTHOR

Cite the organization either in a signal phrase or in parentheses. It's acceptable to shorten long names.

> The U.S. government can be direct when it wants to be. For example, it sternly warns, "If you are overpaid, we will recover any payments not due you" (Social Security Administration 12).

6. AUTHOR UNKNOWN

If you can't determine an author, use the work's title or a shortened version of the title in the parentheses.

> A powerful editorial in last week's paper asserts that healthy liver donor Mike Hurewitz died because of "frightening" faulty postoperative care ("Every Patient's Nightmare").

7. LITERARY WORKS

When referring to literary works that are available in many different editions, you need to cite additional information so that readers of any edition can locate the text you are citing.

Novels: Give the page and chapter number of the edition you are using.

> In *Pride and Prejudice*, Mrs. Bennett shows no warmth toward Jane and Elizabeth when they return from Netherfield (105; ch. 12).

Verse plays: Give the act, scene, and line numbers; separate them with periods.

> Macbeth develops the vision theme when he addresses the Ghost with "Thou hast no speculation in those eyes / Which thou dost glare with" (3.3.96–97).

Poems: Give the part and line numbers (separated by periods). If a poem has only line numbers, use the word *line(s)* in the first reference.

> The mere in *Beowulf* is described as "not a pleasant place!" (line 1372). Later, it is called "the awful place" (1378).

8. TWO OR MORE WORKS CITED TOGETHER

If you cite the works in the same parentheses, separate the references with a semicolon.

> Critics have looked at both *Pride and Prejudice* and *Frankenstein* from a cultural perspective (Tanner 7; Smith viii).

9. SOURCE QUOTED IN ANOTHER SOURCE

When you are quoting text that you found quoted in another source, use the abbreviation *qtd. in* in the parenthetical reference.

> Charlotte Brontë wrote to G. H. Lewes: "Why do you like Miss Austen so very much? I am puzzled on that point" (qtd. in Tanner 7).

10. WORK WITHOUT PAGE NUMBERS

For works without page numbers, including many online sources, identify the source using the author or other information either in a signal phrase or in parentheses. If the source has paragraph or section numbers, use them with the abbreviations *par.* or *sec.*

Studies reported in *Scientific American* and elsewhere show that music training helps children to be better at multitasking later in life ("Hearing the Music," par. 2).

11. AN ENTIRE WORK

If you refer to an entire work rather than a part of it, there's no need to include page numbers.

At least one observer considers Turkey and Central Asia to be explosive (Kaplan).

MLA LIST OF WORKS CITED

BOOKS

1. One author
2. Multiple books by an author
3. Two or three authors
4. Four or more authors
5. Organization as author
6. Anthology
7. Work(s) in an anthology

8. Author and editor
9. Translation
10. Introduction or afterword
11. Multivolume work
12. Subsequent edition
13. Reference-book article

PERIODICALS

14. Journal article
15. Magazine article
16. Newspaper article

17. Unsigned article
18. Editorial
19. Book review

ONLINE SOURCES

20. Entire website
21. Work from a website
22. Online book
23. Online journal article
24. Online magazine article
25. Article in a database
26. Online newspaper article

27. Online editorial
28. Blog entry
29. Email correspondence
30. Online forum posting
31. Online reference article
32. Podcast

OTHER KINDS OF SOURCES

33. Art

34. Cartoon

35. CD-ROM or DVD-ROM

36. Film, DVD, or video clip

37. Interview

38. Letter

39. Map

40. Musical score

41. Sound recording

42. TV or radio program

43. Digital file

SOURCES NOT COVERED BY MLA

A works-cited list provides full bibliographic information for every source cited in your text. Here's some general advice to help you format your list:

- Start the list on a new page.

- Center the title (Works Cited) one inch from the top of the page.

- Double-space the whole list.

- Begin each entry flush with the left-hand margin and indent subsequent lines one-half inch or five spaces.

- Alphabetize entries by the author's last name. If a work has no identifiable author, use the first major word of the title (disregard *A, An, The*).

- If you cite more than one work by a single author, list them all alphabetically by title, and use three hyphens in place of the author's name after the first entry (see no. 3 for an example).

Books

For most books, you'll need to list the author; the title and any subtitle; and the place of publication, publisher, date, and the medium—*Print*. A few details to note when citing books:

- *Authors*: List the primary author last-name-first, and include any middle name or initial after the first name.

- *Titles*: Capitalize all principal words in titles and subtitles, including short verbs such as *is* and *are*. Do not capitalize *a, an, the, to,* or any preposition or conjunction unless they begin a title or subtitle. Italicize book titles, but place quotation marks around works within books.

- *Publication place and publisher*: If there's more than one city listed on the title page, use only the first. Use a shortened form of the publisher's name (Norton for W. W. Norton & Company; Princeton UP for Princeton University Press).

- *Dates*: If more than one year is given, use the most recent one.

1. ONE AUTHOR

Miller, Susan. *Assuming the Positions: Cultural Pedagogy and the Politics of Commonplace Writing*. Pittsburgh: U of Pittsburgh P, 1998. Print.

2. TWO OR MORE WORKS BY THE SAME AUTHOR(S)

Give the author's name in the first entry, and then use three hyphens in the author slot for each of the subsequent works, listing them alphabetically by the first important word of each title.

Kaplan, Robert D. *The Coming Anarchy: Shattering the Dreams of the Post Cold War*. New York: Vintage, 2001. Print.

———. *Eastward to Tartary: Travels in the Balkans, the Middle East, and the Caucasus*. New York: Vintage, 2001. Print.

3. TWO OR THREE AUTHORS

Follow the order of names on the book's title page. List the second and third authors first-name-first.

Malless, Stanley, and Jeffrey McQuain. *Coined by God: Words and Phrases That First Appear in the English Translations of the Bible*. New York: Norton, 2003. Print.

Sebranek, Patrick, Verne Meyer, and Dave Kemper. *Writers INC: A Guide to Writing, Thinking, and Learning*. Burlington: Write Source, 1990. Print.

4. FOUR OR MORE AUTHORS

You may give each author's name or the name of the first author only, followed by *et al.* (Latin for "and others").

Anderson, Robert, et al. *Elements of Literature: Literature of the United*

States. Austin: Holt, 1993. Print.

5. ORGANIZATION OR GOVERNMENT AS AUTHOR

Diagram Group. *The Macmillan Visual Desk Reference.* New York:
Macmillan, 1993. Print.

For a government publication, give the name of the government first, followed
by the names of any department and agency.

United States. Dept. of Health and Human Services. Natl. Inst. of Mental
Health. *Autism Spectrum Disorders.* Washington: GPO, 2004. Print.

6. ANTHOLOGY

Use this model only when you are citing the whole anthology or the contribu-
tions of the editor(s).

Kitchen, Judith, and Mary Paumier Jones, eds. *In Short: A Collection of
Brief Creative Nonfiction.* New York: Norton, 1996. Print.

7. WORK(S) IN AN ANTHOLOGY

Give the inclusive page numbers of the selection you are citing.

Achebe, Chinua. "Uncle Ben's Choice." *The Seagull Reader: Literature.*
Ed. Joseph Kelly. New York: Norton, 2005. 23–27. Print.

To document two or more selections from one anthology, list each selection by
author and title, followed by the editors' names and the pages of the selection.
In addition, include in your works-cited list an entry for the anthology itself
(no. 6).

Hiestand, Emily. "Afternoon Tea." Kitchen and Jones 65–67.

Ozick, Cynthia. "The Shock of Teapots." Kitchen and Jones 68–71.

8. AUTHOR AND EDITOR

Start with the author if you've cited the text itself.

Austen, Jane. *Emma.* Ed. Stephen M. Parrish. New York: Norton, 2000.
Print.

Start with the editor if you've cited his or her contribution.

Parrish, Stephen M., ed. *Emma.* By Jane Austen. New York: Norton, 2000. Print.

9. TRANSLATION

Dostoevsky, Fyodor. *Crime and Punishment.* Trans. Richard Pevear and Larissa Volokhonsky. New York: Vintage, 1993. Print.

10. FOREWORD, INTRODUCTION, PREFACE, OR AFTERWORD

Tanner, Tony. Introduction. *Pride and Prejudice.* By Jane Austen. London: Penguin, 1972. 7–46. Print.

11. MULTIVOLUME WORK

If you cite all the volumes, give the number of volumes after the title.

Sandburg, Carl. *Abraham Lincoln: The War Years.* 4 vols. New York: Harcourt, 1939. Print.

If you cite only one volume, give the volume number after the title.

Sandburg, Carl. *Abraham Lincoln: The War Years.* Vol. 2. New York: Harcourt, 1939. Print.

12. EDITION OTHER THAN THE FIRST

Gibaldi, Joseph. *MLA Handbook for Writers of Research Papers.* 6th ed. New York: MLA, 2003. Print.

13. ARTICLE IN A REFERENCE BOOK

Provide the author's name if the article is signed. If a reference book is well known, give only the edition and the year of publication.

"Iraq." *The New Encyclopaedia Brittanica.* 15th ed. 2007. Print.

If a reference book is less familiar, give complete publication information.

Benton-Cohen, Katherine. "Women in the Reform and Progressive Era." *A History of Women in the United States.* Ed. Doris Weatherford. 4 vols. Danbury, CT: Grolier, 2004. Print.

Periodicals

For most articles, you'll need to list the author, the article title and any subtitle, the periodical title, any volume and issue number, the date, inclusive page numbers, and the medium—*Print*. A few details to note when citing periodicals:

- *Authors*: Format authors as you would for a book.
- *Titles*: Capitalize titles and subtitles as you would for a book. Omit any initial *A, An,* or *The*. Italicize periodical titles; place article titles within quotation marks.
- *Dates*: Abbreviate the names of months except for May, June, and July: Jan., Feb., Mar., Apr., Aug., Sept., Oct., Nov., Dec. Journals paginated by both volume and issue need only the year (in parentheses).
- *Pages*: If an article does not fall on consecutive pages, give the first page with a plus sign (55+).

14. ARTICLE IN A JOURNAL

Bartley, William. "Imagining the Future in *The Awakening*." *College English* 62.6 (2000): 719–46. Print.

For journals that do not have volume numbers, give the issue number after the title, followed by the year of publication and inclusive page numbers.

Flynn, Kevin. "The Railway in Canadian Poetry." *Canadian Literature* 174 (2002): 70–95. Print.

15. ARTICLE IN A MAGAZINE

Cloud, John. "Should SATs Matter?" *Time* 12 Mar. 2001: 62+. Print.

For a monthly magazine, include only the month and year.

Fellman, Bruce. "Leading the Libraries." *Yale Alumni Magazine* Feb. 2002: 26–31. Print.

16. ARTICLE IN A DAILY NEWSPAPER

Springer, Shira. "Celtics Reserves Are Whizzes vs. Wizards." *Boston*

Globe 14 Mar. 2005: D4+. Print.

If you are documenting a particular edition of a newspaper, specify the edition (*late ed., natl. ed.,* and so on) after the date.

Margulius, David L. "Smarter Call Centers: At Your Service?" *New York Times* 14 Mar. 2002, late ed.: G1+. Print.

17. UNSIGNED ARTICLE

"Coal Mine Inspections Fall Short." *Atlanta Journal-Constitution* 18 Nov. 2007: A7. Print.

18. EDITORIAL OR LETTER TO THE EDITOR

"Gas, Cigarettes Are Safe to Tax." Editorial. *Lakeville Journal* 17 Feb. 2005: A10. Print.

Festa, Roger. "Social Security: Another Phony Crisis." Letter. *Lakeville Journal* 17 Feb. 2005: A10. Print.

19. BOOK REVIEW

Frank, Jeffrey. "Body Count." Rev. of *The Exception,* by Christian Jungersen. *New Yorker* 30 July 2007: 86–87. Print.

Online Sources

Not every online source gives you all the data that the MLA would like to see in a works-cited entry. Ideally, you'll be able to list the author's name, the title, information about print publication (if applicable), information about electronic publication (title of site, editor, date of first electronic publication and/or most recent revision, name of publisher or sponsoring institution), the publication medium, date of access, and, if necessary, a URL. Here are a few details to note when citing online sources:

- *Authors or editors and title*: Format authors and titles as you would for a print book or periodical.

- *Publisher*: If the name of the publisher or sponsoring institution is unavailable, use *N.p.*

- *Dates*: Abbreviate the months as you would for a
  Although MLA asks for the date when materials w
  most recently updated, you won't always be able to fin
  if it's unavailable, use *n.d.* Be sure to include the date ᴜᴜ ..
  accessed the source.

- *Pages*: If the citation calls for page numbers but the source is unpaginated, use *n. pag.* in place of page numbers.

- *Medium*: Indicate the medium—Web, email, PDF, MP3, jpeg, and so on.

- *URL*: MLA assumes that readers can locate most sources on the Web by searching for the author, title, or other identifying information, so they don't require a URL for most online sources. When readers cannot locate the source without a URL, give the address of the website in angle brackets. When a URL won't fit on one line, break it only after a slash (and do not add a hyphen). If a URL is very long, consider using the one from the site's homepage or search page instead.

20. ENTIRE WEBSITE OR PERSONAL WEBSITE

Zalta, Edward N., ed. *Stanford Encyclopedia of Philosophy.* Metaphysics
  Research Lab, Center for the Study of Language and Information,
  Stanford U, 2007. Web. 14 Nov. 2010.

Nunberg, Geoffrey. Home page. School of Information, U of California,
  Berkeley, 2009. Web. 3 Apr. 2009.

21. WORK FROM A WEBSITE

Buff, Rachel Ida. "Becoming American." *Immigration History Research
  Center.* U of Minnesota, 24 Mar. 2008. Web. 4 Apr. 2008.

22. ONLINE BOOK OR PART OF A BOOK

Cite a book you access online as you would a print book, adding the name of the site or database, the medium, and the date of access. (See next page for examples.)

Anderson, Sherwood. *Winesburg, Ohio.* New York: B. W. Huebsch,
  1919. *Bartleby.com.* Web. 7 Apr. 2008.

If you are citing a part of a book, put the part in quotation marks before the book title. If the online book is paginated, give the pages; if not, use *N. pag.*

Anderson, Sherwood. "The Philosopher." *Winesburg, Ohio.* New York: B. W. Huebsch, 1919. N. pag. *Bartleby.com.* Web. 7 Apr. 2008.

To cite a book you've downloaded onto a Kindle, Nook, or other digital device, follow the setup for a print book, but indicate the ebook format at the end of your citation.

Larson, Erik. *The Devil in the White City: Murder, Mayhem, and Madness at the Fair That Changed America.* New York: Vintage, 2004. Kindle.

23. ARTICLE IN AN ONLINE JOURNAL

If a journal does not number pages or if it numbers each article separately, use *n. pag.* in place of page numbers.

Moore, Greggory. "The Process of Life in *2001: A Space Odyssey.*" *Images: A Journal of Film and Popular Culture* 9 (2000): n. pag. Web. 12 May 2009.

24. ARTICLE IN AN ONLINE MAGAZINE

Landsburg, Steven E. "Putting All Your Potatoes in One Basket: The Economic Lessons of the Great Famine." *Slate.* Slate, 13 Mar. 2001. Web. 8 Dec. 2007.

25. ARTICLE ACCESSED THROUGH DATABASE

For articles accessed through a library's subscription services, such as InfoTrac and EBSCOhost, cite the publication information for the source, followed by the name of the database.

Bowman, James. "Moody Blues." *American Spectator* June 1999: 64–65. *Academic Search Premier.* Web. 15 Mar. 2005.

26. ARTICLE IN AN ONLINE NEWSPAPER

Mitchell, Dan. "Being Skeptical of Green." *New York Times.* New York Times, 24 Nov. 2007. Web. 26 Nov. 2007.

27. ONLINE EDITORIAL

"Outsourcing Your Life." Editorial. *ChicagoTribune.com.* Chicago Tribune, 24 Nov. 2004. Web. 3 Jan. 2008.

28. BLOG ENTRY

If the entry has no title, use "Blog entry" (without quotation marks). Cite a whole blog as you would a personal website (no. 20). If the publisher or sponsor is unavailable, use *N.p.*

> Gladwell, Malcolm. "Underdogs." N.p., 13 May 2009. Web. 11 Aug. 2011.

29. EMAIL CORRESPONDENCE

> Smith, William. "Teaching Grammar—Some Thoughts." Message to the author. 15 Feb. 2008. Email.

30. POSTING TO AN ELECTRONIC FORUM

> Mintz, Stephen H. "Manumission During the Revolution." H-Net List on Slavery. Michigan State U, 14 Sept. 2006. Web. 18 Apr. 2009.

31. ARTICLE IN AN ONLINE REFERENCE WORK OR WIKI

> "Dubai." *MSN Encarta.* Microsoft Corporation, 2008. Web. 20 June 2008.

For a wiki, cite the date of the last modification or update as the publication date.

> "Pi." *Wikipedia.* Wikimedia Fundation, 6 Aug. 2011. Web. 11 Aug. 2011.

32. PODCAST

> Blumberg, Alex, and Adam Davidson. "The Giant Pool of Money." Host Ira Glass. *This American Life.* Chicago Public Radio, 9 May 2008. Web. 18 Sept. 2008.

Other Kinds of Sources

Many of the sources in this section can be found online. If there is no Web model here, start with the guidelines most appropriate for the source you need to cite, omit the original medium, and end your citation with the title of the website, italicized; the medium (Web); and the day, month, and year of access.

33. ART (PRINT AND ONLINE)

> Van Gogh, Vincent. *The Potato Eaters.* 1885. Oil on canvas. Van Gogh

Museum, Amsterdam.

Warhol, Andy. *Self-Portrait*. 1979. Polaroid Polacolor print. J. Paul
Getty Museum, Los Angeles. *The Getty*. Web. 5 Jan. 2008.

34. CARTOON OR COMIC STRIP (PRINT AND ONLINE)

Chast, Roz. "The Three Wise Men of Thanksgiving." Cartoon. *New
Yorker* 1 Dec. 2003: 174. Print.

Adams, Scott. "Dilbert." Comic strip. *Dilbert.com*. United Features
Syndicate, 9 Nov. 2007. Web. 26 Nov. 2007.

35. CD-ROM OR DVD-ROM

Cite like a book, but indicate any pertinent information about the edition or
version.

Othello. Princeton: Films for the Humanities and Sciences, 1998. CD-ROM.

36. FILM, DVD, OR VIDEO CLIP

Super 8. Dir. J. J. Abrams. Perf. Joel Courtney, Kyle Chandler, and Elle
Fanning. Paramount, 2011. Film.

To cite a particular person's work, start with that name.

Cody, Diablo, scr. *Juno*. Dir. Jason Reitman. Perf. Ellen Page, Michael
Cera, Jennifer Garner, and Jason Bateman. Fox Searchlight, 2007.
DVD.

Cite a video clip from YouTube or a similar site as you would a short work from
a website.

PivotMasterDX, dir. "Storaged." *YouTube*. YouTube, 29 Apr. 2009.
Web. 11 Aug. 2011.

37. BROADCAST, PUBLISHED, AND PERSONAL INTERVIEW

Gates, Henry Louis, Jr. Interview. *Fresh Air*. NPR. WNYC, New York.
9 Apr. 2002. Radio.

Brzezinski, Zbigniew. "Against the Neocons." *American Prospect* Mar.
2005: 26–27. Print.

Berra, Yogi. Personal interview. 17 June 2001.

38. PUBLISHED LETTER

White, E. B. Letter to Carol Angell. 28 May 1970. *Letters of E. B. White.* Ed. Dorothy Lobarno Guth. New York: Harper, 1976. 600. Print.

39. MAP (PRINT AND ONLINE)

Toscana. Map. Milan: Touring Club Italiano, 1987. Print.

"Austin, TX." Map. *Google Maps.* Google, 11 Aug. 2011. Web. 11 Aug. 2011.

40. MUSICAL SCORE

Beethoven, Ludwig van. *String Quartet No. 13 in B Flat, Op. 130.* 1825. New York: Dover, 1970. Print.

41. SOUND RECORDING (WITH ONLINE VERSION)

Whether you list the composer, conductor, or performer first depends on where you want to place the emphasis.

Beethoven, Ludwig van. *Missa Solemnis.* Perf. Westminster Choir and New York Philharmonic. Cond. Leonard Bernstein. Sony, 1992. CD.

The Beatles. "Can't Buy Me Love." *A Hard Day's Night.* United Artists, 1964. MP3 file.

Davis, Miles. "So What." *Birth of the Cool.* Columbia, 1959. *Miles Davis.* Web. 14 Feb. 2009.

42. TELEVISION OR RADIO PROGRAM (WITH ONLINE VERSION)

"Stirred." *The West Wing.* Writ. Aaron Sorkin, Dir. Jeremy Kagan. Perf. Martin Sheen. NBC. WPTV, West Palm Beach, 3 Apr. 2002. Television.

"Bush's War." *Frontline.* Writ. and Dir. Michael Kirk. *PBS.org.* PBS, 24 Mar. 2008. Web. 10 Apr. 2009.

43. MP3, JPEG, PDF, OR OTHER DIGITAL FILE

For downloaded songs, photographs, PDFs, and other documents stored on your computer or another digital device, follow the guidelines for the type of work you are citing (art, journal article, and so on) and give the file type as the medium.

> Talking Heads. "Burning Down the House." *Speaking in Tongues.* Sire, 1983. Digital file.

> Taylor, Aaron. "Twilight of the Idols: Performance, Melodramatic Villainy, and *Sunset Boulevard.*" *Journal of Film and Video* 59 (2007): 13–31. PDF file.

Citing Sources Not Covered by MLA

To cite a source that isn't covered by the MLA guidelines, look for models similar to the source you're citing. Give any information readers will need in order to find the source themselves—author, title, subtitle; publisher and/or sponsor; medium; dates; and any other pertinent information. You might want to try out the citation yourself, to be sure it will lead others to your source.

INDEX

Angier, Natalie	Men, Women, Sex, and Darwin	**132**
Atwood, Margaret	The Female Body	**147**
Ballí, Cecilia	Ciudad de la Muerte	**188**
Barry, Dave	A GPS Helps a Guy Always Know Where His Couch Is	**168**
Barszcz, James	Can you Be Educated from a Distance?	**98**
Bennett, Jessica	The Flip Side of Internet Fame	**272**
Bittman, Mark	I Need a Virtual Break. No, Really	**277**
Chase, William M.	A Question of Honor	**81**
Culpepper, T. Allen	The Myth of Inferiority	**103**
Diaz, Junot	Fiesta, 1980	**63**
Fishman, Rob	The Generation of Generation Q	**253**
Friedman, Thomas	Globalization: The Super-Story	**220**
Friedman, Thomas	Generation Q	**250**
Gabriel, Trip	Plagiarism Lines Blur for Students in Digital Age	**115**
Heaney, Seamus	Mid-Term Break	**109**
hooks, bell	Talking Back	**55**
Iyer, Pico	The Burning House	**226**
Lahiri, Jhumpa	This Blessed House	**13**
Lee, Chang-Rae	Coming Home Again	**33**
Norton	Using Sources in Your Writing	**283**
Ozibko, Michal	iDeath	**311**
Perrin, Anne	Stop Blaming Teachers	**121**
Pollit, Katha	Why Boys Don't Play with Dolls	**183**
Quindlen, Anna	Still Needing the F Word	**172**

Rich, Motoko	Literacy Debate: Online, R U Reading?	**260**
Smith, Paul Chaat	The Big Movie (from Everything You Know About Indians Is Wrong)	**1**
Staples, Brent	What Adolescents Miss When We Let them Grow Up in Cyberspace	**246**
Trebay, Guy	The Vanishing Point	**177**
Walker, Jerald	Dragon Slayers	**46**
Wayman, Tom	Did I Miss Anything?	**112**
Wolf, Naomi	The Beauty Myth	**153**
Zakaria, Fareed	The Islamic Threat	**211**

MICHAL OZIBKO ⎨ *iDeath*

MICHAL OZIBKO (b. 1981), a Czech artist, painted a classmate lost in thought as she apparently listens to something on her iPod. The device is so powerful it seems to light the girl, Jana, from below, in at least a partial visual allusion to the hellish nature of her absorption. (Although she could be meditating or praying, that seems not to be the case.) The title, with its ironic use of Apple's signature lower-case "i," reinforces the artist's message. No clothes or jewelry give her a social identity; all that we know about her is her hair color and the fact that she seems to be held captive by her ear buds. This painting was selected for inclusion in the prestigious BP Portrait Award show at the National Portrait Gallery in London in 2010.

Michal Ozibko, *iDeath*. Courtesy Michal Ozibko.

STUDY QUESTIONS

1. Here is a work of art with a very distinct THESIS. Do you agree with what the painter has apparently asserted here, that we are cut off from one another because of our devotion to technology?

2. Hyper-realism adds to the disquiet the painting creates; some people have to look twice to be sure it is not a photograph. (That is in part because it uses the same shallow depth of field that is typical of photographic portraiture.) Why do you think the artist chose such a painstaking method of making a picture? Would this be the same painting if it were done in a looser, more impressionistic style?

3. If you had been the sitter, would you be flattered to be the subject of this portrait, or instead would you be annoyed, even angry?

4. *For Writing.* Describe the ideal portrait of yourself. What aspects of your personality would you want revealed? What objects might you include? Would you want the portrait to be a closeup or a long shot? Why? What medium and what style would best express the truth of who you are?